On Scottish Ground

On Scottish Ground

Selected Essays

Kenneth White

POLYGON

Edinburgh

© Kenneth White, 1998

Polygon
22 George Square
Edinburgh
EH8 9LF

Typeset in Sabon by Bibliocraft, Dundee,
and printed and bound in Great Britain by
The Cromwell Press Ltd, Trowbridge, Wilts

A CIP record for this book is available
from the British Library

ISBN 0 7486 6237 5

The right of Kenneth White to be identified
as author of this work has been asserted in
accordance with the Copyright, Designs and
Patents Act 1988.

The Publisher acknowledges subsidy from

THE SCOTTISH ARTS COUNCIL

towards the publication of this volume.

Contents

Preface

When George Buchanan came back to Scotland after an extremely creative period in France, he set about 'gathering his papers' and, among other things, produced his *History*.

Here I have done something of the same.

But if there are, very definitely, elements of history in these texts, it is not primarily with history that they are concerned – it is with an itinerary of the mind, going all the way from radical analysis to expressive activity, and with the opening, via projective cartography, of a field, the whole constituting what I think of at the moment as 'an Atlantic enlightenment'.

Some of the texts heregathered were written in Scotland before I left for the Continent (they tell, among other things, why, at one point, I felt the need to leave), some were written in the Atlantic Pyrenees, but the majority in Brittany, on the occasion of my renewed contact with the English-language world in general, and the Scottish scene in particular, from 1989 on. In the context of this book, they have been dechronologised, spatialised.

All in all, the book offers the testimony of what you might call a Euro-Scot, in the line, say, of Duns Scotus, the said George Buchanan and David Hume, to mention only three examples among many in a tradition I value highly and have tried to live up to.

As Hume said, introducing his studies on human nature: 'I was seized very early with a passion for literature, philosophy and general learning . . . I went over to France with a view of prosecuting my studies in a country retreat, and I there laid that plan of life which I have steadily pursued'.

I chose to renew contact with the English-language sphere via Scotland, and I've chosen here in this initial book of essays (the first in a projected series) to talk about Scotland. But what I say of Scotland, with Scottish references, is, I think, with extrapolation, valid for other places. I have always considered my native place neither as nation nor as region, but as microcosm.

Kenneth White
Brittany
April 1998

1

The Alban Project

If I tend to call Scotland 'Alba', it's in much the same way as Walt Whitman called New York 'Manahatta': 'I was asking for something specific and perfect for my city, whereupon lo! upsprang the aboriginal name'. If Manahatta for Whitman was a 'word nested in nests of water-bays', Alba for me is . . . Well, before letting it all get dismissed with something like an 'Och ay, Alba, that's teuchter for Scotland', I propose we look into things with some detail, following out land-lines and word-sense.

On Ptolemy's world-map (Alexandria, second century), the northern part of *Insula Britanica*, up by the *Oceanicus Ibernicus*, the *Duecalledonius Oceanus* and the *Iperboreus Oceanus*, is called *Albion*. On other maps, Albion is the name applied to the British island as a whole. If Albion, Alba is connected with Latin *albus*, white (we'll come back to this), that is easily enough understandable. We can imagine neolithic tribes, maybe mediterranean Azilians, arriving in sight of the white cliffs of Dover and singing out: 'White land!' Then, as they moved up country till they finally saw the white peaks of the Grampians shining above their heads, they may well have thought: 'That other place just *looked* like the white land, this is the *real* white land', or, in other words: 'Down there was preface, now we're into the heights and depths of the text'.

What's sure is that, with the older Albion fading into pale mythology (Blake will try to pick it up again, with eccentric enthusiasm, and Charles Doughty, with his deadly dull epic *The Dawn in Britain*), the word Alba, Alban, Latinised as Albania, was going to be applied more and more exclusively to the northern territories. There's a seventh-century Gaelic manuscript,

1

Senchus Fer n'Alban, 'the tradition of the men of Alba'. Then there's that Latin text, *De Situ Albanie*, describing the seven regions of Pictland: Atholl, Angus and the Mearns, Strathearn and Menteith, Fife, Mar and Buchan, Moray and Ross, Caithness and Sutherland. And when we come to Kenneth MacAlpin, it's as King of Alba that he's first presented. Here's *The Prophecy of Berchan*, calling him 'the first king who ruled in the East [i.e. east of the Grampians, in Pictland] of the men of Ireland in Alba'. And here's the *Chronicle of Huntingdon*: 'Kenneth was the first of the Scots to obtain the monarchy of the whole of Albania which is now called Scotland'.

But we can delve down and reach out farther.

In his *Les Celtes et l'expansion celtique*, Henri Hubert, discussing the word Alba, connects it with those names of towns, rivers, mountains and peoples that can be found all over Europe: Alba, Albona, Albi, Alpes, Albani, that constitute probably 'the most numerous and the widest spread group of geographic denominations'. We're concerned with an arch-word, an arch-name. If, for Hubert, the word is probably Indo-European and connected with the same root as the Latin *albus* (white), it's not originally Gaelic-Celtic, it goes back to Iberian and Ligurian. Pokorny, writing in the *Zeitschrift für Celtische Philologie*, disputes the connection of Alba with *albus*, points out that all the places called Alba in Italy are mountainous, and considers that the root, non-Indo-European, means 'heights', as in Alps. While not caring to engage in the philological debate, I'd say that it seems both easy and justifiable to interpret Alba as 'the white heights', 'the high white place', 'the high white world'.

The question to be met with now is maybe this one: why bother with such erudition? Do we not live nowadays, and is it not more important to write about the contemporary situation than go into all this archaeologising?

The immediate answer is that if a lot of literature can simply mean grubbing about in the contemporary situation, poetics has a deeper task to perform; that a literature without poetics ends up pretty fast as litter-ature; and that a country deprived of a strong poetic world-sense is not only culture-less but future-less, destined for abysmal punkdom.

A country is that which offers resistance. The word itself says it, stemming as it does from *contra* (same thing in the German *Gegend*, region, district, which contains *gegen*, against). But in the course of time, the resistance wears down, the country gets covered with cliché and becomes couthy, or even cruddy. Alba is Scotland un-couthied, un-cruddied, re-discovered. Scotland itself after all is a colonial term, and Scotland has been over-colonised. Post-colonial Scotland means getting back down to Alba, to original landscape-mindscape, and, connecting them, wordscape.

In a couthy context, language is considered only as a means of communication. And in time it becomes that to such an extent it begins to feel like old chewing-gum in the mouth. But language is not primarily communication, it says the relationship of the human being to the universe, it expresses *original* experience, it is the *evidence* of original experience. And it is this which comes across in real poetry.

We're talking about radicality. Radical is a word used here and there, but most of the usages aren't radical enough. They stay at the sociological level, which is the end-point of the chain, instead of getting back into the primal area. If you're talking about radicality, you're talking about roots (*radex*, *radices*), but there's no sense of talking about roots (all you'll get is a lot of ethno-fantasia and identity ideology), unless you talk about ground. Again, radicality means, if not getting back to the ultimate root, at least as far back as possible, in order to begin again. As any botanist, as any gardener knows, if a plant has been damaged, new growth will start, not at the place of damage, but farther down.

This, I submit, is what must happen with our culture in general, and with Scotland, that socio-cultural growth on the ground of Alba, in particular.

Here's Neil Gunn (*The Scots Magazine*, September 1939), moving along the coast of Buchan towards Fraserburgh:

. . . before we entered Fraserburgh we came upon an extraordinary sight, that was surely a portent and a sign: a cemetery of drifters. It was as if a fleet of them, like a school of enormous whales, had run themselves aground, become permanently stranded, and rotted. From some the planking was entirely gone, leaving the gaunt ribs for wind and salt spray to whistle through. They had all taken the ground head-on, some had slewed round, at least one had broken its back. It seemed a tragic end to a story that in every case had been charged with danger and courage, hope and despair, continuous vigilance, ceaseless adventure, in summer seas, in winter's smashing storms. If each skeleton could tell its true story, and tell the stories, too, of those who had walked its decks and of those who waited on shore for a return that brought the welcome news of safety first and of plenty or poverty next, this bay, this cemetery, would be the birthplace of an imperishable epic. Each boat had been deliberately stranded. When a skipper-owner walks away for the last time from a vessel that he has sailed on the right side of death for thirty years, a vessel that he and his crew and their families have depended on, through good fortune and bad, what a parting must be there! Perhaps only those who deal with the sea can understand.

Taking this not only as the image of a socio-economic conjuncture, but as a metaphor for the whole Scottish situation, I propose that we try and move beyond the pathos and the pathology (which Gunn seems tempted to indulge in – so much literature is content to do just that) and get out on to a new path. It is not easy, but what else is there really worth doing? It is certainly the only *radical* thing to do.

The Scottish Renaissance had called vociferous attention to the situation and made a move to give Scotland a sense of being something more than a pathetic and picturesque province of the crumbling British Empire. But seen from a distance, was the Renaissance itself much more than just part of the scene? To come back to our metaphor, you can imagine one of those old drifters converted into a Scottish Revival Pub, with whisky fumes and Lallans poems pouring through the portholes, while at the prow of another, MacDiarmid, arms outstretched, is shouting 'Back to Dunbar!' before going below decks and writing a 35,000-line epistle to Lenin, full of thinly disguised quotations from scientific and philosophical journals, about the vast lost Celtic Empire that stretched from the Dniester in the Russian East

to the shores of Portugal in the West, from the archipelagos of
Scotland in the North to the central part of Italy in the South . . .
And it all piled up.

I was reading MacDiarmid in Glasgow, not without exaltation
(I'm thinking in particular of *In Memoriam James Joyce*), but at
the same time feeling that what I really had to do – still not
forgetting our drifter metaphor – was *get back out into the drift*.

In Glasgow, in those gas-fire rooms with a round red object
in the greyness of the window reminding you vaguely of the
sun, I was reading also Spengler's *Decline of the West*, Céline's
Journey to the End of Night, Toynbee's *A Study of History* and,
more than once, Nietzsche's *Ecce Homo* and *Daybreak*. Anyone
living in Scotland soon has a bellyful of chronicle-history, even if
it's coming at them only through the novels of Scott and Co. (in
Scotland, it's an industry), but conceptual history, theoretical
history, that's something else again. It begins with Hegel's
Phenomenology of Mind (1807), and it's continued both by
Spengler and Toynbee. Hegel had said that night must fall for
Minerva's owl, the incarnation of historical wisdom, to take her
flight. Toynbee sets down as epigraph to his study of the morphology of the twenty-one fully developed cultures that our planet
has known a phrase pronounced by a prophetess in Vergil's hell:
'Night's coming down, Aeneas' (*nox ruit, Aeneas*). Ah, those
Glasgow nights – the screech of trams, and ships' horns on the
river! For Toynbee, every culture, initiated by creative individuals and groups, goes through four phases: genesis, growth,
breakdown, disintegration. With regard to the final phases, part
petrification, part putrefaction, creative individuals, out for
renewal, will adopt a strategy of withdrawal and return, withdrawal and return, while at the same time trying, along their own
life-paths, to 'become what they are' (Pindar's phrase, *genoi
hoios essi*, adopted by Nietzsche).

This is where *Ecce Homo* comes in: 'It was high time for me
to think back to myself – that deepest self, as it were buried
and grown silent' (silent and distant, so as not to turn into just
a 'quirky hedgehog'). *Ecce Homo* is the portrait of an *author*
(I'm thinking of Rimbaud's 'Writers galore, but where's a real
author?') out to 'keep the elevation of my task clean of the many
lower and more shortsighted drives', out to develop 'the most
spacious soul which can stray and roam the farthest into itself',

out to find 'the first language for a new range of experiences', intent all the time on place, landscape, weather, whether it be in the Ober-Engadin at Sils-Maria ('I know of nothing more congenial to my nature than this piece of high land'), the quiet bay of Rapallo ('that little forgotten world of happiness'), the back-country of Nice with its halcyon sky ('many hidden places and heights in the landscape of Nice are for me consecrated by unforgettable moments'), the coast near Genoa ('that confusion of rocks near to Genoa where I was alone and shared secrets with the sea'), or that 'little resort not far from Vicenza where I spent the Spring of the year 1881'.

It was with all this in mind and with, deep down, initial intuitions coming from movements and moments in the back-country of Fairlie or along the coast, that I left on my own *travels in the drifting dawn* (in that 'dawn', you have Alba again – as, by the way, in the title of my very latest book, *Le Plateau de l'Albatros* ...) That meant following blue roads, holing up in self-created hermitages such as Gourgounel in the Ardèche, looking into the face of the East Wind, travelling along the bird path into the diamond country, and so on.

I'm using of course the titles of some of my books, trying maybe to suggest, tentatively, step by step, an answer to the question somebody might conceivably put: 'What does a guy who writes books with titles like *Pilgrim of the Void* have to say to a particular place at a particular time: Scotland now, for example?'

So let's get back to Scotland, and to the development of geopoetics – the large field to which my pathways have led.

It was in Paris I found it, in the rue Saint-Sulpice, practically filling all by itself the window of an antiquarian bookseller's: an elephant-sized volume, bearing the title *Physical Atlas of Natural Phenomena*, put out from Edinburgh in 1850 by Alexander Keith Johnston. I knew of its existence, had been looking for it in a desultory way for years, had practically given up – and there it was. The price was pretty stiff, but I haggled and hummed a bit, said I'd think it over, came back the next morning, hummed and haggled a bit more, laid down the cash, and it was mine. It's been one of the central pieces in my library in Brittany for some time now. I open it at least once a week.

In his Preface, dated Edinburgh, April 1848, Johnston says that the aim of the *Atlas* is 'to present in a graphic form a concise yet comprehensive view of the Physical Geography of the Globe, embracing under that term its superficial structure, the movements of its oceanic and aerial currents, and the distribution of organized existence on its surface'. He insists both on 'the importance and utility of this most interesting branch of knowledge' and on 'the absence in this country of the necessary aids for its study'.

The *Atlas* consists of thirty maps, accompanied by synoptic texts: The Mountain Systems of Europe, The Glacier Systems of the Alps, The Phenomena of Volcanic Action, Physical Chart of the Atlantic Ocean, Tidal Chart of the British Seas, The River Systems of Asia and Europe, Rain Map of the World, The Birds of Europe ...

As I said, I open it at least once a week. There's the sheer æsthetic pleasure of it. But there's also something else: the maps give me a sense of expansiveness, relieving me of the oppression we all feel at one time or another, and some of us all the time, so that we don't even know it's oppression but think it's 'just life'. I love to pore over that rain map of Europe, realising with pleasure – it's written there in a lovely red on a beautiful grey – that I was born in 'the province of the Autumn Rains'.

Now, the *Atlas of Natural Phenomena* is inscribed to Alexander von Humboldt, 'at whose suggestion this work was originally undertaken, and on whose profound and various researches in every department of natural science a large potion of the contents is founded'), and Alexander von Humboldt is definitely one of the principle ancestors of geopoetics (which is why a long chapter is devoted to him in *Le Plateau de l'Albatros*). Here's what Humboldt, quoting his brother Wilhelm, says in Note 23 of the second volume of *Cosmos*:

> It may seem strange to endeavour to connect poetry, which rejoices always in variety, form and colour, with those ideas which are most simple and abstruse: but it is not the less correct. Poetry, science, philosophy, and history, are not in themselves, and essentially, divided from each other; they are united, either where man's particular stage of progress places him in a state of unity, or where the true poetic mood restores him to such a state.

It is the convergence of science, philosophy and poetry that constitutes the basis of the geopoetics project. Whatever the situation, the creative individual can strive towards it in an *opus*. The socio-cultural question is whether the historical context is ready for the energies of that *opus* to radiate out into a culture in any given place.

It's because I think the historical context is ready in Western culture, with various modalities according to locality, that, as an extension of individual *opus*, I started up in April 1989 the International Institute of Geopoetics.

I think also the time is now in Scotland.

There was no science of the whole. It was axiomatic that science dealt with parts, weighing them, measuring them . . . Then, in 1917, along came Einstein with his *Cosmological Considerations* (*Kosmologische Betrachtungen*). Suddenly a new field opened up, a total field. A school report concerning the young Albert Einstein said this: 'Unsociable, permanently adrift' (I refer to what was said earlier about 'drifting' in this essay). Einstein had turned that drifting into a field of research, situated outside the closed disciplines, speaking of the need for science to abandon 'mechanical, specialised logic' and take 'a great intellectual leap', presenting his own 'wildly speculative' manner of thinking. That science should have gone still farther after Einstein, into quantic physics, with chance, disorder, the chaotic, the indeterminate seen no longer as illusions due to our ignorance, but as part integral of the universe-multiverse, leaving Einstein himself in the role of an eccentric classic, an extravagant theologian who still couldn't believe that 'God played dice', substracts nothing from his significance. Especially as Einstein was not only a scientist advancing physics, but a whole man asking himself existential and cultural questions, with a sensation of his own life to be lived. As a scientist, he feels caught tragically in a dilemma between, on the one hand, schematic logic (mathematics), and on the other, what he calls 'the living story', all the 'delightful slices of life'. How to reconcile the two, how to be methodical without losing out on the phenomena of the world? Einstein doesn't have the answer (could it lie in a poetics?), but he has the immense merit of posing the question. As to life-sense, there's

this: 'I feel so much in contact with all of life that it's a matter
of indifference to me to know where the individual begins and
where he ends'.
  In scientific terms, we're moving there from physics to biology.
Here's a biologist, Henri Atlan, writing (in *L'Unité de l'homme*,
Seuil, 1974) about man as an open system:

> The old humanism is no longer tenable, because the
> conventional image of man is breaking up [. . .] That's
> the image of Man as dominating by his discourse and his
> actions a world of nature [. . .] Those who bewail the end
> of humanism can't imagine that anything beneficial could
> emerge from the end of an illusion [. . .] It's not because
> Man is disappearing and being wiped away 'like a face in
> sand at the tide's edge' as Michel Foucault says, that we
> should be shedding tears about our fate. The Man that's
> disappearing is not man in general, it's an imaginary
> absolute that has played its part in the development of
> Western knowledge . . . This Man is being replaced by
> things, but we can recognize ourselves in these things
> because they can speak to us.

Instead of Man considering himself as an absolute agent and as
master of things, at the same time as in reality he is cut off from
them and is gradually enclosed in a schizophrenic world, we are
presented with an image of the human being as bearing a faculty
of auto-organisation *among* things, discovering that the language
of things is not radically different from his own. It's this existence
among and with things that Atlan calls 'a unified existence'. As to
that faculty of auto-organisation he mentions, it's what two
other biologists, Maturana and Varula, call auto-poesis.
  The words 'poetry' and 'poetics' turn up more and more in this
context. In *The New Alliance* (Gallimard, 1979), Prigogine and
Stengers, physicist and science-historian, call for 'a poetic listening in to nature'. In *Mind and Nature* (Wildwood House, 1980),
speaking of the only science that could interest him totally and
which does not yet exist, since it implies an entry into unknown
territory, Bateson (anthropologist, psychiatrist, epistemologian),
talks of æsthetics, saying that the thing to know now is 'on what
surface to map out a theory of æsthetics'.
  This idea of 'mapping out' (this time I refer back to my

evocation of Johnston's *Atlas*), is also frequent. In an essay entitled *Cognitive strategies*, Humberto Maturana presents the acquisition of knowledge as a form of mapping: the projection via our sense organs of external reality on to our nervous system, insisting on the fact that science is not the domain of objective knowledge but a field depending on the subject, defined by a method specifying the properties of the knowing self.

Before I leave the field of science and this section of my essay, I feel the need to insist on the fact that if I'm speaking in favour of 'the whole', of 'the subject' and of 'open system', I am not at all suggesting that the field is open to anything at all. I am very much a proponent of clarity and precision, and what 'openness' means is clearing the decks of the mind of all the inventions, illusions and imaginings of the old figure of Man, not leaving the gates wide open for new variations on them all to rush in as at some gleesome New Age jamboree.

A few years ago, I was invited to a symposium on 'Science and the Imagination' in England. The amount of Platonic ether, etherial fantasia, spiritualistic mush and holy hotch-potch in the name of holism was such as to make me want to intervene now and then with a discrete little remark and a smile. After the proceedings, the organiser came up to me with a Big Brother glare in his eyes and said: 'I think you're a troublemaker'. Me, a quiet Taoist from the outer West, just musing his way along the paths of philosophy and navigating the *nous poetikos*, branded as a troublemaker! Well, in some contexts, if you can put two ideas together, you're a disturber of the peace, if you can put two ideas together and make a third, you're Public Enemy number 1.

I think we can do better than that.

There has been a great deal of intellectual, theoretical ferment in Scotland over the past few years, connected largely with a rediscovery and re-examination of George Davie's *The Democratic Intellect* (Edinburgh University Press, 1961). I'll mention only three titles: *The Crisis of the Democratic Intellect* (Polygon, 1986) by the same Davie, *The Eclipse of Scottish Culture* (Polygon, 1989) by Craig Beveridge and Ronald Turnbull, and *The Revival of the Democratic Intellect* (Polygon, 1994) by Andrew Lockhart Walker.

It was, on the one hand, because Davie's original thesis concerning 'the generalist tradition of Scottish university education', had been misconstrued, under-translated, seen as an excuse for localist complacency if not self-congratulation ('We *are* the democratic intellect'), and, on the other hand, because education as an introduction to the fields of world-culture and as an invitation to explore ways-of-life, was more and more threatened by a market-geared conception of education as techno-minded processing with its cohorts of administration people and its managerial lingo of 'performance indicators', 'cost benefit analysis', 'mission statements', integrated into a system euphemistically entitled 'the enterprise culture', that a need was felt in the 1980s to come back to that thesis and push it as far as possible. Davie himself stated caustically in *The Edinburgh Review* that 'we sometimes have the impression that what the Scots are aiming at is democracy without intellect' (that is, populism), while Beveridge and Turnball, commenting in general terms on Scottish nationalism in the 1960s and 1970s, say that it lacked 'a substantial cultural and philosophical component', and that its aim with regard to Scottish education: the teaching of Scots and Gaelic in schools, the introduction into the programmes of a dose of Scot. Lit., while not being reprehensible (though the question remains: what, how and to what end?), were 'seriously limited'. The move was towards a broader intellectual-cultural basis and a deeper grounding, situated outside and beyond both humdrum home-issues (i.e. the use or non-use of Lallans and Gaelic) inherited from the Scottish Renaissance days and the accumulated ammunition for the ding-dong dialogue with England that rarely got beyond resentment and chip-on-the-shoulderism.

This meant, in the first instance, a cool look at 'English epistemology' and the English educational system as ideally represented by Oxford and Cambridge. Dismissed in the eighteenth-century by Adam Smith of Glasgow as 'sanctuaries for exploded systems and obsolete prejudices' and, in the nineteenth century, by an Englishman, Darwin, as 'intellectually sterile', these institutions are seen by the late twentieth century Scots critics as still based largely on class distinctions, and as fulfilling a conservative social function: finishing schools devoted to the 'polishing' of a certain anthropological type marked by what Walker calls 'decorous mediocrity'. As to the 'epistemology', it is based on

pedantic specialisation, the latest avatar of which is linguistic
philosophy as laid out, say, by Ayer, and continued by Austin
and Moore. Asked, in the course of an interview (see Bryan
Magee's *Modern British Philosophy*, Secker and Warburg, 1971)
why this technical description of prevailing linguistic behaviour
(described by someone, was it Marcuse? as 'meticulous boredom') is so little thought of on the Continent, an Oxford
professor of philosophy replies: 'I'm inevitably rather guessing
about this, because philosophy outside the English-speaking
world is a field in which I'm not particularly well informed'.
Faced with this kind of ignorant, self-satisfied complacency, not
to speak of the dead language employed, one hardly wishes to
attack at all, just to look away.

The Scots critics I'm referring to look first to what they take, in
the wake of Davie, to be the specifically Scottish tradition in
philosophy. Tending to leave Hume aside (simply because he had
his text combed for Scoticisms, which seems a peccadillo rather
than cause for intellectual banishment), their genealogy centres
on the eighteenth-century Common Sense Philosophers: Thomas
Reid, Frances Hutcheson, Dugald Stewart, thereafter going back
to John Mair (sixteenth century) and forward, in the nineteenth,
to John Nichol, in the twentieth, to John Anderson, John Baillie,
Alasdair MacIntyre, John Macmurray, John Macquarrie.

What our critics want, and what they see in this lineage of
thinkers and teachers, is a democratic social openness, the readiness to take on a wide field of experience and reference, a
willingness to go right back to first principles, a kind of thinking
('intuitive realism') that avoids both positivism and absolute
idealism, and an awareness of what goes on in the 'more open
world of the Continent' (Walker). So far, so good – but have we
really got very far? If we do try to go further with these thinkers,
we very soon find ourselves caught in an interpersonalist nexus
with a more or less definitely-contoured religious background.
Too much of it is, ultimately, pulpit philosophy. Rabelais made
fun of it in the person of John Mair when he claims to have come
across in a Paris library a book by Mair entitled *How to make
puddings*, and George Buchanan makes fun of the same Mair
when he says Mair (*maior* in Latin) was major only in name. If
it's said, as proof of its cogency and scope, that Reid's Common
Sense philosophy was adopted in nineteenth century France, the

fact is undeniably true, but the context has to be examined, it's important to see in what circumstances: Napoleon was looking for a philosophy that would play the same role in the schools and universities as the church did in society at large, that is, keep the really radical ideas out. If we take the case of John Nichol, faced with a radical democratic poet like Whitman, he's completely lost: writing in the ninth edition of the *Encyclopedia Britannica* (1875), while he can concede Whitman some occasions of 'uncouth power', he sees in his work not only 'absolute barbarism both of manner and matter', but 'a glorification of nature in its most unabashed forms, an audacious protest against all that civilisation has done to raise men above the savage state'. In other words, with this philosopher, we're in a very circumscribed context indeed. Unless you keep an eye on it, Common Sense will kill all rhythm and idiom and colour, all expansiveness.

Beyond the Common Sense domain, I come back to the *general desires* expressed in the books I've quoted from, for with them we can, I think, go farther, open up a larger context, bring in freer energies, draw different co-ordinates.

What we're all agreed on is the need for 'enlarged investigation' (Davie), for 'a fundamental rethinking of the philosophy, science, ethics, æsthetics, politics and economics of the past 400 years' (Walker), the need to 'redraw the map of knowledge' (Peter Scott, *What Future for Higher Education?* Croom Helm, 1979), and in particular 'redraw the map of Scotland's past and realign the perspectives of its future' (Beveridge and Turnbull), try to attain 'an integrated view of the world' (id.). To do so, I suggest the referential topography has to be extended. Walker refers, not only in passing, but according to the tenor of his argument, to Heraclitus, Erigena and Duns Scot, who all happen to be among my own references. In addition, and here we're coming close to geopoetics, he calls for an 'earth ethic', an 'ethic of the biosphere', quoting the remarks of Freya Matthews (*The Ecological Self*, Routledge and Kegan Paul, 1991) about our 'cosmologically dispossessed culture' and the need for 'cosmological rehabilitation'. This, of course, has to mean a whole lot more than 'greening' (there's red, blue and brown in nature as well as green), and, I submit, it has to go deeper than ecology (and ethics). Here in Scotland we have some of the finest wilderness country in Europe (*Scotia deserta*) and not only can we not let it go to merely exploitative interests, we have to establish a new relationship to it, way outside anything like the rural bucolics of, say, England. The premises for this are there in Scottish tradition: cosmography, even cosmopoetics (think of Buchanan's *De Sphaera*), was part integral of Renaissance education in Scotland, and with his *The Theory of the Earth* (1788), Hutton was one of the initiators of geology.

A word now as to strategies, means and methods. Speaking of culture, Beveridge and Turnbull declare that what makes for the vitality of a culture is 'intensity of debate rather than the security of ideas on which it rests'. Yes and no. I'm all for debate, if need be, and if 'security of ideas' means some kind of comfortable authoritarian convention, I have no time for it. But, back of all debate, what is necessary for a culture is a *grounding*. That's where geopoetics starts.

What we need, badly, is a new grounding.

2

The Archaic Context

If your roots don't plunge into the archaic, you're unlikely to
produce anything powerfully new. (Kostas Axelos)

In *Highland River* (The Porpoise Press, 1937), Neil Gunn tells
the story of Kenn, the story of his search for the source of a river
which is the source of his life. Aware of an opacity in the civilization around him, and in his own civilised mind, he goes back to
the river of his childhood in an attempt to get beyond the opacity
and penetrate through to a light:

> Knowing this, he would like to stop the thickening of his
> mind, to hunt back into that lost land . . . It was intensely
> real and Kenn had a feeling that if he could recapture this
> he would recapture not merely the old primordial goodness
> of life but its moments of absolute ecstasy, an ecstasy so
> different from what is ordinarily associated with the word
> that its eye, if it had one, would be wild and cold and
> watchful as the eye of the gull on the cliff-top. Though that
> is a cold image, conveying only the suggestion of a first
> momentary aspect, of the initial thrill – before translation
> takes place.

In this paragraph, there is not only the motivation of my own
early work, but its leitmotivs. It was full of cold images, in
particular that of the gull, and was based on a triple notion of
primordial contact, ecstatic experience and the search for a logic,
a language to make it all last. The first poem in my first poem
book (*The Cold Wind of Dawn*), was called 'Precentor Seagull',
and it went like this:

You up there
in the lurching church of the elements
mover and moved
white as a ghost and fat
as the paps of the dark earth-woman
with a squawk man in you
would waken wide if there was one
the sleeping gate to paradise
or the white world's thighs
give us the sound at least the note
the initial noise
and it's we will make the psalms we need
with whatever we know and are . . .

The tone was pretty extravagant, I'm willing to admit, and
hardly suited to the strictly domestic culture that was Britain's
way back there in the 1950s and early 1960s. It was coming from
something, somewhere, psychologically and culturally a lot
further back. Since that early outburst, I've spent a lot of time
trying to trace my way back to the things and place I must have
come from to be able to perpetrate such wild ravings. That's
what this essay is all about. But before trying to trace that path
back, a word as to the tone itself. For with writers you might
almost say, by their tone ye shall know them, even before you get
the drift of their meaning. Here's what Henry Thoreau has to say
about extravagance:

I fear chiefly lest my expression may not be extra-vagant
enough, nay not wander far enough beyond the narrow
limits of my daily experience, so as to be adequate to the
truth of which I have been convinced. Extravagance! It
depends on how you are yarded . . . I desire to speak somewhere *without* bounds, like a man in a waking moment to
men in their waking moments. For I'm convinced that I
cannot exaggerate enough to lay the foundation of a true
expression.

1.

The city of my birth, Glasgow, is known mainly for the fact that
it was long an industrial hell, and for its hard-bitten humour.

Everything concerning its foundations, the original lie of the land, the original mindscape tended to get thrust well into the background. But take Mungo, the patron saint of the place. Look into his story and you find his original name was Kentigern (Kenti-gern, the 'head of the house of the moon'). And if you read the text of his *Life*, you'll come across one Lailoken, a 'wild man of the woods', the ancestor of those nature-poets who were later to roam about Strathclyde, particularly in the area of Dumbarton (the 'fortress of the Bretons'). I'm thinking of Taliesin, Llywarch-Hen, Aneurin. Here's Taliesin talking of the 'mysteries' of the world:

> I'm a skilful composer, a clear-sounding singer
> I'm metal, I'm druid
> I'm architect, I'm man of science
> I'm snake, I'm love
> I'm no havering bard
> . . .
> I know the lands of fertile inspiration
> The inspiration I sing
> Comes from the depths

And here he is talking of his 'migrations':

> I've taken on many aspects
> Before coming to my final form
> I remember them clearly:
> I've been a gleaming spear
> I've been a drop of rain in the air
> I've been a word among letters . . .

Here is Llywarch-Hen conjuring up images of snow and while he's at it dropping a little word of wisdom:

> The night is long, bare the moon, white the rock
> grey the keen gull at the cliff's edge
> too many men get lost in vain talk

And here's a phrase of Aneurin's that is a programme of life in itself: 'As long as there are things to be found, there will be searchers'.

2.

I'd left the city long enough for my 'native' landscape to be, not
the urban one, but that territory which the Norsemen, who sailed
along it in their dragon-ships, called the *Skotlandsfirdir*. Haakon
of Norway had had his fleet wrecked by a storm, providential for
the kingdom of Scotland, just a couple of miles along from the
village where I lived, and when I began to interest myself in languages around my early teens it wasn't too hard for me to imagine
the Norse tongue spoken on the very wave-beaten rocks where I
was studying the grammar: '*Tha foru menn milli theira melholm
skotakunungs ok gerdu their sett milli sin skyldi magnus konungr
eignask eyjar aller their er liggja fyrir vestan skotland . . .*'.
   From the grammar I went to the poems, reading Harold
Hardradi, Rognvald Kali, all the scaldic poetry I could get my
hands on:

> Humbled the homesteads
> burning in Scotland
> red flame from smoking thatch

   I liked the guttural sounds, and the wild imagery, where a
snake is a 'moor salmon' and the sea is 'the gull-path'.
   In old records, I came across mention of a Norse brooch that
had been found in the nineteenth century a mile south of the
village. This brooch bore runes of the Viking time that gave the
name of the owner: *malbri-tha a talk thaele i lari* (Malbritha of
Lari owns this brooch). I have seen since a stone in Norway
bearing the same kind of terse and alliterative inscription:

> *ek wiwar after woduride*
> *witadahalaiban*
> *worahto*

– 'I, Viv, to the memory of Vodurid, the giver of bread, made
these runes.' And in the tomb of Maeshowe in the Orkneys there
is an inscription which says, among other things, that it was cut,
with an Icelandic axe, by 'the greatest rune-writer West of the
ocean', the ocean in question being of course the one designated
on the old nautical charts as *mare iperboreum*.
   If the runes were well made, they were supposed to be bearers
of power. Every one of them bore the name of a god. Thus the

rune 't' (written ↑) was associated with the god Tyr. I've seen a
stone in Gotland where the writer cut the rune 't', but wishing
maybe to reinforce its power, added branches to it, giving it the
form of a fir tree ♠. In this case, the resemblance between sign
and tree is no doubt pure coincidence. But in ogam writing, such
correspondences are intended. In that alphabet, the first letter
corresponds to the birch tree, and the first three letters (birch,
rowan, ash) spell out the name of the sun-god Belenos.

I'm not out here to pile up antiquarian erudition. What I'm
trying to do is work out a buried topology. With the references
evoked, we're in a mental space in which writing is a power, a
fundamental activity, and that activity is linked to the phenomena of nature. This is where, obscurely, I begin. And where we
all begin. Which is why when we look, say, at runes on a rock, or
at an Oceanic mask, or at an Amerindian totem, we know we are
in presence of a power that is almost regularly absent from
modern art and modern life.

3.

The books that remain uppermost in my mind from my childhood reading were all concerned with the northern landscape.
Which does not mean going back to imitate, but means going
outward towards something equivalent.

There was *Russian Tales for Children*, told by Alexei Tolstoy
and translated from the Russian by Evgenia Schimanskaya; *The
Romance of Labrador* by Sir Wilfrid Grenfell; and Fridtjof
Nansen's *Eskimo Life*. I think that it was pure chance that made
for this constellation of northern readings at this time (most of
my books were school prizes donated by different people, and the
rest were bought from second hand bookstalls often according to
their price). But it was not pure chance that accounted for my
interest in them. They corresponded to something in myself and
wakened a latency.

Alexei Tolstoy claimed that he had not retold the Russian tales
in a conventional, literary manner, but had tried to maintain the
crispness and originality of the folk style – the contrast interested
me, and I knew I'd have to look into it further. As to the stories
themselves, they were all about animals and birds and trees. I can
recall one or two of them: 'The Crane and the Heron'; 'Father

Frost' ('he crackled in the fir trees, jumping from branch to branch, snapping his fingers'); and a story about the grouse who, after thinking one winter of building himself a hut, decided against it, convinced that 'better than keeping house is to lie in the snow, sit on little birch trees, look over the open fields and meet the Spring with a shout'. There were no cranes in my part of the world, but there were plenty of herons, a lot of forest and frost, and grouse galore. I remember clearly certain of the illustrations in that little book: a rabbit looking at a wintry moon, a wolf howling, a saucer-eyed owl on a tree stump. It was a cold landscape, but there was a hidden, animal life going on in it. I loved it.

The *Romance of Labrador* presented a series of 'pageants'. First of all there was the Pageant of the Rocks, concerning the geology of Labrador, the archaean formations, the granite and the lava. This was followed by the Pageant of the Indians, the Eskimo, the Vikings, all those who had lived out their lives on Labrador land. Thereafter came the Pageant of the Three Kings, the three kings being the principal fish of subarctic waters: the salmon, the herring, the cod. Finally came the Pageant of the Soil, which spoke of phanerogams and cryptogams (the words intrigued me), and went into the growth of larch, fir, willow, alder, ash and white birch. Again, in addition to the text, I was attracted to the images: photographs of Cape Blow-me-down, the Great Kaumajets (Shining Tops), an Eskimo grave. There was a lot of sheer information in these pages, but interwoven with it, inseparable from it, a way of being in the world.

This became more explicit with Nansen's *Eskimo Life*: 'It is poor, this land of the Eskimo, it has neither timber nor gold, it is naked, lonely – but how beautiful!' I was particularly interested in the chapter on religious ideas, my introduction to the comparative history of religions. It was here I first heard of *angekok*, shamans, of *tôrnat* (spirits) and of *tônârssuk* (master of the spirits). 'When Christianity was introduced among the Eskimo, the *tôrnârssuk* was changed into a devil.' I began to feel a certain sympathy for all poor devils. I even began practising a kind of home-made shamanism. It was in the woods and on the moors up behind the village. I ate berries religiously. I stood still under waterfalls. I made love to trees. I ran with the white hare. I talked with the owls and the crows . . .

I must have been about nineteen when I wrote the aforequoted 'Precentor Seagull'. Years later, in Rasmussen's *Report of the Fifth Thule Expedition*, I came across this, the 'magic words' of an Eskimo shaman:

> The gull, it is said
> the one that cleaves the air with its wings
> the one that is usually
> above our heads
> *keeya! aya!*
> *keeya! aya!*
> gull you up there
> steer down towards me
> your wings are red
> up there in the coolness
> *ayaya! ayaya!*

If you take the trouble to refer back to the bit of my poem I quoted, you'll see the resemblance, which amounts practically to an identity. That first poem of mine was a shaman-poem. I was a shaman without a tribe.

4.

At some time during this early period, somebody gave me a book in which there was an old poem concerning Finn and his companions, the Fianna: 'When Finn lived, and the Fianna, moor and shore were dearer to them than any church.'

There was another track to follow up.

The Finn tradition had been strong in Scotland, as in Ireland. For centuries, it had marked people's minds, and there were still traces of it in the landscape: the Fianna cliff (*Sgor nam Fionnaidh*) and Ossian's cave in Glencoe. On every crest of those mountains, says the legend, there's one of Finn's men sleeping – the wind is their breathing. Nowadays, we tend to see this tradition only in terms of its eighteenth-century romantic revival or its funny funeral by that garrulous literary undertaker, James Joyce. But if you trace it back far enough – up beyond Gaelic pieties – you come to something like an archaic deer-cult (Ossian, Finn's son, means 'fawn' and Oscar, his grandson, means 'deer-lover'), something close to the caribou cult of the Indians and

Eskimo of Labrador. So much for distant origin, but by the time
you come to the beginning of our era, the Fianna were a group of
warrior-poets. To be a 'companion of Finn', you had to give up
clan and family ties, be an accomplished athlete (run and leap
faster than the normal), and know by heart the twelve books of
poetry. For political reasons, but mainly because of the arrival of
Christianity, the whole thing disappeared about the third century. But the poems remain, and some of them are very beautiful.
Here is one:

> Your song is sweet, blackbird, nowhere in the world have I
> heard music sweeter than yours. You, priest, would do well
> to listen, you can always go back to your prayers later. If
> you knew the real story of the blackbird, priest, you'd weep
> tears, you might even stop for a moment thinking about
> your God. It was in the blue-streamed land of Norway that
> Finn caught the bird you now see. And he put it in a wood
> of the West, in a wood of fine trees where the Fianna loved
> to take their rest. Finn loved to lie there listening to the
> blackbird sing or the stag roar. He also loved the song of
> the grouse, the sound made by the otter as it slips into the
> water, and the screech of the eagle. He delighted in the
> noise of the waves in the morning as they rolled over the
> beach of white pebbles.

As the recipient of a good Scottish education, I had lengthy
screeds of the Bible by heart, and wasn't insensitive to its rhythm
and its grandeur, but from then on, I knew I preferred 'the noise
of the waves in the morning as they flowed over the beach of
white pebbles' to any talk about God. Take this, from Revelation:

> His eyes were as a flame of fire, and on his head were many
> crowns; and he had a name written, that no man knew, but
> he himself. And he was clothed with a vesture dipped in
> blood: and his name is called The Word of God . . . And
> out of his mouth goeth a sharp sword, that with it he should
> smite the pagans: and he shall rule them with a rod of iron:
> and he treadeth the winepress of the fierceness and wrath of
> Almighty God. And he hath on his vesture and on his thigh
> a name written, King of Kings, and Lord of Lords.

That's a pathological nightmare. And we've been wrapped up in it for too long a time. The world has been left numb and dumb by it.

Yet even when God Almighty came to the Finn country, when the song of the blackbird gave way to the ding-dong of bells, something of the old feeling remained. Here's one of the hymns of St Patrick, in which one finds a cosmic naturalism very rare in Christianity:

> I bind myself today
> to the power of the sky
> to the light of the sun
> to the whiteness of snow
> to the force of fire
> to the brightness of lightning
> to the swiftness of the wind
> to the depths of the sea
> to the steadiness of the earth
> to the hardness of rocks . . .

It must be said that those early Celtic Christians were pretty headstrong with regard to the conventional fold. Not only did they insist on cutting their hair a certain way, not only did they have their own baptismal practices and fixed their own Easter date, but in general they had a highly individualistic way of looking at things that did not please at all the ecclesiastical authorities in Rome. The Roman envoy at the Synod of Whitby in 663 had this to say: 'The only people stupid enough to be in disagreement with the whole world are those Scots and their obstinate allies the Picts and the Bretons who live on two islands lost at the far ends of the ocean . . .'

I was beginning to feel I had companions.

5.

I was engaged in archaeological and anthropological studies concerning my 'territory' on the West Coast of Scotland, when I came across a book (I'm telling it the way it was, chance after chance) by a certain J. Kevan McDowall called *Carrick Gallovidian* (Ayr, 1947). This was the presentation of a forgotten tongue, referred to by the author as Pictish Gaelic or Iberian

Pictish, and by the Scots Gaelic dictionaries as 'ancient' or 'obsolete' Gaelic, surviving only in place-names. For McDowall, this tongue was in all likelihood the aboriginal tongue of the British Isles.

We go back to a fertile district – Iberia – between the Black Sea and the Caspian whence, probably under pressure from further east, a migration of people moves west, forming the basic populations of the Balkans, Italy, Gaul, Spain and Lusitania. From south-western France and northern Spain, they take to the sea, touching on Ireland and moving up through the primeval forests of Britain, right up into Caledonia. They live in caves and hollows, use stone (Old Stone, paleolithic) implements, hunt, fish and gather wild fruits and grains. They have no domestic animals, no agriculture, no pottery. Later, about 10,000 years BC, comes another wave of people, with domestic animals this time, also pots and urns and implements of polished stone (New Stone, neolithic). They live in caves and huts, or build lake-dwellings (crannogs). They also raise up stones and build stone circles.

According to my informant of the time, these peoples, paleolithic and neolithic, were the basis of the Pictish tribes that roamed Scotland before the arrival of the Scots, that is, the Gaelic Celts. After the Gaels had conquered Ireland in the sixth century BC (sending the Tuatha de Danaan underground) and thereafter parts of Wales and Scotland, there was a two-way cultural influence between them and the pre-Celtic aboriginals. The latter absorbed Gaelic elements and became Celticised, while the Gaels were more than a little in awe of the earlier inhabitants, whom they considered as possessing the secrets of nature, in particular their wise men, the druids. The traditional picture of these is of rather solemn white-toga'd gentlemen cutting mistletoe in portentous oak woods with a golden sickle. But in fact they were probably closer to the medicine-men of the American Indians or the *angegok* of the Eskimo, dressed in animal skins and with bird-caps on their heads. There's an old Hebridean tale which speaks of the arrival in Lewis of those who set up the standing stones: 'Once there was a king who was also a holy priest. He came to Lewis with many ships and on the ships were lesser priests and great stones and dark men to handle them. *The holy man wore robes made of the skins and feathers of birds*' (my italics).

The Gaels themselves had nothing like these druids. The Celtic institutions were Indo-European, like, say, the Vedic society of India, with priest king and official poets to remember genealogies and compose eulogies. But the shamanising Druids attracted the Gaels as much as did the beauty of the Pictish women, and perhaps also the independence which was theirs in the pre-Celtic matriarchal society. Both these elements were a force of change in Celtic culture. The women countered the brutality of the Celt, while Druid practice instilled in the culture a sense of naturalism. Both these forces of change met with resistance. The Druids in particular were anathema both to the official poets of the Gaels and, later, to the Christian missionaries.

Leaving the official poets and the Christians, let's come back to the druid-shaman and the Pictish tribesmen. They resisted Celticisation longest in Scotland north of the Grampians, so that this area became the centre for druidic studies.

Right through Irish literature, we hear of men being sent to Scotland for instruction. In the old Irish text *The Talk of the Two Scholars (Imacallan in da thuarad)*, for example, we hear of one Nede, son of Adnae. This Adnae was, in Ireland, an *ollamh*, that is, a head-man in science and poetry, but it was to Scotland that he sent his son for learning. In addition to amassing knowledge, Nede spent a great deal of his time walking by the edge of the sea ('for the shore was always a place of revelation for the poets') as a kind of meditation exercise. Here's how Nede speaks of the 'complete way' he was following:

> I am a son of poetry, and poetry is the son of reflexion, and reflexion is the daughter of meditation, and meditation is the daughter of science, and research is the daughter of the great learning, and great learning is the daughter of great intelligence, and great intelligence is the daughter of understanding, and understanding is the daughter of wisdom, and wisdom is the daughter of the three gods of Dana.

6.

The Greeks had wind of something wild and weird going on out there in the West:

Opposite to the coast of Celtic Gaul [writes Hecateus of Abdera, fourth century BC, a pupil of Pyrrho the Sceptic and philosopher at the court of Ptolemy] there is an island in the Ocean, not smaller than Sicily, lying to the north. It is inhabited by the Hyperboreans, so called because they dwell 'beyond the North wind'. The inhabitants venerate Apollo more than any other god. They have a remarkable temple to Apollo, of a round form, adorned with many consecrated gifts. There is also a city, sacred to the same god, most of the inhabitants of which are harpers. The Hyperboreans speak a strange tongue and have a remarkable attachment to the Greeks, especially to the Athenians and the people of Delos, saying this friendship goes back to ancient times.

References to the Hyperboreans abound in Greek literature, from Homer and Hesiod right up to Pindar, Strabo and Diodorus of Sicily. Plutarch refers to the island of Britain and to the islands off its coastline, saying several of them 'bear the names of demons'. More than one Greek or Phenician sailor – one thinks mainly, of course, of Pytheas of Marseilles – must have ventured out beyond the pillars of Hercules in order to explore that other world, the world of that god the Greeks called the Hyperborean Apollo (was it Belenos?). An archaic and labyrinthine mind such as Pindar, however much attached he was to Athens (writing it, archaically, *Athânes*) and Delphi, nevertheless had an eye towards the Hyperborean world, as well as to the 'nomad Scythians' and the wide spaces of Asia: 'Heart of mine, towards what distant cape are you leading my steps?'

The Romans, too, at least some of them, were able to think of something other then imperial triumphs and military occupation. Julius Solinus evokes the 'island of the Silurians', which he describes as being separated by a narrow firth from the 'coast that is in the hands of the Dumnonii' (that part of Britain I lived in was inhabited at one time by the Dumnonii; they gave their name to the town of Dunoon, a favourite holiday resort for Glaswegians).

In AD 306, Constantius Chlorius made an expedition to North Britain, among the Picts and Caledonians. An anonymous orator delivered a panegyric on him in the presence of the emperor

Constantine, and the following passage indicates the general
fascination in the Greco-Roman world for the North and its
'eternal light':

> It was not British trophies that he sought, as was generally
> supposed. But at the moment when the gods were already
> summoning him, he advanced towards the uttermost limits
> of the world. The man who accomplished such a prodigious
> exploit was not dreaming of conquests. Fulfilling a plan
> which he had revealed to none, he went to gaze upon the
> Ocean. Before enjoying life eternal, he wished to see, while
> still on earth, the light that never dies.

It would be possible to pursue these references. But enough of
Athens. Let's go to Delphi where, as Heraclitus says, the oracle
does not talk, therefore cannot lie, but shows by signs. What kind
of signs in the present instance? Well, when in Greece, do
geometry.

If you draw a line on the map between Delphi and Athens (the
temple of Athena at Delphi is next to that of Apollo) and continue it, you hit Delos, where the Hyperboreans, according to the
legend, sent girls as worshippers of Apollo (were they temple
prostitutes?) Now, if Apollo was supposed to have come from
the North, from among the Hyperboreans, he was also supposed
to have come from Crete, Mount Ida being the reputed birthplace
of Zeus, of whom Apollo was the 'dauphin' – the dolphin was
sacred to him. What connection between Crete and the Hyperboreans? If, continuing with your geometry, you connect Delphi
to Athens, and Athens to Tegee, where there was an important
sanctuary to Athena, you get an equilateral triangle. A rough
centering of this triangle, on the line from Delphi to Mount Ida,
gives you Corinth, where there was a temple to Apollo, and if,
from Corinth, you draw a line parallel to the line Delphi-Athens-
Delos, you hit, eureka! Leucade, the White Rock. Because the
sun god seemed to die there every day, Leucade was dedicated to
Apollo and part of the ceremonies enacted there consisted in
priests jumping suicidally off the rock into the sea. Now (pursu-
ing our logic . . .), if the high white cliffs of Leucade in western
Greece seemed to be the point where the sun god died, would not
further explorations west discover that there were more white
cliffs over there, thus pushing Apollo's death-place further out?

And as the explorers sailed further up the shores of this white-cliffed island in the ocean, would they not come finally to regions of midnight sun where the sun never died at all? And would not that be a good reason for placing there, rather than in Crete, or at least as well as in Crete, the birthplace of Apollo?

But if we may have found what connects Cretan-born Apollo with Hyperborean Britain, it looks from the old texts as if the myth of the Hyperboreans may have antedated the actual Greek discovery of Britain, so we still have to find the source of the Hyperborean myth itself.

7.

To the Egyptians, the Greeks were ignoramuses. We recall what Solon heard from the lips of the Egyptian priest: 'You Greeks are like children. You think you are very knowledgeable, but you know nothing of the history of the world'. According to Egyptian tradition, the first dynasties originated in a race out of the West, the *Shemsu Haru* (the Companions of Horus). They were guided to Egypt by the dark god, Osiris, who was the 'original inhabitant of the Western Lands' and king of 'the Fields of Yalu' situated in the extreme-West. The Egyptian funeral rite contained the formula 'to the West' and implied the crossing of water in 'the ark of the sun'. In certain other Egyptian traditions, the Fields of Peace (*Sekhet Heteb*) are situated in the North.

In India also we find a Hyperborean myth. The sacred mountain, Mount Meru, lies to the North, and there is a tradition relating to a northern people, the Men of the Northern Continent (*uttarakurudvipa*), who live according to nature, without laws. This 'anarcho-atopian' tradition is not incompatible with the origins of the Indo-Europeans, who moved southwards down into India via the Iranian plateau. But is it possible to go even further and posit the existence of some great Hyperborean or Atlantean culture in the Arctic, destroyed by a tremendous flood that left no trace except vaguely in people's memories? This might account for the existence of the myth in so many diverse cultures. Plato himself, the man who wanted, as he says in *The Sophist*, to 'tell no tales', thought it useful, at least in the bygoing.

Whether or not we speak of some lost Atlantis (and I certainly wouldn't be one to harp on it), there is, or was, in the arctic and sub-arctic area, a culture of which we can find traces among the Amerindians, the Eskimo, the Siberians, the northern Japanese – and the Celts, which was of far-reaching influence. It is characterised by naturalism and shamanism. If it came to be associated, in historical times, with the Celts, its origins are further back: it is not only pre-Celtic, it is non-Aryan, non-Indo-European.

It is possible that the pre-paleolithic aboriginals of the British Isles belonged to those great Hyperborean tribes which dominated north-western Europe long before the first Indo-European set foot there. Speaking before the Anthropological Society of Vienna in 1907, Julius Pokorny said that in the population of Ireland he saw traces of a northern race probably related to the Lapps, the Finns and the Samoyeds. Alexandre Bertrand (*La religion des Gaulois*, Paris, 1897) had a similar theory. According to him, before the Celtic period there was frequent contact between the inhabitants of Gaul and the northern world. These 'French' aboriginals he refers to by the term 'Touranian', which includes the Scythians. The religion of these aboriginals was, to quote Bertrand, 'the shamanism of the boreal lands'. Now, the word Scyth sounds close to the word Scot, and we know that western Scythians and eastern Celts were in close contact. What Rice says of the Scythians could also apply to the Celts: 'The Scythians were not primarily sensualists; rather were they realists for whom the abstract and the sinuous had an irresistible appeal.'

Whatever be the various strands, they all came together to make the cultural texture of pre-Christian Britain. In the *Book of the Dun Cow*, we read: 'The demonic power was great before the faith'. In that demonic power we can recognise shamanism. Much more than sorcery and witchcraft, which is the degenerate state of shamanistic naturalism, much more than demonology, the world of the *daimon*. It is this *daimon* (extravagant poetic energy) that we carry in our archaic bones, however much the rest of our bodies has been civilised and bemoralised. It breaks out now and then, in a William Blake, a D. H. Lawrence, an Artaud, a Delteil. In fact it's possible to see at a glance writers in whom the archaic root can still flourish and others who do no more than manipulate counters in an impoverished context.

8.

The last century or so, while seeing a massive increase of one-dimensional Man, has also seen various more or less desperate attempts to get back to the archaic ground and make a new start from there. The most significant of these attempts, both for scope of vision and vigour of thought, was that of Nietzsche. The essential text remains for me the one we come across in the first pages of the *Antichrist*:

> We are Hyperboreans. We know very well in what remote-ness we live. 'Neither by land nor by sea will you find the way to the Hyperboreans' – already Pindar knew that. Beyond the North, beyond the ice, beyond death itself lies *our* life, *our* happiness. We rediscovered happiness, we know the path, we found the way out of millenia of labyrinth. Who else found it? Modern man perhaps? 'I don't know whether I'm coming or going', moans modern man. We were mortally sick of that kind of modernity. Rather live amid the ice than among modern virtues and other South winds! We were courageous enough but for long we didn't know where to go with our courage. We had no way. But here now is the formula: a yes, a no, a straight line, an aim.

Rimbaud is to poetry what Nietzsche is to philosophy. Disgusted by the civilisational 'shit-pen' he sees around him, Rimbaud goes all out to recover what he calls his 'primitive state of a child of the sun'. If Nietzsche's happiest time was up in the Grisons where he was 'six thousand feet above humanity', Rimbaud was probably happiest when he made his long walks through the Ardennes, along 'the purple streams'. An early poem ('My Bohemia') shows him on those roads. It is in the first instance a humorous self-portrait: here comes the poet with poverty-stricken pants and there he is sitting at the side of the road using the elastics of his boots in place of a lyre and examining the 'soul' of his foot. But there is an exhilaration in it all that goes beyond self-irony and the need to kick out at the more phoney aspects of 'poetry'. At one point the humour takes on cosmic proportions, and that's where it becomes really interesting. Sleeping out under the stars, Rimbaud says his inn was 'at the sign of the Great Bear'. Why the Great Bear? First of all, Rimbaud certainly knew that his own 'Christian' (rather pagan) name, Arthur, was derived from that of the bear, *arth*. The same root is to be found in *Arcturus*, the northern star. As to the constellation of the Great Bear, it is situated close to the North Pole, and it was to just such an extreme 'Hyperborean' situation (the 'polar chaos' of the *Illuminations*) that Rimbaud's erratic journeys·in search of 'the place and the formula' were to lead. But we can go still further. If we remember what Heraclitus says of the Great Bear, that it is 'the boundary line of evening and morning', the Bear constellation appears as that twilight area between night and day, or between the unconscious and the conscious, which is the mental area from which so much of Rimbaud's hallucinatory writing proceeds. 'The domain of bright Zeus', to quote Heraclitus again, 'lies opposite the Bear'.

Surrealism continued Rimbaud on these lines. Here's André Breton writing from 'the petrified forest of human culture':

> I salute you from the petrified forest of human culture
> Where nothing has been left standing
> But where great gleaming fires whirl and prowl

Despite appearances that might make it seem to the superficial observer a purely modernistic phenomenon (and God knows for some who have a culinary conception of culture simply a new recipe for writing 'pomes'), surrealism was essentially an attempt to get back into the living forest, the archaic ground. Here's Breton again referring to the mental processes of 'primitive' Indians: 'There is no separation between the natural and the supernatural (the real and the surreal). No hiatus. One continuum'. But if he refers here to the Indians of North America, he was later to turn to the 'Indians' of Europe. Deploring in the Westerner 'a shameful repression of his past, owing to the "might is right" imperialism imposed nineteen centuries ago by the legions of Rome', Breton looked to Celtic art, seeing in it 'a distant light' as well as a cosmic consciousness in which the self was not separate from the world, in which animate and inanimate were conjoined, and he quotes Taliesin:

> I am the wind that blows over the sea
> I am a wave of the sea

> I am the roaring of the sea
> I am a bird on the sea-cliff . . .

From surrealism through Taliesin to John Cowper Powys is but a step (once the real perspectives have been opened up!), and from Powys to MacDiarmid is but a short step further. André Breton picking up grotesque lumps of rock from the bed of the river Lot is the same as old Powys laying his brow on a rock at the top of a Welsh hill, which again is the same as MacDiarmid, in his 'stony limits', reading Ifor Williams' *Canu Aneurin* 'in difficult days' and 'trying to see again in a stark winter wood'.

9.

To 'see again', which means both perspective and clarity of vision, is, at least for a start, to open up the whole northern circumpolar cultural complex which I have been trying to get at, erratically, and from various angles, throughout these pages. Since it may seem all too extravagant, it is good to have allies among the scientists. Here is the ethnologist Lévi-Strauss speaking in *Sad Tropics* (Plon, 1955):

> Today we are quite certain that communications between Alaska and the Aleutians on the one hand, Siberia on the other, were never interrupted. Although there was no knowledge of metallurgy, iron tools were being made in Alaska at the beginning of the Christian era. The same ceramics are to be found from the region of the Great Lakes to Central Siberia, likewise the same legends, the same rites, the same myths. While the West was closed in on itself, it seems that all the Northern peoples from Scandinavia to Labrador through Siberia and Canada kept up the closest contacts. If the Celts borrowed certain of their myths from this sub-arctic civilisation, of which we know practically nothing, it is easier to understand how the Graal cycle is closer to the myths of the Forest Indians of North America than to any other mythological system.

Exactly.

Over the years, I have come to see a connexion between Celtic naturalism, Eskimo vision, Siberian shamanism, Amerindian religion and Japanese Shinto continued into Zen. If I use various words here: naturalism, vision, shamanism, religion, Shinto, it is not because any of them is to be exclusively attached to its ethnic adjective (in fact they are practically interchangeable), it is simply to offer a congeries of words that give a basis to the word 'poetry' as I understand it. Without that basis, art, as Rimbaud said, is just tomfoolery.

I am not speaking of symbols, and I have no time for esoteric flapdoodle. I have referred to symbol systems, to religious institutions and to mythologies, but what I am ultimately concerned with is direct contact, immediate association, outwith system, institution, mythology. Which is why at the end of all these explorations I suggest we take a walk in the woods. Here is the sub-arctic forest as described by naturalists (F. Fraser Darling and J. Morton Boyd, *The Highlands and Islands*, Fontana, 1972):

> The birch woods are golden on the mountainsides in the Autumn sunshine and in Winter they are a purple-brown mist merging into the grey-green tops of the alders in the bottoms of the glens. In sparkling February sunshine the shadows of the exquisite tracery of branches are cast upon the mountain snows, showing the intertwined tracks of rabbit, hare, mouse, vole, roe, red deer, fox, badger, wild cat, otter, weasel and ermine. In the dripping thaw the woods look faded and impatient for the Spring, which comes suddenly in April with returning tits, warblers, wrens, thrushes, robins, pipits, finches and others. There is an extraordinary feeling of joy in being among the birches when the leaves are opening from the bud.

Confronted by scenes like these, I have often felt like the poet Saigyo standing in front of the Shinto sanctuary at Ise and saying:

> What it is
> that dwells here
> I know not
> but my heart
> is full of gratitude
> and my eyes brim with tears

But knowledge is possible. And the paths of this essay have, I hope, opened it up at least in part. I would say, in conclusion, that if this birch wood and its birds touches us so, it's because, ultimately, the birch is at the centre of Hyperborean culture. For the Siberian tribes, it's 'the forest girl'. The woman *par excellence* of all northern Eurasia is Diana, which is a latinisation of Tanaïs, the name of a Scythian goddess whose principal symbol is a birch tree in a clearing. References to the birchtree are frequent in Celtic poetry. The Welsh poet Dafydd ap Gwilym (fourteenth century) knows the erotic connotations ('the forest girl') when he chooses a birch-grove as a trysting place. So there is the tree, but there are also the birds. The old Scottish earth-goddess, the *Cailleach*, appears most often in the guise of a bird: crow, gull, cormorant or heron. The Irish expression for supreme knowledge is 'crow wisdom'. The Siberian shaman has bird symbols on his costume, and he fixes a bird's wings to the door of his cabin. The American Indian puts feather in his hair, and the fringes of his shirt symbolize wings. Like the Eskimo, he indicates a burial place by planting a post on the top of which he sets a bird's skeleton. In certain shaman ceremonies of the Altaï, the 'sky road' is represented by a line of trees (birches, of course) all surmounted by bird images. But the 'bird path' is also a Ch'an expression. In Ch'an Buddhism, to 'tread the bird path' means giving up all merely egoistic attachment and being open to 'original nature'.

I end this initial culture-analysis with the feeling that, even if as yet I don't have it absolutely all together, at least the elements are there, at least the groundings. Without such a ground and grounding (permitting developments that can go from the most concrete to the most abstract), the word 'culture' has no valid meaning at all.

3

A Shaman Dancing on the Glacier

When, at one point in the lead-up to the symposium, 'Burns, Beuys and Beyond – the figure of the artist in (modern) society', I was asked what was going to be the title of my lecture, the words 'A shaman dancing on the glacier' leaped in to my mind with all the inevitability of dictation from the subconscious. Which is another way of saying that my title may sound a bit surrealistic. I didn't understand it very well at first myself, but, as I worked away, I came to understand it more and more. A good part of what I have to say will consist in an attempt to demonstrate the relevance of that title in the context which is ours today.

I'm fairly certain I'm not the only one to have been fascinated by Mircea Eliade's book: *Shamanism – The Archaic Techniques of Ecstasy* (Payot, 1951). But maybe nobody read it with such a jolt of recognition as I did when I first came across it in Paris around 1959.

At that time I was living, quite spartanly, off a post-graduate scholarship from Glasgow University, working at a thesis (which I later abandoned), on 'Poetry and Politics', but mainly wandering around the streets and backstreets of Paris and writing bits and pieces that were later gathered into a book called *Incandescent Limbo*. I say 'bits and pieces' not in any pejorative sense. On the contrary. What later became *Incandescent Limbo* (it took me years to find a satisfactory shape) was written with no ready-made notion of what a book should be, with no preconception of unity. It consisted in random explorations of external reality (places, encounters, conversations), but also in explorations of inner reality (dreams and memories). And among the latter were a great many flashbacks to my childhood on the West Coast of Scotland.

35

When I was about eleven or twelve years old, I was much concerned with an area I called 'up the back'. This area took in about ten square miles of territory in Ayrshire, comprising field, wood, moor and hills. After a period of belonging to gangs, which was my introduction to politics, I was then entering a long period of isolation, and I was up to all kinds of solitary practices, all of which were connected with the territory I've just evoked. Before going into any interpretation, before trying to open up any perspectives, let me just describe them.

What marked, and still does, the North end of the village of Fairlie was a great outcrop of stone called the Craigie Rock. Up alongside this rock rose a winding path lined with hawthorn. I'd climb up that path till I came to a fence that really marked the beginning of the Territory. In one of the posts of that fence, in a slit in its wood, I'd inserted a bit of quartz – I'm eleven or twelve years old, remember – and before I entered the Territory I had to get myself ready for it by concentrating at that point, with my hand on the piece of quartz, counting out four sequences of sixteen, which was the most complete figure I could think of. Once into the Territory, after that little piece of ritual, I had all kinds of possibilities open before me.

A lot of my time was spent in just standing and staring, or in a meditative kind of wandering. But I'd also take in a lot of particular objects and occasions. There would be the animals: complacent cattle, solemn horses, maybe some plodding, determined hedgehog. But there were mainly birds: first of all the gulls circling and caterwauling round the cowp; hordes of crows in a sycamore wood; and, in a beech copse farther up, a band of heron – in spring, the ground would be strewn with broken pale-blue shells, blood-smeared, smelling of the sea. I'd done a lot of what we used to call 'nature study' in earlier years, and there was still an element of this in my habits, but something more ancient, more archaic, more radical, seemed to have taken over. This manifested itself in a fascination with bones, skeletons, skulls (of animals and birds) that I picked up in the fields, in the woods and on the moors. And in something that might better be called ornithomania than ornithology: I remember, at nights, 'talking' with owls, whose cry I imitated not too badly – my attempts at least aroused response (I did the same thing with seals on the shore). I had favourite places too: a certain clump of birch, a rock on the moor, where I felt some kind of special concentration. And I had some rather special practices. One consisted in stripping down and standing for a pretty long stretch of time under a waterfall. And I had chosen trees with conveniently shaped branches where I undertook something that Sigmund Freud, had he known of it, might have called arboreal masturbation. I'd climb up the tree to my 'climax' branch and there enjoy an ejaculation that opened out on to a contemplation of space: the blue-green Firth of Clyde, the Cumbraes, Arran, Kintyre. At other times, I might guddle for trout in the Glen burn, but mostly I'd just be watching the water, almost hypnotised by its ripple, whirl and flow. And there'd be the moor: the wind and the emptiness. There was a long stretch of it leading up to the Kaim, a great mass of frontal moraine marking the termination of some quaternary glacier. In winter as I tramped towards it, I loved to watch the snow smooring off its heights. And up there, made from the rubble of stone, I had a hut. In the beginning, in that hut, I had a mirror, a length of red thread and nine pebbles. I had no definite idea as to the purposes of those items, I just liked to have them there – till I threw them away one day as no longer necessary to me, mere encumbrances.

This is where Mircea Eliade's *Shamanism – the archaic techniques of ecstasy* comes in.

As I read through that book, I came across more and more correspondences between what he was laying out and my own early experience. In other words, I realised I had stumbled on to shamanism, had practised a kind of home-made shamanism, that is, an immemorial tradition going back to neolithic, paleolithic and prelithic times, elements of which can be found all over the world, from Siberia to Australia via the Americas and Oceania. This isn't really so surprising as it may sound. It's almost certain that, given enough scope, enough freedom, a child will go through all the past phases of humanity, from fishes to philosophers.

Let me give a few concrete examples, to corroborate what I've just been claiming, and to lead us farther into the field (the field of feeling, technique and symbol) of shamanism. Eliade tells, for example, how, among the Buryats of Siberia, the shaman will sit by a sick person, beside him an arrow from the head of which a red thread leads to a birch tree outside – it is along this thread, along this life-line, that the soul of the sick man will come back

into his body. So much for the red thread. Likewise, to purify and
fortify himself, the ancient practitioner of Shinto stood under
waterfalls. And while we're in this therapeutic context, let's
mention the fact that in his 'bundle', the American medicine-
man will have pieces of quartz or rock-crystal. But beyond
medical or magical therapeutics, I was much more interested
in the general cosmology. It must never be forgotten that if the
shaman is a 'medicine-man', concerned with individual sick-
nesses and collective problems in the tribe, he also practises
simply 'for joy'. What the shaman, or the 'dawn-man', as the
Ojibwa call him, is out for, is an ecstasy (getting outside one's self
as well as outside history), and a de-conditioning. Starting out
from a reduction (renunciation of social identity, etc. – he is in
fact invited to see himself reduced to his bones), the shaman
achieves a transcendence, a capacity for experiencing (and also
expressing) total life. By separating himself, at least temporarily,
from the community (and to a certain extent he always remains
outside), the shaman comes to know an identity larger than the
one coded in the community, and it is precisely this which
enables him to do the greatest good to the community, by giving
it breathing space. If the shaman imitates the movements and
voices of animals and birds (I recall my owls and seals), it's in
order to learn the language of the whole of nature, this desire for
complete language leading eventually to the practice of incanta-
tion (providing enchantment) and/or the development of a jargon
(the language of the *jars*, that is, the wild duck).

The total experience of the earth is also a *luminous* experience,
which is to say that it is uranian as well as telluric. The uranian
and the telluric may be represented by deities: Mother of the
Animals, Supreme Sky Being, but they may also be de-theolo-
gised, if I may say so, and reduced to 'white light' (*ak ajas*, among
the Altaï Tatars), or 'the girl of the forest', the birch tree. It's with
the 'forest-girl' that the sexual element comes in, sexual relation-
ships with 'the powers', outside the reproductive (family-domes-
tic) chain, being part of the shaman thing. As to the light
elements, it's there right at the inception of the shaman's career
when, in certain ceremonies, pieces of quartz or rock crystal (i.e.
sky-stones, stones of light, solidified light) are actually thrust into
his body (as I thrust my bit of quartz into the post). Another sign
that the shaman is now indeed recognised as a shaman is the

erection of a post, surmounted by a bird-sign, outside his house. This is the sign (the totem, if you like) that he is able to undertake the metapsychical journey that will take him from hell (the kingdom of the dead, the land of shades) to heaven (the land of supreme potentiality) and all over the earth.

A whole mystic geography, cosmic topography is involved. In ceremonies, in symbolic performances, this metapsychical journey may begin with the shaman climbing up a birch-tree (nine degrees or stages will have been marked on it) till he 'flies off'. In this performance and in others similar, he will sometimes be 'helped off' by hallucinogenics, but mostly simply by drumming, dancing and leaping. Performances apart (it's there, obviously that charlatanry and trickery plays its role – trickery willingly accepted by the onlookers, via a kind of willing suspension of disbelief), what gives the shaman his inner power is a sense of connection, and what enables him to give 'artistic' manifestation to this power-sense is his skill in body-movement and, above all, his voice, his words. To give just one example of these, here's an Eskimo poem illustrative of the ornithophany just evoked:

> The gull
> he who
> cleaves the air with his wings
> above our heads
> you gull up there
> steer down towards me
> your wings are red
> up there
> in the freshness
> *ayaya! ayaya!*

And to point out once more the correspondences between this ancient shamanism and my own early experience, here again are the first lines of the first poem I ever wrote to keep, 'Precentor Seagull':

> You up there
> in the lurching church of the elements
> mover and moved
> white as a ghost and fat
> as the paps of the dark earth-woman

with a squawk man in you
would waken wide if there was one
the sleeping gate to paradise
or the white world's thighs
give us the sound at least the note
the initial noise
and it's we will make the psalms we need
with whatever we know and are . . .

Let me just insist on the fact that I wrote 'Precentor Seagull' about fifteen years before I came across the Eskimo invocation.

Now, it may be thought that all this is very well, but that it is much too idiosyncratic to have any bearing whatsoever on Scottish literature, presumably what we're concerned with when there is mention, say of Robert Burns. I can well imagine, if not in the present enlightened company, at least in the near vicinity, cultivated citizens with, on their faces, that irony which is so often the veneer of an ingrown despair, who will be saying that, having always taken me for an outsider, they now know I'm also a throwback and that my exotic talk of Siberians and Amerindians, not to speak of Polynesians and Bushmen, while, of course, fascinating, has precious little relevance to the Scottish context, Scottish culture and identity. We all know what Scottish culture is, don't we? That mixture of common sense and sentimentality, of social realism and airy-fairy, of Gaelic piety and Lowland pawkiness, etc., etc. We all know about Scottish identity: porridge and the People's Friend and all the rest of it. And if you write ten neat lines in Lallans about the whooping-cough of your baby boy when you were on holiday in the Mearns, that is Scottish literature, is it not? I'm reminded at this point of a talk I did once in Edinburgh on the subject of Scottish culture, a lecture in which I suggested it needed both radical re-reading and enlargement of scope. After it, a woman came up to me and said: 'But I *like* my Scottish identity'. I said I liked mine too, but it wasn't the same one. She looked at me as if I had horns. So I'm back on the subject today, suggesting again the necessity of re-reading and enlargement. What I've been saying about shamanism, for example, seems to me to shed quite a lot of new light on our long-lost, long-caricatured and sentimentalised background.

Let's go right back into the Celtic past, to one of the finest pieces of Celtic archaelogy, the famous Gundestrup cauldron discovered only a few years back in a Danish peat bog. On it you see represented many figures, not all of which are easy to identify. But one of them is certainly the god Cernunnos, whom you see seated in a kind of yogic posture, horns on his head, a torque in one hand, a snake in the other, surrounded by animals, mainly deer. The Gundestrup cauldron probably stems from south-east Europe, and dates to about the first century before our era. Now, just compare the figure of Cernunnos on this cauldron with, say, a stone engraving (it's just come to my attention), made by an Eskimo woman at Baker Lake, North-West Territories, Canada, in 1971. The connection, I submit is obvious, the correspondences clear. Well, the Eskimo engraving is of an Inuit shaman surrounded by his auxiliaries, his familiar spirits. In other words, I am suggesting that the figure of Cernunnos, one of the most ancient and most central in the Celtic pantheon, is part of the shamanist tradition.

And what has this to do with art and literature? A great deal, I think. I suggest that the Cernunnos theme is continued in the mythology (and the literature) of Finn. The name of Finn himself means 'the white one' (as if he was a white shaman), but the names of his immediate family: Ossian, Oscar, are both con-nected with names for deer. It will be remembered too that the Companions of Finn had to abandon all clanic ties, that they had to be exceptional physically (excellent at running and leaping), and that they had to know by heart the twelve (essential) books of poetry. I suggest that something like this is a good basis for culture, a real basis for a (Scottish) literature: devoid of romantic sentimentality, Gaelic piety and Lowland reductiveness – a ground we lost long ago, which went subterranean.

Once this shamanist element is recognized, you can follow the line. It's there in the ballad of Thomas the Rhymer, which is the shaman's subterranean epiphany, as in, for example, the Yakut vision of the realm of the dead. It's there in 'Tam o' Shanter', which is an eighteenth-century remake of Thomas the Rhymer and which contains obvious shamanist elements: the visit to the dead, the passing of the bridge which means the move from one mode of being to another – but if 'Tam o' Shanter' has all the trappings, Tam doesn't make it. And Scottish literature wasn't going to make it, owing to the lack of an energy-field, for a long time afterwards.

One who felt the dearth of so-called Scottish culture, and the narrowness of so-called Scottish literature, at the beginning of this century, and who was out to change things, summed up his programme as 'back to Dunbar'! That was the Scottish Renaissance, but I don't think it's enough. What I'd say, for a start at least, is: 'Back to Finn', and that what we need is a wide-ranging *reconnaissance* as well as a new grounding. Back to Finn, and, via that figure, into that Hyperborean 'white world' from which, as Lévy-Strauss has shown, the Celts derived so much of their myth, and over to the Caucasus where, as Dumézil (Eliade's master) has suggested, Scot meets Scythian (there was a direct connection between Celtica and Iran via Bohemia and the Danube) and we open out on to the whole of the Eurasian steppe. Doing so, we will not be losing roots and identity, we will be extending them, enlarging them, recovering scope and energies, able to apply them within any specific socio-cultural context, for example, the one now called Scotland.

Let me make it quite clear (caricatures are so facile – and so reassuring), I am not advocating any kind of neo-shamanism, to be practised in and around Glastonbury or Glasgow. I am speaking of a *basis*, and a basis on which all kinds of *developments* are possible. Even within the specific context of shamanism, election is followed by instruction, the ecstatic is followed by the didactic. I'd extend that on to a larger scale. On the basis of this fundamental experience (it's the *experience* I advocate, not the imitation of forms), let us both expand and intensify – into, for example, ecology and philosophy and poetics and politics (that way, we may get depth ecology, lightning philosophy, live poetics and, who knows, even enlightened cultural politics). This has already happened in the history of world culture. The rock crystal in the shaman's body becomes the 'diamond body' of tantric Buddhism. The 'bird path' of the shaman, which was originally a line of bird-crested birchtrees, becomes the 'bird path' of Zen (the trajectory of the non-ego self) – even before that, the Rig Veda says 'intelligence is the bird that flies fastest', the *Panîaviṃa Brahmana* says 'he who understands has wings', and in Taoism, the Tao-man is called 'the feathered host'. As to Boehme, the man of 'the morning redness in the sky', he speaks of 'the bird language' universally forgotten. To continue on these lines, Zoroaster was almost certainly a shaman in the Iranian tradition, so that when the shaman-philosopher Nietzsche chose to use his name in the title of one of his key-books, *Thus spake Zarathustra*, he was working on a sure intuition: 'We are Hyperboreans, we are well aware in what remoteness we live . . . Beyond the ice and snow lies our life, our happiness'. In general, throughout all this there is the fundamental notion that if Man is Man-in-history (and God knows if Scotland from Scott on has lived on that), he is also, and more radically, Man-in-the-cosmos. Certainly, history always creeps in, but the need to leap out of it is what renews it, gives it fresh impetus. And I suggest that some such move as I am describing is necessary for art to get beyond the merely socio-personal and the mere juggling with ciphers or forms, all sorts of trifling non-entity, to become what it always is potentially: mind-expanding, world-forming.

I come now to Joseph Beuys.

It was in Basel that I first saw a sculpture, or rather an installation, by Beuys. It consisted of a heap of grey felt and a scattering of withered branches. I don't remember what it was called. Maybe, 'November'; maybe 'The Shaman was here', or maybe 'The Day after Postmodernism'. What I do remember is that on the ground floor of the Modern Art Museum I'd been both bored and irritated by a temporary exhibition full of pathology, craftiness and inanity. Up there on the top floor, in that room, there was just this bit of thing, where craft had no part at all. It was a mixture of brute physical presence and intellectual idea. I'd been glad to get rid of the noise and garishness downstairs. Here was nothing but grey felt, and wintry branches – pointing to something, opening on to something, inviting one to enter into a space . . . I was interested. Interested enough to want to know more. The more I got to know, the more I was convinced here was someone who had a grasp of the matter, the whole matter.

If we consider the German cultural force-field in the last couple of centuries, certain figures come to mind: Goethe, of course (especially, from our point of view here, in his essays); Schiller with his notion of 'æsthetic education'; Hölderlin with his 'free use of the national'; Nietzsche with his forceful and clairvoyant move through nihilism; Benn with his *provoziertes Leben* (provoked living) . . . There has been no strong poetic

figure since. But in art, in the culture-field in general, there has
been Beuys.

Beuys was born in that dune and marsh country where the
Rhine and the Maas come together, in the district of Nordheim,
at Cleves – just across the Dutch Border from Nijmegen, roughly
on a line with Rotterdam. It is an area in which borders are
effaced, a territory crossed and recrossed by all manner of
peoples, a landscape that seems to have maintained some linea-
ments of an archaic past. 'I had a very close relationship to the
Lower Rhine landscape', says Beuys of his childhood, which
appears also to have been extremely imaginative, bringing in
games concerning 'Stagleader' or 'Genghis Khan's Grave' that
have to do with early readings, perhaps a collective unconscious,
and a sense of space. Those games concerning myth images gave
way in time to nature study:

> Then came the interest in plants and botany which has
> stayed with me all my life. It started as a kind of catalo-
> guing of everything that grew in the area, all noted in
> exercise books. We would go off hunting for anything we
> could find, then build tents from rags and bits of material
> so we could show our collections. There was everything
> from beetles, mice, rats, frogs, fish and flies to old farmyard
> machines or anything technical we could get our hands on.

This again developed, when Beuys built himself a laboratory at
home and later undertook scientific studies at the University of
Posen. He might have ended up a pure scientist but for a
realisation that came to him during the course of a lecture in
1943: 'I experienced it as a vivid shock in the middle of a lecture
on amoebae by a professor who had spent his whole life
pondering a couple of fuzzy images of single cells somewhere
between plant and animal structure. It gave me such a fright I
said: "No, that's not my idea of science".' He would, then, not be
a scientist, but an interest in growth processes, growth patterns
would remain with him throughout his life, coming together with
other elements to produce something *sui generis*.

The date 1943 gives us the historical context and a reminder of
the ideological indoctrination any German mind was then subjected to. This mainly centred round Nordic mythology – a
subject which ever since has been taboo, leaving a blank in the

cultural process and hence in mental development. Thanks largely to an enlightened teacher, and to his own interests, Beuys's reading of this mythology was different from that of national-socialist ideology. In fact, what he saw through it was shamanism. Think of the *Yuglinga Saga* and what it says of Odin (Odin with his two crows: Huginn, thought, and Muninn, memory), that 'sleeping, his body became a bird or an animal, a fish or a dragon and travelled to distant lands', and the connection is obvious. Think of the story of Hadingus in the *Historica Danica* by Saxo Grammaticus, how he's at dinner when a woman appears and invites him to follow her underground, where they cross a dark, wet region, a river and a bridge . . . It's the shaman's trip, it's 'Thomas the Rhymer' and all the rest. But there was more, and even closer. Rising above the town of Cleves was the Schwanenburg, a castle surmounted by the figure of a swan. 'I always had the swan before my eyes', says Beuys. Now, as Mullenhoff points out in his *Deutsche Altertumskunde*, d'Arbois de Jubainville in his *Les Premiers habitants de l'Europe* and Déchelette in his *Manuel d'archéologie préhistorique*, to mention only three of the classics in this field, the swan cult is one of the oldest cults in Europe, with a very strong poetic tradition that goes, so far as well-known names are concerned, from Hesiod, who has the swan cry out 'on the edge of the ocean' right up to Yeats, with his 'wild swans at Coole'. Beuys was later to look for ways to express his own relationship to swan, as well as to stag, hare and other animals: 'The figures of the horse, the stag, the swan and the hare constantly come and go – figures which pass freely from one level of existence to another'.

Once again, let me insist, I am not advocating any overt mythologising art, nor suggesting that Beuys was open to any such temptation. What I see in him is something I evoked with regard to my own experience: the connection with an archaic tradition, allied to an anarchic use of it – let's say an *abstract* shamanism, away outside any antiquarian reproduction. Beuys is quite clear about it: 'I take this form of ancient behaviour as the idea of transformation through concrete processes of life, nature and history. My intention is obviously not to return to such earlier cultures but to stress the idea of substance and transformation . . . the deepest root of the idea of spiritual life, deeper than the mythological level.' And he stresses the necessity of a kind of *gai savoir*, rather than any solemn mythologism in the handling of this material, speaking of an understanding of life that is 'expansive enough to project beyond personal problems and feel a kind of Homeric laughter running through the whole structure of life and natural powers'.

So, on a shamanistic basis, partly intuitive, partly learned, Beuys worked out a practice for the modern situation comprising theory, education and negotiation: 'I need an educational concept. I need a theory of perception, and I must negotiate. Those three things belong under one roof'. This practice was political in the large sense, while overflowing normal political stances, and it was artistic, while going outside anything like the history of art and the normal art-scene: 'I could not find a starting point in art history'. So this kind of artist will go back to chaos, outside any system of rules, and he'll use materials not usually associated with art, in order to transform 'cultural life as a whole'. If I don't think all of Beuys's artefacts or performances work, I am very much in sympathy with the whole enterprise. I like his vocabulary (at least a lot of it): 'threshold-signs'; 'a new energy field'. And I like his titles ("I really do need the spoken language"): From the Intelligence of the Swans, In the House of the Shaman, Eurasia.

When Beuys came to Scotland in 1971, he was imbued with an interest in Scotland's pre-Renaissance culture, an attraction to a landscape he considered as 'the last European wilderness', and the intention of producing a total art work. That work came to be entitled 'Celtic Kinloch Rannoch, the Scottish Symphony'. It is not one of his best titles (surely simply 'Rannoch Moor – a symphony' would have been much better), and it is probably not one of his best works. When it was finally mounted in a large studio in Edinburgh College of Art, it consisted of a 16-mm film of the moor projected on to a 25-foot long wall. In front of this stood a piano, that was never played; a microphone into which Beuys occasionally made unsemantic noises; an axe and some planks; a metal tray with lumps of gelatine; two tape recorders; a blackboard on which Beuys made drawings, all subsequently erased. This nomenclature no doubt sounds ludicrous, and I don't think the work in any way reached the wished-for coherence. This is the risk of performance, perhaps its limit, perhaps even its impossibility. But what interests me is the *idea*, the conception: the attempt to achieve a total experience, a total expression of Rannoch Moor

All this leads me up to my glacier.

Beuys's choice of Rannoch Moor was singularly felicitous. This bleak plateau was where the last ice sheet to cover Scotland began to develop about 25,000 years ago and where it died away about 10,000 years ago. You have to imagine snow piling up on this granite floor, piling up and turning into ice, till the ice formed a glacier 3,600 feet deep near Glen Coe that moved north-east into the Spey basin, south into the Firth of Clyde, westward to the Hebrides. Now, a glacier is one of the greatest geomorphic (land-transforming) powers there is, and if it is no longer believed that this quaternary ice-sheet deeply changed the *structure* of Scotland, already laid down in tertiary times, signs of its grinding and erosion are everywhere on Rannoch Moor, that highly irregular surface with its profusion of lochans and its innumerable hummocks of what were glacial debris.

There is, then, the spectacular scenery itself. But there is more. From the plateau of Rannoch Moor, you plunge down into Glen Coe, and Glen Coe is *the* resting place in Scotland of the companions of Finn earlier mentioned as bearers of a shaman tradition – on every summit there, one of them is supposed to be lying asleep, and the wind of the heights is their breath. That is the legend, and it is not without grandeur. But we can try to read *back beyond the legend*.

What I suggest is that shamanism began when man began moving over the earth after the retreat of the last glacier. He is on the hunt for animals, but it is with reverence, and he has great awe of the glacier, remains of which still lie up there on the heights – the original 'white goddess'? I can't prove this, it's only an intuition, but I can cite two instances, both from America, that maybe give me some kind of corroboration. One concerns Tsimshian mythology, in which a clear distinction is made between fictions and stories called *adaorh* that carry tribal memory of actual movements, events and figures. In these *adaorh*, frequent mention is made of glaciers, notably the Stikine Glacier, and one story in particular tells how the ancestors of the Wolf Clan passed under one of its last ice-bridges . . . So much for the North Pacific Coast. The other instance concerns Arawak

Indians down in Columbia. When the anarcho-geographer Elisée Reclus visited Columbia (then New Granada) about a hundred years ago, he was out to explore the Sierra Nevada de Santa Marta. At a little pueblo called San Miguel, he saw Arawak shamans facing the glacier lit up by the setting sun and celebrating the mountain goddess . . .

Again, I am not suggesting that we celebrate any mountain goddess. I am suggesting that we try and get back an earth-sense, a ground sense, and a freshness of the world such as those men, those Finn-men, knew when they moved over an earth from which the ice had just recently receded.

This is the dawn of geopoetics.

4

'Tam o' Shanter': A New Reading

'Tam o' Shanter' has generally been considered as a convivial and boisterous piece of comic realism, an extravagant fantasia, to which readers can abandon themselves with relish and with no thought as to ulterior meaning. It is only when we realise the possible overtones of the word 'Shanter' that the 'witch-story' takes on new dimensions, and a closer reading becomes imperative.

It is known that Burns derived the word from the name of a farm. But let readers once look on it with linguistic imagination and even a modicum of poetic thought, and it will become involved in their minds with other words: *chanter*, *chantre*, *shanty*. It then becomes evident (or, for the moment, highly possible) that the title of the poem means something like: Tom of the Chanter, Tom the Singer, Tom the Poet.

The first thesis of this essay, then, is that, far from being a mere tale, 'Tam o' Shanter' must be read as a poetic odyssey, the approach of an eighteenth-century Scottish poet to the fundamental theme of poetry, which goes back to the psycho-cosmic journey of the shaman.

The secondary thesis is that, as an exploration of this traditional theme, 'Tam o' Shanter' stands in intimate relationship to the thirteenth-century ballad of 'Thomas the Rhymer'; is, in fact, the eighteenth-century version of the old ballad, deriving from the same sources, parallel in situation and content, though differing (for historical reasons) in æsthetic, morality and perspective.

In the ballad 'Thomas the Rhymer', pagan transnaturalism and Christian supernaturalism come together to produce a poem of a distant eeriness. While in the eighteenth-century poem (apart from obvious Gothic horror laid on with humour) the keynote is homely presence. Whereas, too, the ballad is built up on symbolic conventions, realistic detail is the mainstay of Burns's poem; in fact, the 'meaning' is almost completely immersed in it, so much so that thousands of readers have been able to accept is as a mere yarn, or a *genre* painting. That the overtones are there is, however, indubitable, as I shall try to show.

All this is by no means to suggest that Burns was writing consciously a symbolist poem, or even knew he was echoing the ballad. What I'm suggesting is that Robert Burns was so immersed in the folk-lore, poetry, song and legend of early Christian and pagan Scotland, that he could not help reflecting it whenever he was writing with inspiration.

The ballad plunges straight into its story:

> True Thomas lay on Huntlie bank,
> A ferlie he spied wi' his e'e.

But in the eighteenth-century poem, we are treated to a long prologue, painting the picture of a country town at evening, the domestic life of Tam, and his character as seen by his wife. Where, then, we know nothing of Thomas the Rhymer, bar that he is 'true', 'a rhymer' and is lying on Huntlie Bank – the man has no history, exists in a timeless presence, only one adjective of quality to 'label' him, and that rather a tribute to his trade, or a secret sign of allegiance, than any reference to his character – Tam is there in a full psycho-social context. He is married, he has a 'hame, where sits our sulky sullen dame', the very personification of moral righteousness. Tam is honest, too, indeed he is a man after Robert Burns' own heart, for whom the 'honest man' was the ideal of humanity. But Tam is not only 'honest', he is weighed down with a whole load of qualities, the sum-total of another's opinion of him:

> a skellum,
> A blethering, blustering, drunken blellum.

The only hope, with this body of carping judgement about him, that Tam (in this a representation of the reformed, strait-jacketed Scot) has of the 'timeless presence' I mentioned as being the privilege of Thomas the Rhymer, is, quite simply, to get drunk. Which he does, roaringly.

The prologue ends with the prophecy of Tam's wife: that this

immoral and irreligious rascal will be 'deep drown'd in Doon', or
'catch'd wi' warlocks in the mirk, / By Alloway's auld, haunted
kirk'.

The scene is laid, the threat is in the air, the suspense is on.

We are now given a picture of one particular night, a night of
comradeship at the inn, with a blazing fire, songs, talk, ale and a
woman – in short, Burns's earthly paradise (compare the anar-
chistic revels of the 'jolly beggars' at Poosie Nansie's). But the
dream, or illusion of social pleasure and freedom is short-lived:

> The hour approaches Tam maun ride.

It is twelve o'clock, 'o' night's black arch the key-stane'. This
'key-stane' we will meet again, in a more concrete form. The
whole central part of the poem takes place between two limits of
time and place: the key-stone of the night, and the key-stone of
the bridge.

From the time we leave the inn to the time he crosses the bridge
and returns to the safety (and the ills) of his home, Tam is on his
own. But in fact he is not alone, or at least, 'he is never less alone
than when alone'. The whole of Scotland, reflected in his sub-
consciousness, is with him.

Robert Burns is now riding into his deepest mindscape.

As is appropriate, at its very entrance stands the Deil, with
whom Robert Burns felt many affinities: indeed, the Deil was as
much a brother to the poet Burns as Soutar Johnnie was to Tam.
But Burns the man was somewhat wary of this affinity, dared not
openly avow the relationship. Burns the Exciseman, despite his
song, could not *afford* to dance away with the Deil. His
conscience (rationality, morality, sentimentality) would not let
him. Unlike True Thomas'–

> That weird shall never danton me

– he did not care to venture into the deep region, except in terms
of public devil-may-care swashbuckling, or when in drink.

That Burns often approached the personal catastrophe is
obvious from his biography – and from this poem. That he
dodged it, leaving behind only the tail of his horse, is also shown
in this work.

But let us enter with him now the dangerous territory.

Tam's horse is a 'gray mare', which suggests that the ride is no ordinary one. We are in the region of the 'dark gods', the collective unconscious, the land of Magog, the Earth-Mother (the whole West Coast of Scotland is, or was, rich with her presence, the Paps of Jura being her breasts). White-grey horses were always associated with her. She ruled the storms:

> The wind blew as 'twad blawn its last.

What we have now is a coalescence of all the poetry and myth of Scotland, a pouring forth of all that the fertile mind of Burns had in store. Beyond Christianity and social morality we penetrate into an archaic region. Is it a coincidence? Several of the hills, rounded, breast-like hills to be found in Ayrshire and Kintyre, were called *Meg's* or *Mag's Hill* – Meg, the name of Tam o' Shanter's mare.

> Tam skelpit on thro' dub and mire,
> Despising wind, and rain, and fire.

We are in Beltane country (Bel – god of the powers of nature) where the 'guid blue bonnet' and even the 'auld Scots sonnet' have little significance.

We pass the ford where the pedlar was smothered, the birch tree (grey) and the great Stone (the Cailleach, Scottish name of the Earth-Mother, could turn herself into a stone). From the scene where drunken Charlie broke his neck, we pass the gorse bush and the cairn (a seat of the Cailleach?), where the murdered child was found. And then on to the well with the thorn tree on which 'Mungo's mither hang'd hersel'.

Ballad scenes all of them, reaching well back into pagan Scotland.

Before Tam o' Shanter now is the river, the crossing of which means safety, but, before the river lies the centre of the struggle, Burns's *Walpurgisnacht*, which takes place in Kirk Alloway:

> Thro' ilka bore the beams were glancing;
> And loud resounded mirth and dancing.

Here Burns inserts an interpolation in praise of whisky ('Inspiring bold *John Barleycorn*!'), which is a clue as to his own poetic inspiration. It is whisky alone which enables Tam to look without fear on the 'devilish' scene, it was whisky alone which enabled Burns to penetrate into the very recesses of his mind, right into the pagan core, after having thrown off the hindrances of Christian morality and, in this case, its particularly drastic form, Calvinism. Whisky, or *usquabae*, was the real Water of Life to many a Calvinist; drinking it allowed him to escape the moral death which he otherwise endured; drinking it freed his imagination, let him enjoy some natural being, some thalamic (if I may say so) consciousness:

> What dangers thou canst make us scorn!

Cautious honesty is thrown to the winds. The way is open to poetry and the deep lust of life (the devil): 'And, vow! Tam saw an unco sight!' It is only now that we arrive at the second line of the ballad of 'Thomas the Rhymer': 'A ferlie he spied wi' his e'e'.

Tam sees 'warlocks and witches in a dance', but they are Nationalist witches, scorning the imported French dances. Burns foists his own particular social preoccupations, those of a very conscious small farmer of the eighteenth century, on to those representatives of natural, supra-national powers.

The man that plays the tunes for all this festivity is the Deil himself, Auld Nick, the arch-musician, the arch-poet – Pan ('in shape o' beast'), earthy, dark, shaggy:

> He screw'd the pipes and gart them skirl,
> Till roof and rafters a' did dirl.

All around him are emblems of death, each one of which is described. Is this mere mortuary picturesqueness, the gothic horror effect? The dead folk in their coffins hold lights in their hands – it may well be that Burns thought he was merely indulging in the gruesome and the macabre, laughing up his enlightened sleeve, but that here we have a remembrance of some old mythology is evident: perhaps the dead as the powers that preside over the earth, each dead man 'a man in the moon', reigning over seasons and fertility.

Follows the enumeration of the emblems of death, piled upon the 'haly table' – black magic, black mass, is in progress: a murderer's bones in gibbet irons, two unchristened children, a thief just cut down from the hangman's rope, five bloody tomahawks (is the 'New' World present at this northern orgy?), five scimitars (and the East? – and why five of each?). With these, a garter that had strangled a baby, a knife that a son had used to murder his father:

> Wi' mair o' horrible and awefu',
> Which even to name wad be unlawfu'.

All this would seem to represent the degeneration of some early cult – a degeneration caused in part by the Church, whose propaganda turned the pre-Christian pagan mythology into something 'horrible and awefu', making witches (in close association with the Earth-Mother cult) into disreputable old hags.

It is as old hags that Tam, through his eighteenth-century eyes, sees them. Remember that what Thomas the Rhymer saw was completely different:

> a ladye bright
> Come riding down by the Eildon Tree.

There is a far cry from 'the Queen of fair Elfland' to

> wither'd beldams, auld and droll,
> Rigwoodie hags . . .

The little phrase following, 'wad spean a foal', while apparently 'thrown away', a gratuitous and humorous insult, is significant. Witches were originally connected with horses (only later did the horses degenerate into broomsticks). Epona (Magog, the Earth-Mother) was a Gaulish horse goddess, said to have been fathered by a mortal man on a mare.

I have already mentioned the Cailleach. Cailleach means 'old woman', or, if you like, 'wither'd beldam, auld and droll, rigwoodie hag'. As also mentioned before, she controlled the winds, seas and seasons. But what is more, she kept a beautiful maiden (Spring, or the New Moon) in a cave in Glencoe. This girl ran away with Diarmid, the Gaelic Adonis, or, the Poet (Christopher Grieve knew what he was doing when he chose his *nom de plume*, and when he wrote his *A Drunk Man Looks at the Thistle*, he was turning Tam o' Shanter, alias Thomas the Rhymer, into a semi-psychotic Scottish nationalist).

Tam gazes on the old witches (the Cailleach, the Earth-Mother in her old woman phase) and feels desire for a woman younger and more beautiful. And just as a problem is never raised without the possibilities of its solution being at hand, so this desire does not exist in a vacuum, but is rather a presentiment of reality. The reader who remembers what was said above about the Cailleach's imprisonment of the maiden Spring in the cave of Glencoe is quite prepared for the appearance of Nannie, a young and beautiful witch.

Tam-the-Poet wishes to be naked with her, the representative of nature, the bringer of fertility.

Remember, too, what was said above about the Cailleach (the young witch is the Cailleach in another phase) as the Goddess of Storms, and there will be no surprise at the powers of Nannie:

> Lang after ken'd on Carrick shore;
> For mony a beast to dead she shot,
> And perish'd mony a bony boat,
> And shook baith meikle corn and bear,
> And kept the country-side in fear.

What is to be noticed as giving the eighteenth-century (and social-realist) cachet to the text is the minute description (in economic terms) of the sarks of the old witches and of Nannie. Tam wishes, for example, that the shifts of the beldames were of 'snaw-white seventeen hunder linnen'. While Nannie's sark 'o' Paisley harn' was made by her Grannie out of cloth costing 'twa pund Scots'. The difference is vast between this and the description in the ballad of Thomas the Rhymer:

> Her shirt was o' the grass-green silk,
> Her mantle o' the velvet fyne.

Social conditions have changed, the economic context is entirely different, but both ballad and tale derive from the same sources. Both Thomas and Tam are inspired.

Tam gazes:

> bewitch'd,
> And thought his very een enrich'd,

as Nannie performs her wild and lascivious dance.

At this point, Burns feels he has to be careful, he is on the borderline:

> But here my Muse her wing maun cour;
> Sic flights are far beyond her pow'r.

The mention of the Muse shows Burns's limitation. As Lorca says in his *Theory and Function of the Duende*:

> Angel and muse come from without; the angel gives radiance, the muse gives precepts . . . The *duende* has to be roused in the cells of the blood. We must repel the angel and kick out the muse, and lose our fear of the violet fragrance irradiating from eighteenth-century poetry, and of the great telescope in whose lenses sleeps the confining, ailing Muse. The real struggle is with the *duende*.

Robert Burns knew that struggle with the *duende*, but his century foisted a muse on him, the muse of Reason. And too often he worshipped and bowed down.

But here the lust of life is so great and overpowering:

> Even Satan glowr'd, and fidg'd fu' fain,
> And hotch'd and blew wi' might and main,

that Tam is quite beside himself, out of his mind and

> tint his reason a' thegither,
> And roars out, 'Weel done, Cutty-sark!'

He has made his cry, the cry of the *duende*: free of his muse, of his reason, he has called to the deep natural powers, but there is no possibility of union between them and him:

> . . . in an instant all was dark.

The vision of the dancing powers, of free life and fertility is gone.

It was not so in the ballad of 'Thomas the Rhymer' where, quite naïvely:

> She mounted on her milk-white steed;
> She's ta'en true Thomas up behind:
> And aye, whene'er her bridle rung
> The steed flew faster than the wind.

Perhaps if Tam had not shouted his admiration as one standing *outside* this reality, perhaps if he had simply joined in the dance and told the piper to play his favourite tune, all would have been well, and he would have come back to 'outer reality', in due time (seven years or so) enriched. But Tam spoke and, as the ballad says:

> if you speak word in Elflyn land
> Ye'll ne'er get back to your ain countrie.

Tam has no wish to remain in Elfland, to go beyond that barrier of darkness:

> O they rode on, and farther on,
>   And they waded through rivers aboon the knee,
> And they saw neither sun nor moon,
>   But they heard the roaring of the sea.

> It was mirk mirk night, and there was nae stern light,
>   And they waded through red blude to the knee,
> For a' the blude that's shed on earth
>   Runs through the springs o' that countrie.

> Syne they came on to a garden green,
>   And she pu'd an apple frae a tree.
> 'Take this for thy wages, True Thomas,
>   It will give thee the tongue that can never lie.'

Tam o' Shanter will never obtain the apple of wisdom. He will remain, in the minds of his contemporaries (and his descendants)

> a skellum,
> A blethering, blustering, drunken blellum.

He turns tail.

And that tail remains as Nannie's trophy in hell. While the poem ends on a (humorous) morality from the rational muse, that rational muse who was to go on talking for a long long time in Scotland.

Into the White World

My head is incandescent, on the point of bursting. A world it
conceals is asking to be born. (Paul Klee, *Journal*)

This essay is written on the assumption that, to understand
something about poetry (and poetry speaks ultimately of the
white world), it is better to read, say, Knud Rasmussen's *Intellectual Culture of the Iglulik Eskimos*, or Shirokogorov's *Psycho-
mental Complex of the Tungus*, than the ruck and run of our
literary production.

It assumes also that poetry is meant neither for weak stomachs
nor soft brains – and that it is more than 'something' (liberally
vague) done by individuals, professionally (according to some
economico-cultural nexus) entitled poets, working on the nau-
seatingly incoherent data of an ego-limited conscience, with
more or less skill, taste, sensitivity, etc., etc . . .

Poetry signifies the transcendence of the individual conscience
and the introduction to a world (a cosmos, a beautiful whole in
movement). It is the absence of these two notions (transcendence,
and penetration) which makes for a degraded state of poetry
where, for example, observations (more or less 'deep') on this,
that, and the next thing, event, person, thought, feeling, imagin-
ing, pass for poetry – when in fact they are only the literary sub-
products of individuals, psycho-physiologically in a larval state
(even, and perhaps more so, when they're 'distinguished') crawl-
ing more or less contentedly about a decomposed environment of
which they constitute the 'literary world', a hideous caricature of
the real world of poetry.

Real poetry, and the life it implies, begins a few thousand

miles, as the gull flies, as the wind blows, away from this 'civilised' compound.

Nietzsche, at Sils-Maria, lived '6,000 feet above men and time'. The Chinese say (or used to say) that to know what real poetry is you have to meet a man distant from you by 3,000 miles (I'm quoting from memory, and may have got the figures wrong, but you get the idea).

1.

All of our European culture has for long been moving, under an excruciating tension that has been growing from decade to decade, towards something like a catastrophe: with anxiety, violence, precipitation; like a river that wants to reach its *end* and which no longer thinks, which is afraid to think. The man who speaks here has on the contrary done nothing up till now but think: a philosopher and a solitary by instinct who . . . found his profit in isolation, in the outside, in patience and biding his time; a mind ready to take risks, who has already ventured into all the labyrinths of the future . . . The first perfect European nihilist, but who has already lived out nihilism in himself, who has it in him, beneath him, outside him . . .

Thus wrote Nietzsche, in the Preface to *The Will to Power*.

By now, the catastrophe has occurred. Life goes on, cultural manifestations are still made ('the show must go on' – much of our culture being reduced in fact to the level of a show); but it all happens, as Gottfried Benn put it, against a 'sinking background' (*einen versinkenden Hintergrund*).

By the early decades of the twentieth century, Hofmannsthal has the taste of 'decaying mushrooms' (*vermodernde Pilze*) in his mouth; Eliot is moaning liturgically in the Wasteland; Breton is decrying the lack of reality (*Discours sur le peu de realité*). The 'obscure disaster' which Mallarmé situated sidereally has become a world phenomenon.

A technologised science meanwhile makes tremendous headway – preparing perhaps a definitive catastrophe. The House of Being (which language was before it turned into what a romantic

poet called *babylonische Sprachenverwirrung*, Babylonian confusion) is reduced to a villa, an asylum, or a sanatorium at the
side of the technological Highway, containing much wailing
and gnashing of teeth, some cynical laughter, some last-minute
speeches, some 'avantgarde' experiments, some whimperings,
many death-croaks . . .

The picture could be enlarged, details could be added. But this
is not the subject of the present essay.

The subject of this essay is the real ground, the real world of
poetry.

                                   2.

The mind cries out for unity, for a unitive experience, for the
knowledge of something large and yet which is more, and other,
than the massive confusion which is our only alternative to the
smallnesses of all kinds that relentlessly beset us and maintain the
mind in restricted activities culminating, detail after detail, in
unbearable tension. Psychic health being, apparently, impossible,
to escape the torture of the mind we have recourse to all kinds of
temporary tranquillizers or, finally, to madness, when the mind,
at the limit of tension, snaps abruptly.

There is a burning need of an intellectual culture, centred
around some unifying myth.

But to speak of myth is perhaps to show contempt for,
despair of, the human intellect, and to invite a regression to
a pre-rational, pre-logical mentality? Is it not an obvious step
backwards, rather than those 'steps forward' we hear so much
about?

In fact, the process of rationalisation in the human mind has
not meant a surpassing of the mythic conscience, but only its
suppression. Which is why (like so much else in the mind that
civilization has forced underground), it breaks out in degraded
and distorted forms. Modern life is rank with degraded mythic
conscience – witness the avid interest in horoscopes, the desperate indulgence in all kinds of more or less absurd religion, the
highly irrational state of political activity . . .

To propose a myth, or rather (to avoid all sorts of mythological
clutter) a complex of images with an idea of life both personal
and social, is to invite, first and foremost, the development of the

human mind as a whole, and the development of a life, personal and social, corresponding to it. It is to reawaken the sense of a fully and harmoniously developed humanity.

It seems unnecessary to insist on how far from such plenitude and harmony humanity is at the present moment. The only solution, the 'logical' conclusion in the present state-of-things and on present lines of thought (the image of 'lines' is used conventionally – harmonious development being manifested rather in wave-shape or constellation) is to amputate humanity entirely of its faculties and turn the human being into 'one-dimensional Man,' where the word 'Man' is nothing more than a euphemism. That way he will function more efficiently in the machine – and who but a madman would deny that it's the machine that counts, and that Man's happiness depends on his utter adaptation to it.

The poet is a 'madman' (marked first by extravagant energy, then with a large logic) in this sense.

The desire of a whole world, the nostalgia for unity and unitive experience, can only appear as mad and aberrant in a civilization which, while it satisfies many desires (most of which it has pre-viously fabricated) leaves unsatisfied the one fundamental need, of which the poets, above all, the wide-ranging, deep-plunging poets, are aware.

It is the expression of this need that runs like a white thread through modern poetry, like a faster, more urgent current in the general turgid or trivial mass of literature.

3.

Hölderlin, that always exemplary figure, knew it, with his nostalgia for Greece, that Greece which his friend Hegel de-scribed as 'an immaculate world, unadulterated by any scission':

> And if your soul leaps
> With nostalgia outside your own times
> You remain alone on a cold riverbank
> Beside your fellows and know them not . . .

paying his desire for that world, and the penetration of his knowledge of it, with isolation and alienation from his own society.

Whitman knew it. What Hart Crane was to call the 'American psychosis', eminently illustrated by Whitman, is the desire of the same white world – a desire which between its own impulsion and the resistant inertia of actual society, can become pathological.

The 'American psychosis', which is the desire for the whiteness and the white world, is to be seen right through American literature at its intensest levels.

If Whitman had it (sometimes concealed under a more superficial stars-and-stripes Americanism), Melville had it, concealed by nothing (hence the madder nature of his work): '. . . a white whale. Skin your eyes for him, men; look sharp for white water; if ye see but a bubble, sing out'.

Hart Crane had it:

> How many dawns, chill from his rippling rest
> The seagull's wings shall dip and pivot him
> Shedding white rings of tumult, . . .

In a less powerful sense, but no less unmistakably, William Carlos Williams has it: '. . . the difficult thing to realise is that the thrust must go through to the white, at least somewhere'.

Jackson Pollock had it (see the white confused mass of his 'mappa mundi').

Robert Duncan, sometimes, has it:

> White white white like
>   a boundary in death advancing
> that is our life, that's love
>   line upon line
> breaking in radiance . . .

But the white world desire is not only American. We find it at the other pole of the modern world, in Russia, where its most obvious representative is Dostoevsky, towering above the moralistic mud-flats of the later 'social realism'. Dostoevsky's Russia of saints and prophets is also the desire, the search for the white world.

It's there in Raskolnikov, Rogoshin, Dimitri – those multiple characters moving through a welter of feeling and soul-complexity, beset by a chaos of questions with no fixed answers,

penetrating through humanity social and individual towards a
naked-elementary truth, an elementary-ecstatic state of being
which Stefan Zweig, in his essay on Dostoevsky, calls 'white-
glowing feeling' (*weissglühende Empfindung*), and which he says
is the lyrical element in the novels, their fundamental energy-
field.

4.

Having shown the presence of the white world desire in the
modern world, we can try now to look closer at the experience
itself. For, before being an idea (with philosophical developments), and a field of existential poetics (containing, potentially,
a social programme), it is an experience, centering on the real
body – a psycho-physical experience that can be of the utmost
intensity. To this writer, it is *the* principal experience of poetry,
without which no real poetry exists.

In this context, Robert Graves' book *The White Goddess*
(Faber and Faber, 1948), which purports to be an exploration
of the essential theme of poetry, must come to mind.

For Graves, real poetry is muse-poetry, implying devotion to
and worship of the White Goddess. While in no way denying the
White Goddess, there is something beyond muse poetry, white-
goddess poetry, something without which muse-poetry itself
degenerates, and which is white-world poetry. Beyond the goddess, there is the world:

'Love takes God as being sweet', writes Meister Eckhart, 'but
intellect goes deeper, and conceives God as being.'

What is the white-world experience, and what can we say of
the state of being it realises?

To say world is to say, first and foremost: earth.

If rationalization has meant for modern man separation, in the
mind, from primal conscience, it has also meant, for the life of his
body, separation from the earth.

'The incandescent reality of the earth', writes Georges Bataille,

> cannot be touched or possessed by those who fail to recog-
> nize it. It is the failure to recognize the earth, the neglect of
> the star on which they live, the ignorance of the nature of its
> riches, that is to say the incandescence enclosed in this star,

which has made for man an existence at the mercy of the
merchandise he produces, the more important part of
which is devoted to death.

Note that this experience of the earth is an experience of the
incandescence (the whiteness) of the earth, and is more fundamental than any naturalism (or nature-worship).

It is the kind of earth-experience, extremely difficult, if not
inconceivable to modern Man (who can still accept at least a
measure of naturalism – in the form of gardens, parks, reserves)
which Artaud describes in his account of the Tarahumara
Indians: 'They have the highest idea of the philosophical movement of Nature'.

The earth-experience, which is where white-world knowledge
begins, is physical-metaphysical.

To see it, first, at its most physical: 'The attributes of the poets
of the kosmos', writes Whitman, 'concentre in the real body', and
in 'the pleasure of things.'

The real body, or, to put it more fundamentally still, the erotic
flesh – for the experience in question is, largely, sexual.

What is later the white world idea, intuition, philosophy – and
the vague premonitions of which may be nascent at the initial
experience, concentre primarily in the erotic flash, in contact
with things and the elements: . . . swirling water, the sheer flight
of birds, the little body of the hare, wet earth, opening flowers,
the silver birch's slender and cryptic trunk, the heavy berry-
clusters of the rowan, the breast of a girl . . . at the centre of the
universe, gathering into itself as much as possible of the real
world, towards unlimited marriage, a sheer experience of the
nakedness and loveliness of everything, an ecstatic existence,
expanding to a sense of cosmic unity.

The erotic experience, then, leads to a sense of cosmic unity,
or, to put it in another way, *eros* leads to *logos*, physics to
metaphysics, the relationship to things to a relationship to being
itself.

The 'logos' we speak of here, with its roots in erotic experience, has little to do with what we know as 'logic', which is only
a desiccated version of the real thing. If poetry is 'illogical', it's
because it's concerned, not with logic (and still less with mere
illogicality), but with the *logos*.

But what is the *logos*, what is the entity to which we refer by this 'barbaric' term?

5.

If we wish to discover the meaning, or, more narrowly, find a definition of the *logos*, we have to go back, in Western civilization, to the pre-socratics, those poet-philosophers with a tragic sense of separation and the affirmation of unity: 'Although men are in perpetual relationship with the *logos* that governs all', writes Heraclitus, 'they are not in harmony with it, and everything appears alien to them'.

The *logos*, then, 'governs all', it is that 'cosmic unity' we spoke of above. The aim of the pre-socratics, and it is the aim of poetry, was to recover the sense of that cosmic unity, set humanity in relation to it by creating or re-creating a language based on analogies (to the *logos*) in the existent world – to recover the lost relation, the primordial contact.

The *logos* implies a language based on 'what is clear to the senses and the soul' (Whitman), expressing the white world of cosmic unity, and able to lead Man to it, so that, instead of turning round himself dizzily in a vicious circle as *animal rationale* (with a logic that only further imprisons him), he may become, or re-become, *animal poeticum*, in harmony with the *logos*; not a victim of his (degraded) environment, but an inhabitant of his world.

6.

But if we refer the word *logos* to the pre-socratics, and to early Greek civilization, the beginnings of our own, it is in Eastern thought that we find the fullest development of the notions we are discussing.

The East . . . The culturally blasé will smile. We hear rather a lot about the East: Zen is on the town, and the subways crawl with swamis. In order to scotch the myth of the 'mystic Orient', Arthur Koestler went East, with bag and baggage, and came back with the conviction that the whole thing is a romantic wash-out, the reality of the East being wretched and sordid: Indian yogis are soft-headed, superconsciousness is a disguise of the death-wish, and Japanese Zen monks goggle before television sets. There is, apparently, nothing in the East worth intelligent notice.

And yet.

And yet, despite the manifestations of Western Buddhism and its succedanea (in his analysis of Western culture, Nietzsche predicted for Europe, in the twentieth century, a tepid flood of sentimental Buddhism and that such pulp-Buddhism, sub-Zen, etc., bulks large on the cultural scene is obvious enough), the conviction remains, with some, that the East contains something which may not merely be an exotic *addition* to the West's already vast accumulations of dead culture (and stillborn 'creations'), but a *confirmation* of what is most alive, and most essential, in its own existence. There remains the conviction that, beneath the ritualistic irrationalism of the East, and the mechanical rationalism of the West, there lies something of the first significance, something essential to the human being, something which, grasped and incorporated, could change a man's life, something the lack of which makes the idea of a fulfilled human existence impossible to realise.

One may not find it by trekking across India, or by residing in a present-day Zen monastery, or by getting all worked-up about occult wisdom; one may, however, at least have intuitions of it on reading, say, a poem by Bashô or on looking at a painting by Sesshû – enough to be determined to look further.

Analytical, rational thought, which we see entering with Socrates (and perhaps culminating in Kant) means the loss of a concrete totality which suffers no separation, and the establishment of that radical dualism which characterises the abstract totality of the West. Practical, empirical Western reason, which has technological achievements to its credit, prevents any penetrating study of ontological being. What Chinese taoist thought offers us is ontological re-sourcing.

It is with 'ontological being' that we are concerned in poetry, which is why poetry, in its higher instances, has always seemed to be on the edge of Western civilization, not an integral part of it.

Kant affirmed that the 'noumenal world', as he termed it, was unknowable, and that the life of Man must be one of practical reason. But it is knowledge of the 'noumenal world', which we call the white world, that is the passionate research of poetry, and its supreme realisation.

It is this idea (based on the *experience* referred to above) which is absent from so much of Western poetry (returning to it, however confusedly and obscurely, with romanticism), but which is forever present in the poetry of the East. 'The ultimate excellence of poetry', writes Yen Yu (China, thirteenth century) 'consists in one thing: *entering the spirit*. If poetry can succeed in doing this, it will have reached the limit and cannot be surpassed.' The word Yen Yu used for 'the spirit' is *ju shen* (spirit of life). To enter the spirit is to enter the world (the 'real life', the absence of which Rimbaud was to decry in the West).

We are badly in need of poetry that 'has a world'.

P.S. (Three months later.) Just came across (in William Power's translation of the *Hyaku-nin-Isshiu*, Clarendon Press, 1909) this seventh-century Japanese poem by Yamabe no Akahito:

> *Tago no ura ni*
> *Uchi-idete mireba*
> *Shirotae no*
> *Fuji no takane ni*
> *Yuki wa furi-tsutsu*

which, speaking of walking along the Tago shore and seeing the white peak of Fuji glistening through the falling snow, expresses pretty well what the writer of this essay feels with regard to his, still approximate, perception of the 'white world'.

6

The Birds of Kentigern

The seabird passes no marks on the waves but that doesn't mean
it's forgotten the way. (Dôgen)

The original title of this essay was 'Zen and the birds of Kentigern'.
It was because I could imagine somebody saying: 'Oh Christ, here
comes another Zen-addict, talking strictly to the birds', that I
decided to drop the Zen reference, at least in the title. One learns to
be wary of reflex reactions and reductionist mentalities.

Let's get it straight, right from the start. I was 'into' Zen, or
let's rather say, the higher reaches of Mahayana Buddhism, a
long time ago, and I've been so long in it, so far into it, that I've
come out of it – at the other end. And it's at this 'end' that the
birds of Kentigern come in. It's just that a little detour through
Zen Buddhism (which was not exhausted, except for very tired
and mode-orientated minds, by certain American poets of the
1960s) helps to see them *in an original light*.

'Zen and . . .' I know of at least three books with such a title:
R. H. Blyth's *Zen and English Literature*, Thomas Merton's *Zen
and the Birds of Appetite*, Robert M. Pirsig's *Zen and the Art of
Motorcycle Maintenance*. Now I'm coming up with 'Zen and'
the birds of Kentigern. What kind of a bird is that anyway?

The birds in question are gulls, ordinary, common gulls (*larus
canus*, according to ornithology); and Kentigern (his Gaelic name
meaning: head, *ceann*, of the house, *tigh*, of the moon, *ern*) was a
Celtic saint with still, as was the case with so many Celtic saints,
a good deal of the pagan in him. In the (Protestant) church I
frequented as a child, there was a glorious stained-glass window
devoted to the legend of Kentigern. It showed him doing penance

on the shore, the penance consisting in his reading aloud from a book to the heedless, scavenging and caterwauling gulls. This window, which was so often my refuge during the long-winded sermon, fascinated me, and it constitutes one of the primitive psychic ideograms in my mind: man, book, seashore, gulls.

What does it all add up to? What might be the outcome of it all? And what has Zen got to do with it?

1.

If R. H. Blyth could find Zen in English literature, how much the more might he have found it in a literature more specifically Celtic. As Kuno Meyer writes:

> In nature poetry the Gaelic muse may vie with that of any other nation. Indeed, these poems occupy a unique position in the literature of the world. To seek out and watch and love Nature, in its tiniest phenomena as in its grandest, was given to no people so early and so fully as to the Celt. Many hundreds of Gaelic and Welsh poems testify to this fact. It is a characteristic of these poems that in none of them do we get an elaborate or sustained description of any scene or scenery, but rather a succession of pictures and images which the poet, like an impressionist, calls up before us by light and skilful touches. Like the Japanese, the Celts were always quick to take an artistic hint; they avoid the obvious and the commonplace; the half-said thing to them is dearest. (*Über die älteste Irische Dichtung*, Prussian Academy, 1913).

Kenneth Jackson, in turn, comments on these same characteristics:

> The most striking quality about the early medieval Celtic literatures, the more striking when one compares other contemporary literatures of Europe, is their power of vivid imagination and freshness of approach; as if every poet, gifted with a high degree of imaginative insight, rediscovered the world for himself. Where other medieval literatures are conventional and even hackneyed, early Celtic literature is capable of being highly original. This is not true of that genre which was most esteemed by the Celtic

peoples themselves, the official 'bardic' poetry; though even there the irrepressible vividness of Celtic thought breaks through. Fortunately other types of poetry were composed apart from the bardic, and it is there that the qualities referred to are mainly found. (*Studies in Early Celtic Poetry*, Cambridge University Press, 1935)

The key words in these passages are 'quick' and 'fresh'. Practically the same terms are used by Asô, writing of Bashô: 'In the Sanzôshi it is stated: "Freshness is the flower of haiku art". What the deceased master sought above all was this sense of freshness . . . We are always looking for freshness which springs from the very ground with every step we take forward into nature.'

A Zen *koan* puts it this way: 'At every step the pure wind rises'.

2.

A few examples before proceeding:

Birchtree smooth and blessed
proud and melodious
full of grace the mingling branches
that rise up to your crest

Now it is winter, the sea is pale
the salt perch of the gulls is angry

Ah, blackbird, happy you are
with your nest in the bush:
a hermit that clangs no bell

I have news for you; the stag bells, winter snows, summer has gone.

Wind high and cold, the sun low, short its course, sea running high.
Deep red the bracken, it has lost its shape; the wild goose has
    raised its accustomed cry.
Cold has seized the birds' wings; season of ice; this is my news.

Arran of the many stags, the sea reaches to its shoulder; islands
    where companies are fed; ridge on which blue spears are
    reddened.
Wanton deer upon its peaks, mellow blaeberries on its heaths,
    cold water in its streams, nuts on its brown oaks.

Gleaning of purple lichen on its rocks, grass without blemish on
    its slopes, a sheltering cloak over its crags; gambolling of
    fawns, trout leaping.
Smooth is its lowland, fat its swine, pleasant its fields, a tale you
    may believe; its nuts on the tips of its hazel-wood, sailing of
    long galleys past it.
It is pleasant to be there when fine weather comes: trout under
    the banks of its rivers, seagulls answering each other round
    its white cliffs; delightful at all times is Arran.

                                3.

I spent all my childhood on that western seaboard, on the mainland just opposite the Arran of the poem, and my aim from the
beginning was to see into it, feel out its lines – psychocosmo-
graphically, one might say.

We are concerned here with the extreme west of Europe, a
highly characteristic region that stretches, say, from the Gulf of
Gascony to the Scottish archipelagoes. The only *unity* in this area
is the sea, the Celtic Sea, the *mare celticum*. For the rest,
fragmentation is the rule: peninsulas and islands separated by
difficult waters. Other associated features are an edge-of-the-
worldness (*finis terrae*) and, with regard to the 'positive' of the
Continent, a kind of negative destiny. Eastern Europe is the
region of vast continental space, moving between monumental-
ism and nihilism; middle Europe is a congeries of nations, with
all the pettifogging narrowness that nationalism so often implies;
the West is scattered, precarious, fragmented – yet each fragment
is *exact* in itself, there is no vagueness in this plurality. I am trying
to move, by degrees, the way it happens, from physical to mental
geography, from landscape to mindscape.

Whatever be the origins of the people who inhabit these
regions: European aboriginals driven westwards by migratory
hordes from the East; elements of these Eastern peoples who
came all the way across the continent; Mediterraneans coming
up by the sea-route, among them people, Syrians for example,
from farther back in the Orient (before the Arab conquest out off
communications) – whatever be the origins, by the time we come
to the early Middle Ages, the time of the poems referred to above,
the region, humanly considered, is characterised by a type of

Christianity that has little in common with its Roman continental form. It is not only a question of quarrelling about the date for Easter, or the practice of baptism, or how monks should wear their hair. The conflict goes deeper than those details might suggest, and it might be summed up, in a phrase, as: the archipelagical versus the institutional. The bishop has no jurisdiction or authority, what counts is the individual monk, and the monastic communities are scattered all over the landscape, with no central bishopric, and with no notion of hierarchy.

So much for the organisation and the general 'anarchist' mentality. As to the practice, it culminates in a notion of *askesis* which takes the form of a wide-ranging *peregrinatio*: the abandoning of one's-self to the 'winds of God'.

A taste for physical adventure allies itself with a natural mysticism.

4.

To go further into the ways of this 'natural mysticism':

In his *Early Welsh Gnomic Poems* (Cardiff University Press, 1961), Kenneth Jackson makes a distinction between 'nature gnomes relating to universals' and 'descriptive statements about nature relating to particulars'. If this distinction is valid, it is possible also to conceive of a poetry that would unite gnomic sentence with natural description, fusing them into a higher synthesis. It is this gnostic naturalism which we find, for example, in the poems of the hermit Marban when he speaks of his 'shieling in the wood':

> Fair birds come there
> herons, seagulls
> and the sea close by
> makes a pleasant music
> brown grouse rise
> from the red heather . . .

'It was not only', writes Robin Flower,

> that these scribes and anchorites lived by the destiny of their dedication in an atmosphere of wood and sea; it was because they brought into that environment an eye washed

miraculously clear by a continual spiritual exercise that they, first in Europe, had that strange vision of natural things in an almost unnatural purity. (*The Irish Tradition*, Oxford University Press, 1947)

It is at this point that the birds of Kentigern first enter the territory of Zen, for where else (apart from some Amerindian and Eskimo poems?) do we find such a 'vision of natural things in an almost unnatural purity' but in haiku:

> A wild sea
> and the Milky Way bounding over
> to the island of Sado!

> My eyes have seen everything
> but they keep coming back
> to the white chrysanthemums

> In the evening breeze
> the lake water laps
> against the heron's legs

5.

It is far from being a rule, but I find that it's often minds with a Celtic background that get closest to the Far East. We need only think of Segalen, the Breton, in China. As to Japan, there is Lafcadio Hearn, who was at least part Irish.

Here is Lafcadio reflecting on life and death:

I cannot convince myself that even that grosser substance of vanished being ever completely dies, however dissolved or scattered – fleeting in the gale – floating in the mists – shuddering in the leaf – flickering in the light of waters – or tossed on some desolate coast in a thunder of surf, *to whiten or writhe in the clatter of shingle.*

I have emphasised that last phrase, and I shall return to it, because it has a peculiar fascination for me, but all the words Hearn uses here: *dissolved, scattered, fleeting, floating, shuddering, flickering* are typical not only of the perceptions of the Japanese mind, tuned in as it is to the notion of precarious passage outlined so in the Prajnaparamita Sutra:

So must you look upon the fleeting world
a star at dawn, a bubble on a stream
a flash of lightning in a summer sky
a flickering lamp, a ghost, a dream

they are typical of the Celtic mind also. A Celtic monk copying out a manuscript interrupts his labours to note on the margin of his page: 'Pleasant is it indeed to see the sun glittering and flickering so on these margins'. And nowhere other than in Gaelic poetry is there such quick delight in the shimmering of leaves, the leap of a fish in the stream, the flash of sunlight over a loch – and Burns, it will be remembered, sees the snow falling on a river: 'a moment white – then melts for ever'.

To come back now to that last phrase of Lafcadio Hearn's concerning a substance 'tossed on some desolate coast in a thunder of sorf, *to whiten or writhe in the clatter of shingle*'. Here we go beyond appearance and perception into the very nerve of things. So much so that I find it difficult to disengage all the 'lessons' implied for me in such a phrase.

The erotic implication of this 'white writing' is clear enough – it's what Melville felt in the pages of Moby Dick, in the fluking and flurry of the whale. Perhaps too there is some connection in my mind between 'writing' and 'writhing' as if to my mind the *logos* of writing is, or should be, in close conjunction with the *eros* of living.

6.

To speak of '*eros* of living' in connection with Buddhism, Zen or no, may seem like a flagrant contradiction in terms, and indeed for the sense of *eros* one must look, in Japan, rather to the pre-Buddhist period, that is, to Shinto. In some sense I'd like to take the Buddhism out of Zen and maintain the Zen touch on more primitive territory – associate Zen, which is highly intellectual mindscape, with the archaic landscape. Zen, taken to the limit, can do without Buddha, but the body-mind, if it is to remain erotically-logically active, cannot do without the archaic ground.

Behind the Buddhist physiognomy of Japan, and behind the conventions of its civilization, there is Shinto, more secret, a direct inheritance from pre-history, taking us into a foreworld

and concerned, not with Buddha, but with the natural phenomena, or perhaps rather the cosmic principles, of sun, moon,
storm, sea, wind, thunder, lightning, rock, tree . . . The reposi-
tory of primitive Japanese thought, it is certainly one of the best
representatives, at least so far as the records go, of primitive
religious psychology in general. Writing of it, not very approvingly, G. W. Aston speaks of its 'rudimentary character', saying
that it is 'perhaps the least developed of religions which have an
adequate literary record'. When we see what Aston means by
'development': the conception of a supreme and personal deity, a
panoply of images, a moral code, and the recognition of a future
state of life, we may feel grateful that Shinto is 'undeveloped'.
Here is a religion (or should we get rid of that word too, and
speak only of global apprehension?) which has no dogma, no
metaphysical system, no moral code, no eschatology and, far
from evolving the concept of a personal godhead, welters in a
perfect orgy of pagan sacrality, with about 800 polymorphous
divinities to 'cover', or put a halo over, practically every phenomenon in nature. Absolutely non-formalist, Shinto works with
an unrestricted field of energy, a total cosmic economy.

Its principal book (there are two others, the *Nihongi* and the
Yengishiki) is the *Kojiki*, or *Record of Ancient Matters*, which
was compiled about the eighth century, for institutional reasons,
in order to strengthen the unity of the various tribes (from the
North via Korea, from South China, from the Malay peninsula)
existing within Japan, and to establish the ancestral origins of the
imperial family that was trying to bring them together and
consolidate a dynasty. But if it was compiled for institutional
reasons, and with a concern for ancestors, its matter is a heterogeneous mass of poetic material culled from the scattered
Japanese archipelago, and concerned more with natural powers
(the solar field) than with ancestors (the imperial family).

Its first and most interesting part is the description of a genesis:
the birth of the Nipponese islands themselves. Izanami and
Izanagi, the aboriginal couple, stood on the Floating Bridge of
Heaven, which 'is' the rainbow, and stirred the sea with a spear.
It was the salt water dripping from the spear when they drew it
out of the sea that formed the islands

Then there is the beautiful story of the sun-goddess, Amaterasu
Omikami, who, angered by a relative of hers, the storm-god, holed

up in a cave, thus darkening the world, and refused to come out –
till Uzume, another goddess, after placing a mirror to attract the
light, did an obscene dance at the cave's mouth, baring first her
breasts, then her sex, in a kind of divine striptease. This naked
dancing of Uzume provoked the laughter of the assembled gods
and goddesses, and hence the curiosity of the sun-goddess, who
thereupon re-appeared, and there was light in the world again.

Now this sun-story has a curious equivalent in Celtic myth.

It will be remembered that at one point in the tales of Finn,
Finn's wife, Grainne, flees with Diarmid and hides away in a cave
– and if it is recalled at the same time that Grainne means 'sun'
(modern Gaelic: *grian*, which is of the female gender), the
parallel is evident.

This not only points to that area in which, to quote the terms
of my title, Zen (which absorbed the genius of Shinto) and the
birds of Kentigern have something in common, it points again
to the existence of general 'hyberborean' or circumpolar culture
that may have stretched, say, from North America through
northern Europe and Siberia down to the Japanese archipelago.

Frithjof Schuon (*Images de l'esprit*, Paris, Flammarion, 1961)
puts it clearly enough: 'It may well be that Shinto is the most
intact form of that traditional current which we might call
"hyberborean shamanism" and which stretches across Siberia
and the adjacent Mongol territories to North America'.

If the Japanese are by no means 'hyberborean' in the ethno-
logical sense of the word, being much more than half Malayan-
Polynesian, there is no doubt that a northern element exists in the
population. It came down probably from North-East Asia via
Korea, and it may well have been this element that brought
Shinto with it, or rather that hyperborean mentality which, on
Japanese soil, was to become Shinto. There is a notion, within
Shinto, that the North is the most honourable quarter, corpses
being laid with their heads in that direction.

The main feature of this hyperborean mentality is what
Schuon calls 'transcendental immanence', that is, the idea that
nature is not only all that one has, it is all that is necessary –
provided one is able to *see into it*. To see into nature, including
one's own nature, is to reflect the origin, which is the sun
('breathe the spirit of the sun', said the nineteenth-century
Shintoist, Kurozumi).

The red gateways, the *torii* (*tori-wi*, bird perches) stand, as invitations to insight, at the entrances to the Shinto shrines, or mark the direction of some distant object or space (say a rock of peculiar shape, or a stretch of sea). And the shrines themselves, rude and archaic constructions, are almost empty, containing, in their innermost sanctum, two symbols only: a mirror and a sword, that represent the ultimate perfection. The accent is on the primordial and the pure. But this primal purity is not 'moral' in the life-denying sense. The world of Shinto is, on the contrary, drenched with what we might call a cosmic eroticism.

We have already witnessed the naked dance of Uzume, and Shinto goes, at least in its approaches, with a sexual dialectic. This is its link with primitive religion all over the world: we need only think of *phallos* and *kteis* in Greece; *linga* and *yoni* in India; the cross and ring symbolism of the *crux ansata* in Egypt . . . In Shinto, these symbols are coloured red – like the entrances to the shrines themselves. It is as though the way to the 'white' (white is the auspicious colour of Shinto) were through the 'red':

> Among the dark sand
> and the rosy seaweed
>
> the deep-curved
> sea-white clam shell
>
> she is scattered
> over all the earth

7.

To return now, after these 'exotic' excursions, to these Euro-Celtic shores:

Neil Gunn was a natural mystic in the sense I've been trying to define. In that story of a Scottish childhood already referred to, *Highland River* (The Porpoise Press 1937), he talks of 'little entranced flicks of vision'; of a 'quality of loneliness . . . that is perhaps more native to man's essential nature than any other quality'; of 'the visible flash of a salmon leap . . . with the aftermath of the dark swirl and the circles lipping up excitedly to the mind'; of the 'purity' of the coastal landscape, 'stainless as the gull's plumage, wild and cold as its eye'; of thoughts that 'however strange and haunted . . . were never really introverted, but, rather, lifted into some new dimensions of the purely objective, where internal heats and involutions pass out upon, without tainting, the wind and the sea'; and of an 'inner rhythm', caused 'by no more than the quick wave of the gull-cry or the slow wave of the sea – yet the time of his rhythm was different from these and had within it something that went out and away without end, as if indeed it were the rhythm that underlay or interpenetrated all other rhythms, and bore upon it – or was itself – ultimate reality'. All of these remarks are deeply germane to what I am trying to get at in this essay, but it is not *Highland River* I want to go into here, it is a lesser known text entitled *Light*: an essay on meditation in the course of which Gunn speaks directly of Zen.

Gunn talks in this text of 'the vivid, flashing light of livingness, the extra intensity that irradiates life and being, that indeed seems to bring life to being for the first time', and he associates this immediately, though not exclusively, with Zen and the Zen *koan*. Before going further into Gunn's essay, here are a few examples of the *koan*:

Walking alone in the red heavens

A single pine tree murmurs in the breeze

Ten years of dreaming in the forest!
Now on the lake's edge laughing,
laughing a new laugh

For years I couldn't go back,
now I've forgotten the road by which I came

My single peal of laughter
startles heaven and earth

When you get to the top of the mountain
keep climbing

Now I've shed my skin completely
one reality alone exists

The flute without holes is the hardest to play

How can the chaffinch know the wild swan's aspirations?

The enlightenment to which these *koan* are witness and which they can provoke – an experience that comes 'like a lightning-flash' and is the birth of a new life – Gunn then sees paralleled in the very origin of life itself, referring to a chemical experiment at a research centre in California wherein a duplication of the atmosphere of Jupiter was subjected to a continuous barrage of man-made lightning, and the result was nine amino-acids, probably the most common form of energy on earth before the appearance of life:

> I hope you have been struck by the remarkable parallelism between the birth of what we may call physical life on earth and the birth of what I have already called spiritual life . . . I had the sensation of vast sweeping dimensions of space and time in which something central to the universe was being glimpsed – air, sunlight, lightning and the birth of life. Then, thousands of millions of years later, the same again. But now, in a psychic sense, the birth of the spirit, Dim apprehensions in which words like 'meaning', 'purpose' simply have no place – indeed I feel fairly sure that in the aftermath of the lightning they continue to have no place, for the state of being achieved will be itself the meaning and the purpose.

Gunn then goes on to say that this space-of-being he's touching on here is too big for him. To think it out abstractly would require an energy that he feels is beyond him. But might he be able to make some headway through meditation? Even if he did not attain to complete understanding, there would be lightning flashes all along the way, and who knows, the accumulation of these little flashes might lead to the great light itself.

This brings Gunn to the triple path of concentration, meditation, and contemplation (though he tends to neglect the term contemplation as 'too solemn'). If the first step is concentration, that is, the centering of one's mind on any given object or theme, its continuation into meditation means, for Gunn, writing: 'It's easier to keep concentration going when you can follow it up by not only noticing the particular characteristics but also by writing them down . . . Well, when doing all that you would be engaged in an act of meditation.'

In concentration and meditation the whole mind is engaged,

and the experience is one of great psychic density, but it's the
final stage of this process that fascinates Gunn:

> Let me revert for a moment to that last stage in a meditation
> when you find yourself, after minutes, unable to produce
> one more thought. In the end thought itself gets choked and
> the mind becomes a void. It's at this point that the miracle
> happens, and the void, the void itself, gets lit up: the light
> spreads, burgeons; it is suffused with wonder, delight, a
> miraculous sense of freedom. And then you become aware
> of your self there, aware of a rare self, the self that
> interpenetrates all, sees and knows with a final certainty.
> I know some such self has been spelt with a capital S, just as
> the word certainty has been called Truth or Reality. But I
> don't want in this practical exercise to use capitals, or
> words like Mysticism, Transcendance and so on. There is
> no need; only a little application, persistence, failure and
> more persistence. The way is open. But one must go along it
> far enough for thought to get blocked and the void of no-
> thought to open out, for only then can enlightenment come.

The 'void of no-thought' . . . Gunn had come across in his
Eastern readings references to the void or emptiness, without
ever fully understanding what the terms meant. They had seemed
to him to refer to a complete negation and he had tended to
dismiss them from his mind. But now he begins to see more
clearly into this area, and he links this new insight to a Zen
dialogue which I want now to go into in some detail.

8.

I do not know what was Neil Gunn's source for the story which
he refers to as 'the wild geese', but the original source is the *Pi
Yen Lu* (Blue Cliff Records), one of the principal books of
Buddhism and a favourite with Zen adepts, compiled by a
Chinese Ch'an monk, Hsuah-tu, in the eleventh century. The
story is recorded there as Model Subject No. 53, under the title
Hyaku-jô's Wild Duck. As follows:

> Attention! Ba Tei-shi was once out walking with his
> disciple Hyaku-jô, when he saw a wild duck fly up in front

of them. Ba Tei-shi said What was that? Hyaku-jô said:
that was a wild duck. Ba Tei-shi said: Where did it go?
Hyaku-jô said: It has just flown away. Ba Tei-shi was
irritated by such a commonplace answer and suddenly
gave Hyaku-jô's nose a sharp tweak. Hyaku-jô cried out
with the pain. Ba Tei-shi said: You said it flew off? It's been
there all the time!

Back from eleventh-century China to twentieth-century Scotland and Neil Gunn:

What had flashed into my mind was a glimpse of wild geese
flying out of sight from a Zen koan. So I deliberately recall
the koan and see a Zen master and his pupil watching the
geese until at last the pupil says, 'The wild geese are gone'.
At that the master gives the pupil's nose a hefty tweak and
says, 'They are not gone'. Whereupon the pupil suddenly
and overwhelmingly achieves *satori* (enlightenment). When
I first read that koan I found it pretty far-fetched. I could
see a certain confusion in the use of terms that wouldn't
need much logic to comb out; but beyond that, what?
Nothing, really; though the very lack of logic might be
amusing in an absurd way . . . Did I use words like rich,
absurd, delicious? But that's not the small revealing point
which I must pin down at once and it's this: the pupil being
a pupil would have had quite a long experience of concentrating and meditating. I hadn't thought of that. If he
hadn't had he wouldn't have been walking with the master.
But he had never, poor fellow, at the utmost stretch got
beyond thought. He would have been near it, very near it
and now the total unexpectedness, the sheer astonishment,
of the nasal tweak turned his mind blank, void – and into
the void flashed the light, enlightenment, *satori*, and the
geese became immortal.

Now, however sympathetic all Neil Gunn has said so far, and
however close to it he is, I don't think he quite got the point – and
in acute areas like this a miss is as good as a mile.
  Certainly he himself hastens to say that what he has just
written is 'not an explanation of the koan', and he continues
in more general terms:

There are no explanations of koans. To analyse a koan
would be like analysing a living cell: after the analysis the
parts are all there, but life is gone. Logic is a marvellous
tool, but its uses are limited. Thought is meditation's prime
mover, but the movement is directed to an end or an
ultimate beyond it . . . as the Arts make clear.

There is truth in this statement, so far as it goes – but it doesn't
go far enough, for it leaves the way open to a lot of floozy
thinking and 'artistic', 'creative' flummery. Buddhism is to my
mind first and foremost a logic (the logic of 'emptiness' in fact),
and it is much more satisfying, both intellectually and æstheti-
cally, to get into a logic than to plough through so much that
passes for 'creativity', 'art', 'poetry'. That said, poetry, a certain
poetry, will always be the end-point of the logical process. And
clear thought is not its enemy.

To get back to the Zen dialogue. Neil Gunn didn't quite 'get it'
for the simple reason that those wild geese aren't immortal.
There's no place in the Buddhist logic for eternalism. That
'immortal' of Gunn's is more Grecian urn than Zen.

When Ba Tei-shi asked about the wild duck: Where did it go?
Hyaku-jô might have answered something like: 'It hasn't gone
anywhere', or 'It's still there'. How so? What's this dialectic of
'going' and 'still being there'? The fast answer is that nobody
goes anywhere, first because there's no 'body' (no self), secondly
because there's nowhere to go, thirdly, but it's a deduction from
the other two, there's no going.

This is the sword's edge. It's the *sunyavada*, the path of
emptiness, which is central to Buddhism and hence to Zen. In
fact it would be better to speak no more either of Buddhism or of
Zen, and speak only of the *sunyavada* – or better still, travel it,
but the travelling doesn't work without the understanding
(you've got to get your *mental* feet on it).

9.

The story is well enough known:
When the Indian *dhyana*-Buddhist Bodhidharma, after his
arrival in South China, was called before the emperor Wu,
who was an enthusiastic Buddha-Buddhist and had had several

temples built for the establishment of the faith, the talk between the two, the defender of the faith and the wandering monk-meditator, went like this:

'I have built temples and given much aid to monks', said the defender of the faith. 'What is the sum of my merit?'

'Nil', said Bodhidharma, who was a laconic kind of character.

'What exactly is Holy Awakening?' asked the emperor, moving from good deed to religious terminology and metaphysical speculation.

'Sheer emptiness, no holiness', said Bodhidharma.

'Who are you?' asked the emperor, or maybe rather, since he may well have been a trifle irritated; 'Who do you think you are?'

'I've no idea', said Bodhidharma.

End of conversation. The emperor went on, no doubt, building temples, though maybe with less conviction than before. As for Bodhidharma, he went off to live in a cave. Although they were both Buddhists, they weren't talking the same language.

To put it succinctly, Bodhidharma had killed the Buddha and was walking the *sunyavada*. A koan sets it out this way: 'When you kill father or mother you confess to the Buddha, but when you kill the Buddha, who do you confess to? Nakedness!'

Another has this: 'What happens when no thought (including the thought of Buddha) arises in the mind? Mount Sumeru!' Mount Sumeru is, in Indian myth, the mountain at the centre of the world, and the implication is that if one is really 'centred' one sees, at one's centre, not Buddha, not the self – but a nakedness, an emptiness, a nothingness. This is not nihilism. One might, for linguistic amusement, call it a *super*nihilism (a *high* emptiness). It is the space in which the wild duck fly.

10.

We've come a long way from the birds of Kentigern, but we haven't left them. Maybe its only now we're able to see them in their true light.

What I started out to do was to show a relationship between Buddhism and Celticism, or rather (getting rid of the -isms) walk on the *sunyavada* through Celtic territory. The Celtic territory seemed to me open to the *sunyavada* on two counts. First, that territory never knew a state-system with all the institutional hang-ups such a system entails. Second, in this territory there is no *ontological* state-system, the mind, as we saw in Celtic poetry, delighting in flickerings, scatterings, dissolvings, shudderings, all kind of sharp, momentary movements and sudden glimpses.

But we have talked enough for this once. The thing is to get it all down to 'tea and rice', that is, the simplest essentials.

Which means poetry, that other poetry we've been trying to get at all along.

11.

A short time ago I made a trip back up to Scotland, and re-travelled the whole of the West Coast. During that trip I wrote a series of haiku. If these poems are 'right', if they are to get us on to the 'path of emptiness', where the wild duck fly, they ought to have the qualities known in Japanese as *sabi* (solitari-ness, quietness); *wabi* (an unpretentiousness, unfulsomeness, a 'poverty' in the sense of disencumbrance); *aware* (a deep sensa-tion, something like a nostalgia); and *yugen* (a sense of un-definable unity). I quote poems from the sequence here as examples of Zen-Celtic poetry, and as an (open) conclusion to this essay:

> Watching the frost-world
> while my fellow travellers
> talk about management

> Why did he return
> to that empty island?
> bog-cotton in the wind

> A blue-grey stillness
> where the dark waters flow –
> night of the heron

> Frost and blue sky –
> walking between them
> on a ragged road

> That branch among the fern
> was a red stag
> sheltering from the rain

Village of smoke
hills in white mist
mountain whiteness

A grey shore
and a battered herring-box:
Scott of Stornoway.

7

Scotland, Intelligence and Culture

I would like, in the first instance, to thank the organisers of the 1989 symposium on cultural perspectives in Scotland for inviting to give the 'keynote talk' one whom some at least of our fellow-citizens would like to see written off or at least marginalised as French, that is, 'unScottish'. Before actually moving into the field of our concern, let me just evoke briefly the names of some Scottish intellectuals, among the liveliest of the type, who, for one reason or another, chose to live a good part of their lives if not all of it outside Scotland and particularly in France: Duns, Scot, Richard of St Victor, George Buchanan, David Hume . . .

Why did I in my turn leave for France? Because it was more and more apparent to me that British culture, of which Scottish culture was, willy-nilly, a part (with its own particular hang-ups) since 1745, had gone into a slump after the end of the Second World War, and that the situation was in all likelihood going to get worse. 'Getting out' was not 'abandoning a sinking ship', as some kind of pukka sahib morality or sticky localism would have it, it was necessary tactics and strategy. I may as well make it clear right from the start that, for me, a creator's responsibility is first and foremost to his work, not to any community – the individual endowed with energy and intelligence can always go faster and farther than the community and it is by following the paths of his intelligence, looking for the field adequate to his energy that he will, in the long run, do most for that community (as well as others), perhaps by extending the very notion of community. That is one principle, the individualist principle. The other is social-revolutionary: to stay obstinately in a situation which is not ready for change is just to batter your head against a wall – Marx at one point got out of Germany, Lenin got out of Russia, etc.

Exile of one type or another (and intellectual exile is the most interesting, if not the most soul-tearing and tear-jerking) is part and parcel of every powerfully creative life. It is the lesser poet who is anxious to appear as part of a community: for his song he needs to belong. As for the novelist, he can always drag his mirror down the boulevard. If he be working in the nineteenth-century naturalist style he will describe, in psycho-sociological terms, a context in which, say, a frustrated individual will have his 'useless' books thrust into the dustbin by his tough, utilitarian wife. If he work in the more modern (let's say Beckettian) style, he will have the protagonist monotonously talking his head off from *within* the dustbin. In both cases (and others similar – you can have the protagonist paint the bin yellow and talk through a tube) you will have more or less 'amusing reading', you will *not* have the forces and forms that arise from an individual energy that says no and leaves on its own paths, forces and forms that may, eventually, given a modicum of desire, wakefulness and intelligence within the community, actually *change* the culture.

There is a desire for radical change today, but, in many quarters, little wakefulness as to real possibilities and necessities, little intelligence as to means and methods. What one sees rather is an apparently inveterate propensity to mistake ruts for roots, an obsession (understandable, for historical reasons, but still not defendable) with identity, which prevents all increase of the scope of energy, any attempt at new co-ordination, allied to political thought totally devoid of intellectual content – what I've called 'Oor Wullie marxism', a poor alternative indeed to ruthless right-wing private enterprise. Some of the articles I read on my own work (which I chose to re-introduce to the English language via Edinburgh) were such a hotch-potch of feeble argument and reductiveness that I hardly care to spend time analysing them. One recent piece in a respectable Scottish literary magazine concerning my relationship to French culture was not only totally inadequate, it was ridiculous. Let me just say here, rapidly, that I have always been known in France as a *Scottish* writer; that when I left for France, I took a great deal of Scotland with me and that I have never lost touch with what I consider to be the fundamental landscape-mindscape of the country nor with the finest fields of energy, individual or collective, that it has known throughout its history. In my home on the Breton coast I have a fairly extensive Scottish library (gathered together since I was about fifteen). I may even mention in passing that the coastal path along which I walk most evenings is lined, at this season of the year, with bushes of the little white rose of Scotland, known in France as *rose pimprenelle* or *rose d'Écosse*. It was walking along that path those last few days that I thought out what I want to say here now.

The white rose takes us straight, of course, to the door of Hugh MacDiarmid, who must be saluted in any context such as this of ours here today as one who did his utmost to get some sense of what live, high culture means back into a socio-political-psy-chological context which he saw as a vast football pitch and nothing happening – nothing, that is, essential, just a lot of dribbling drivel. Without, of course, going here today into an exposition of MacDiarmid's politics and poetics, I'd like to quote what he wrote in his essay *Aesthetics in Scotland* (Mainstream, 1984):

> Worst of all is the continued absence of competent modern philosophising in Scotland, and above all the absence of æsthetic thought of any such value as might realign Scot-land with other Western European countries and induce æsthetic developments based on Scottish roots and yet able to withstand comparison with the contemporary æsthetic of other countries. The omens are not auspicious. All we can hope for, it would seem is, as in the past, an occasional voice crying in the wilderness.

This essay goes back to 1950, but I don't think that much, as yet, has fundamentally changed. On the contrary, not only are all the old soporifics still there, but a few new ones have been added, some of them stemming from a reductive comprehension of what MacDiarmid himself tried to put in place. I get the impression, in fact, that if a great deal of lip-service is done to MacDiarmid, there is little sense abroad of the higher reaches of his work. On the contrary, there is in some circles a downright rejection of those higher reaches. I read the other day what was presented in another forefront Scottish magazine as a MacDiarmid memorial lecture. It began sympathetically enough, but ended up sounding like the notes for his Sunday sermon of a not very talented parish minister, as if this were some kind of mould the Scottish mind has got itself irrevocably fixed in. MacDiarmid in his grave must have had a little revolution all to himself.

MacDiarmid speaks of 'aesthetics', which to many in Scotland today (those who think they are being radical when they reduce everything to the lowest common denominator) will seem altogether too abstract, altogether too elitist. I think myself it is a fundamental word, the full force of which is carried along a line that goes, say, from Plato to Bateson, via Plotinus, Ficino and Schiller's *Aesthetic Education of Humanity*. A lot of MacDiarmid's work enters that high field, but so much of it is confused and contradictory. In fact, I think it will be more and more evident that MacDiarmid is a kind of John-the-Baptist figure, and that the so-called Renaissance will have to yield to a new, wide-ranging and deep-sounding reconnaissance, and the working out of a new simplicity, which of course means a finely co-ordinated complexity. Among Scotsmen working in that field, alongside MacDiarmid at his best (which is not *A Drunk Man looks at the Thistle*, but, say, *The terrible Crystal*), I would put the great socio-æsthetic projects of Patrick Geddes, the morphological investigations of D'Arcy Thompson and the work of Edward MacCurdy on the notebooks of Leonardo da Vinci, outlining and highlighting Leonardo's 'cosmic vision'. These are energy-points, the nodes of an emergent field.

Here is a beautiful page from D'Arcy Thompson:

The waves of the sea, the little ripples on the shore, the sweeping curve of the sandy bay between the headlands, the outline of the hills, the shape of the clouds, all these are so many riddles of form, so many problems of morphology . . . the road of physico-mathematical or dynamical investigation in morphology has found few to follow it; but the pathway is old. The way of the old Ionian physicians, of Anaxogoras, of Empedocles and his disciples in the days before Aristotle, lay just by that highway side. It was Galileo's and Borelli's way, and Harvey's way, when he discovered the circulation of the blood. It was little trodden for long afterwards, but once in a while Swammerdam and Réaumur passed thereby. And of later years

Moseley and Meyer, Berthold, Errera and Roux have been
among the little band of travellers. We need not wonder if
the way be hard to follow, and if these wayfarers have as
yet gathered little.

There is a programme: æsthetic, epistemological – potentially
cultural.

Before going any farther, let us try and be quite clear exactly
what we mean by 'culture'.

I propose the following definitions. 'Culture', in the general
sense, is the manner in which a human being conceives himself,
works over himself and directs his life. In other words, there is a
conception of existence, a work-process (agriculture: care of a
field; human culture: care of the field of being) and some notion
of what is the acme of human achievement. You have *a* culture
when, in a social group, there is a consensus as to motifs and
motivations. In the Middle Ages, everything revolves round the
image of the Virgin Mary and the divine child; there is an icono-
graphy common to the peasant in the field and the philosopher in
his study. Same thing in the high period of Athens: the politics of
the Agora and the poetry of Homer. And, going farther back in
time, same thing in a paleolithic tribe: everything depends on
hunting, gathering and shamanising. Once you define your terms
in this way, it becomes evident that, in the strict sense of the
word, we do not have a culture at all, except in the merely
sociological sense (where 'culture' means football, bingo and the
daily paper). What we do have is a mass of cultural (most often
pseudo-cultural) production, in which you can find the best (but
you need to have good eyesight), and the worst, but mostly great
wads of mediocrity, what Paracelsus called a *cagastrum*, de-
fended ideologically for its very mediocrity, which turns it into
mediocracy, the biggest political power there is. Under this kind
of culture, the world is lost, world-lines are forgotten.

Before coming back to the actual lie of the land, and to
attempts to read it, and to see the potential emergence of a
world arising from the meeting between live minds, intelligent
bodies and the earth, I'd like to take a bird's eye view of Western
civilisation.

At the top, you have God – a bad idea, but a fixed idea, and
which has had a very long-winded, mind-benumbing career in

Scotland. The first 'line' under the God-point is the Christian
line, that goes from the birth of Christ to a hypothetical return of
the same Christ along a process of history seen, in moral terms, as
a vale of tears, a time of trouble and trial. This line once bore
thought, now all it bears is belief. Below the Christian line, you
have the humanist line, that goes, say, from Plato via Hegel to a
Super-Future seen either as the Perfect State or, in more liberal
terms, as the happiness of the greatest number. For Plato, ideas
are in the air – outside the cave, according to the myth, and that is
metaphysics, which has marked Western thought for centuries.
For Hegel, they are no longer in the air, they are in history,
history is rational, it is going somewhere – to the Great State or
the Supermarket of happiness. The nineteenth century was full of
this, so was a great part of the twentieth.

Nowadays, I don't think anyone any longer believes that the
autobahn of Western civilization is leading to something marvellous. People see it rather as leading to an enormous platitude
covered with Disneylands, or to a sequence of catastrophes:
Plato, in *The Republic*, imagines 'the plain of Lethe, void of
trees and of all that a land can grow'. The countries of eastern
Europe, who went at this in a heavy way, have recently shown
they want no more of it. The result, for a while, will be a throwback to the Christian line, which represented the only transcendence there was in a world totally devoid of transcendence.
Other reactions have taken place in more liberal contexts. In
the face of cosmopolitan, multinational sterility, there has been a
turning back to local community and parochial identity, pieties
of all sorts. But since about the second half of the nineteenth
century, there have been those who realised early on that the
autobahn was leading to . . . something not very interesting.
They considered it was high time to leave the autobahn and move
into areas, territories the autobahn had neglected, if not almost
destroyed. Sometimes they identified themselves with the large
line at the base of Western civilization, which is the pagan line –
hence resuscitation of Pan, Dionysos, ancient earth-cults, etc.,
from Nietzsche to D. H. Lawrence. But there were also the
beginnings of something else among these 'intellectual nomads'.
What is interesting in Western thought over the past century has
consisted in attempts to perceive, to work out that 'something
else': it is a great work-field in regard to which most of our

inherited epistemologies, most of our ingrained dialectics, not to speak of the great bulk of our literature, are quite beside the point.

All my own work – be it in the field of prose-writing (way-books), essays or poems – is involved in the exploration of the area neglected by the autobahn of Western civilization and in the elaboration of new concepts, ways of being, elements of a potential culture.

Obviously, this is not the place to go into detail. We would need a whole series of seminars. Here, I'd just like to evoke an idea of the culture-morphologist Frobenius. In *The Destiny of Civilisations*, he says there have been four great cultural periods: the mythological, which flourished on the shores of the Indian and Pacific Oceans; the period of the great religions, whose domain is Asia; the philosophical period, which began in the western Mediterranean before spreading throughout Europe; then, finally, the 'techno-economist' period, based on French rationalism, British realism and North-American materialism. At this latter period, myth is muddy, religion is routine and philosophy is flattened-out – but a world-economy is in place. To this world-economy ought to correspond a world-culture. After the mechanical conquest of the globe, there has to come a 'turning'. And since world-economy and mechanical conquest rose largely from the shores of the Atlantic, it's on those self-same shores that the critique of mechanical conquest and the creation of a world-culture could initially come about. The world-culture here evoked will be marked by: (1) a spirit of synthesis – it will be 'an orchestration of all cultures'; (2) the move from 'the tyranny of facts' to the 'liberty of the real'; (3) an openness to direct sensation, direct intuition, which demands 'an oriental attitude', an attitude of contemplation.

Now, I think, given scope for its energy, which means endowed with autonomous, well-staffed, well-organised institutions, Scotland could play a part in this. Certainly, for it to do so, it will have to jettison a great deal of what it considers part and parcel of its 'identity'. But this jettison of some aspects will mean the discovery of deeper ones, and the opening of the way to greater freedom of usage. When Frobenius speaks of 'a spirit of synthesis', who doesn't see it in a whole group of polymathic minds born in these parts? I think it is a Celtic trait (witness the polyglot text of the *Hisperica Famina*). As for the openness to nature, think of early Celtic poetry, with which there is nothing to compare except Far Eastern poetry, and think of pelagianism, of the 'there are lights' of Scot Erigena, the multi-veined realism of Duns Scot, on up to D'Arcy Thompson. Think also of the very morphology of the country, so intricate and so beautiful: Humboldt, in *Cosmos*, points out how great a rôle the shape of the Greek coast played in the development of Greek philosophical thought: 'The march of events, the direction of nautical undertakings, and changes in the possession of the empire of the sea, reacting on the enlargement of the sphere of ideas, have all been influenced by the physical configuration of coasts.' There was the beginning of that on the Western seaboard in the early Middle Ages, in people like Brandan, following in the wake of the *immrama*, under the impulsion of a new wind of ideas from Asia. This movement was lost owing to imposition from monolithic Rome. But something like it could come again: a reading of the coast, a reading and roading throughout the territory in terms Brandan and his like could never know, I mean with a sense of fine configuration, infinite ramification. I'm thinking, as an example, of that complex hydrographic network you find on the continental platform of Scotland's Atlantic coast.

There is much talk at the moment of the Atlantic Arc, that stretches from Scotland to Portugal, forming the 'Great West' of Europe. So far, this has only been seen in technical and economic terms. But it could also be a cultural question, it ought to be so.

Instead of being obsessed with England, and in opposition to it, which drives it into narrow, oppositional definition, Scotland should feel itself linked to Atlantic France and Portugal. Instead of thinking of national identity in historical terms, it might think now in those geographical terms.

Here, of course, I am talking geopoetics, which I see as the possible basis of a new culture, in Scotland as elsewhere. To put it in a nutshell, what geopoetics is saying is that at the centre of every live culture there is a poetics, and that the most necessary poetics comes from contact with the earth, following out world lines. I've already mentioned Greek culture, with Homer at the centre. Think too of Chinese culture, where at the centre you have the Book of Odes, bearing 'the wind of the regions'. Without such an active core, you have pseudo-cultural agitation, pseudo-cultural production, pseudo-cultural expenditure. In short, and to put it a little provocatively, but not only provocatively, by all means let's have a Scottish National Theatre (while maybe saying quietly to ourselves that theatre is no more a *fundamental* activity than is the novel as normally practised), but let's insist on the felt presence of the Caledonian Forest, a strong ideational field and a fundamental poetics, able to enliven education, enlarge life, give a sense of open world.

It is, I submit, more with fresh ideational wind blowing over the land than with ministerial mechanics that any real culture change comes about. At least, the beginning is there. To see how this ideational meteorology would apply to education and to the arts, how it could be implemented and fostered by institutions, would take time and more detailed consideration. I would simply suggest as a general principle that they should be as much outward-looking as inward-looking. Let us not forget that one of the best overall histories of Scottish literature these past few years was done by a German, and that the best geo-morphological study of north-west Scotland is the work of a Frenchman. Every attempt should be made to foster and spread the finest studies, wherever they come from, instead of merely abetting internal production.

The media, of course, have an important rôle to play in all this, though in many countries they have practically given up the ghost, preferring to provide the public with pabulum of the lowest possible order. This sometimes goes with an ideology of non-elitism, on a basis of ill-disguised contempt. But another philosophy of public communication is possible, and another practice. It only takes decision to make use of radio and TV talents already there, eager to do better work than they are often asked to perform. No need to fall into sophisticated boredom. Intelligence can be full of laughing wisdom and high culture (which is also grounded culture) is full of joyance.

8

The Scot Abroad

The persistence of the wayward, antinomian Scottish type –
versatile, erudite, filled with wanderlust physical and spiritual.
(MacDiarmid)

My theme here is 'the Scot abroad'. As anybody who knows my
predilections and propensities will suspect, I'll be talking less
about what comes to mind immediately under such a heading in
the customary Scottish context we all know: exiles in Canada or
Australia, whole genealogies of colonial administrators, long
lines of Bible-toting missionaries, and more – via the evocation
of travelling monks, wandering scholars, intellectual nomads,
poetic loners, and pilgrims of the void – about broadening of
outlook, extension of concept, expansion of being. But since
exiles aren't always just exiles, out to found a Burns Society in
the desert (sometimes they go native and become interesting,
sometimes they actually take a look at the desert), since mercenary soldiers are often in the game for more than money and since
colonial administrators quite frequently have side-interests (such
as studying local languages, literature and thought) going beyond
the call of imperial duty, I'll be mentioning also, at least in
passing, these categories, along with merchants, mercenaries,
doctors, engineers, and even missionaries. And – I may as well
put all my cards on the table at once – I'll be coming round in the
end to an apology for erratic Europe, in which, as I see things,
Scotland has played, and can continue to play, an interesting part.

1. The Exportation of Energy and Intelligence

One can sympathize, deeply, with the victims of history, while
feeling that to harp on history is probably not the best way to

advance thought and give breathing-space to the world – may, indeed, serve as an excuse (in addition, one is sure of immediate applause), for not doing so. Which is why, instead of listening in to renderings of the Skye Boat Song or Scots Wha Hae in Saskatchewan, I prefer to think of those Scots you'd find around Hudson's Bay or alongside the French-Canadian *voyageurs* on the long trail between Grand Portage on the edge of Lake Superior and, say, Fort McMurray on the Athabasca River – with a backward thought to the semi-mythical expedition lead by Henry Sinclair, Lord of Rosslyn and Earl of Orkney, who, in 1398, took twelve ships out and over, via the Faroes, Iceland, Greenland, to Newfoundland and Nova Scotia (then, Estotiland), from where they reconnoitred and explored the coast of Massachusetts and Rhode Island, mingling with the Micmac Indians.

I can sympathise, too, at least in part, with so many of the mercenary soldiers Scotland has bred over the centuries. My own grandfather was still in that line. He was neither cash-crazy nor trigger-happy, just eager to be out of the bit for a while, able to play dice, play the pipes, and get a whiff of the world. It was the same kind of motivation: the poverty of the country, a disinclination to confine themselves to humdrum tasks, a liking for wandering and adventure, that had taken so many Scots – David de Berclay, Adam de Hepburn, Sir William de Duclos (that is, Douglas), and the one called 'le bastard d'Escoce' – out to the Baltic where, alongside the Teutonic Knights, they rode the lands of Prussia, Lithuania and Russia. There were Scots roaming all over those northern territories, from Bergen to Dantzig via Stockholm and Königsberg. When, in the sixteenth century, Ivan the Terrible was on the rampage in the Baltic, he picked up hundreds of Scots in Stockholm, who later fought for him in his campaigns against the Crimean Tatars. Catherine the Great's army and navy were chock-a-block with Scots: Tam Dalyell (general), Patrick Gordon (who served the Tsar for thirty-eight years), Thomas Gordon (admiral), Samuel Greig (admiral), Peter Andersen (vice-admiral), Thomas Mackenzie (rear-admiral of the Black Sea fleet) . . ., and when the 'American Scot' John Paul Jones (I remember seeing a pay-roll of the French navy at Fort-St-Louis, near Lorient, in Brittany, and there, beside an American from Virginia, was 'John Paul Jones, Escossais') turned up in 1788, he was made a rear-admiral too. I could continue the army

and navy list of honours, but I prefer to look at more intimate
things – there are papers in the archives that reveal what went on
in these men's minds. Patrick Gordon wrote back home asking
for books on a wide range of subjects. One Matheson, a colonel
in Russian service, in his seventeenth-century testament, lists
among his possessions, along with a couple of rapiers and a
Russian sabre, 'seven books'.

There were the soldiers, then, but there were also diplomats,
merchants, engineers, industrialists and architects. I'm thinking
(still keeping within the same geographical area) of Peter David
('Petrus Davidis de Scotia Aberdonensis'), a Master of the Sorbonne who went in 1479 to Copenhagen in order to help on the
new university there, and who found himself Danish ambassador
to the Duchy of Muscovy in 1495. I'm thinking of the merchant
houses that were being set up in Russia, with ships plying
between Leith and St Petersburg. I'm thinking of Baird's iron
foundry, and his sugar-refinery, and his steamships you could see
on the Neva and on the Volga. And then there was Charles
Cameron, who laid out gardens and raised buildings at Pavlovsk
and Sophia, and William Hastie, who built cast-iron arched
bridges galore and also planned towns. They did all this while
keeping their eyes open and taking notes. William Richardson,
who was among them (later, he was Professor of Humanities at
Glasgow University), brought out his *Anecdotes of the Russian
Empire* in 1784.

There were the medics too. Among them, Robert Erskine, who
studied at Edinburgh, Paris and Utrecht before making for
Russia, where he ended up as Peter the Great's chief physician.
While looking after Peter's health, Erskine found the time to
collect plants, minerals and shells as well as the elements of a
prodigious library, and laid out plans for an expedition in natural
history to the Caucasus and Siberia. Thomas Garvine, born at
Ayr in 1690, studied at Glasgow before making for St Petersburg,
from where he left on a mission to China (1715–18). Another
doctor, John Bell, was entrusted with missions to Persia and
China, bringing out in 1763 an interesting book: *Travels from St
Petersburg in Russia to Diverse Parts of Asia*. John Cook of
Edinburgh also did a lot of travelling along with his doctoring,
telling of it all in *Voyages and Travels through the Russian
Empire, Tartary and Part of Persia*. James Grieve, another Scots

doctor with a lively brain, translated Krasheninnikov's *History of Kamchatka* and gathered in information concerning new natural history discoveries in Siberia and on the shore of the Sea of Okhotsk. Matthew Guthrie, physician to the Imperial Cadet Corps at St Petersburg, wrote, in French (these people were talking French as much as Russian), his *Dissertation sur les antiquités de Russie* (1795), and, in English, monographs on *A Tour through the Countries of the Black Sea* and *Natural History of the Taurida*. Another Scots doctor out there in Muscovy and Tartary, John Grieve, 'physician to the Russian army', got very interested around 1780 in *kumis*, that potent beverage made by the Tartars from fermented mare's milk, seeing in it a cure for 'consumption, digestive disorders and various nervous illnesses'. Nobody else seemed very excited by the prospects till another Scots doctor, George Carrick, came along a hundred years later and not only wrote a treatise on *kumis* but set up a sanatorium-village in the steppe country near Orenburg entirely devoted to its use. There must be something to that *kumis*. In an old French text, I've seen the word transcribed as *kosmos*. Either it was just a slip of the pen, or else drinking that stuff may seem like absorbing the Milky Way itself.

Although a nineteenth-century text describes him as having 'sought relief in liberal potations', I don't think the missionary Henry Brunton, from Selkirk, ever got round to *kumis*, otherwise God only knows what kind of kumical-kosmical extravaganzas he might have penned for our delight. Anyway, 'liberal potations' or not, he did manage to complete his translation of the New Testament into Tatar-Turk, which was some undertaking, though it did not have much effect on the Tatar-Turks. That was in 1813, at a missionary station in the foothills of the Caucasus, known in the Russian annals as the *Shotlandskaia koloniia*. Another Scotsman, by the name of Swan, with the aid, it must be admitted, of an Englishman, one Stallybrass, went one better by translating the whole Bible into Mongolian. That was at Selenginsk, on the East Bank of the River Selenga, 100 miles east of Lake Baïkal.

Before I leave this kind of area of endeavour, I'd like to evoke the careers and itineraries (in doing so, I'll also be shifting geographical position) of two other wideflung Scots: John Leyden and Robert Brown.

As his name suggests, Leyden was of distant Dutch origin (as those other Scots, the Flemings, were of Flemish origin, and the Cummings, the Frazers, the Grants, the Melvilles, the Menzies, the Bruces, the Mowats, the Boyles and the Sinclairs were of French origin), but he was born as the eldest son of a shepherd on a farm near Hawick, in 1775. Some tales from the *Arabian Nights* he read in a chap-book maybe sparked off his interest in foreign countries and foreign languages. At a local school, he picked up some Latin and Greek, to which he added, thanks to an eight-language dictionary that had come his way, smatterings of Hebrew, French, Italian, German and Spanish. In 1790, he went up to Edinburgh University where to his Hebrew he added Syriac, Arabic and Ethiopian. No doubt thinking that he might more easily earn a living that way, he then took to medicine, also finding time to edit the old sixteenth-century text *The Complaynt of Scotland* and write *A History and Philosophical Sketch of the Discoveries and Settlements of the Europeans in North and West Africa at the close of the Eighteenth-Century*. He planned to make a journey of discovery in Africa on his own, but the plan fell through – and it was for India he left, as a doctor in the East India Company. In Madras, he improved his Arabic and learnt Persian. He then left as 'physician and naturalist' on the Mysore Survey, his mission being to collect information on agriculture, mineral resources, diseases, medical practices, races, languages, etc. As a result probably of total exhaustion, he fell ill, tried to recover on the Malabar coast, then at Penang in the Malay peninsula, picking up in the bygoing another handful of languages, and thereafter, strong enough to continue on his way, went back to India, settling this time in Calcutta. In 1807, he handed in to the government authorities at Calcutta a detailed report on 'The Indo-Persian, Indo-Chinese and Dekkani Languages', before becoming Professor of Hindustani. Later on, we find him as judge to a region in the province of Bengal, where he sometimes spoke seven languages in the one day. He died in Batavia, in 1811, on an expedition to Java, leaving in manuscript *A Dissertation on the Languages and Literature of the Indo-Chinese Nations, A History of Modern Persian Literature and Poetry* and *A Prakrit Grammar*.

As to Robert Brown, he was born in Montrose in 1773.

Starting out as an army surgeon in 1794, his interests soon spread to natural history in general. It was as a naturalist aboard *The Investigator* that he took part in the Flinders expedition, spending ten months in Tasmania gathering the material that was to go into his *Prodromus Florae Novae Hollandiae*, which presented 2,200 species, 1,700 of them absolutely new. But what he's best known for is of course the Brownian movement, which he discovered in 1827.

If I wanted to close this first section with Brown, it's maybe because the Brownian movement represents fairly well the kind of diaspora and dispersion I have been describing.

2. Wandering scholars and travelling monks

Having given their due to the practical professions (with their extensions), I want now to look at more specifically intellectual, spiritual and poetic activities.

In the year of the Word 1955, at the University of Glasgow, Kennetus Iohannes Dewarius White (that's me in a semi-Latin guise) was awarded, as part of a prize for Humanity studies, Helen Waddell's *The Wandering Scholars*, written between Paris and Oxford in the years 1922–5. It is a fine book, still occupies an important position in my library, and has attracted round it a host of other books on similar and adjacent themes. Waddell realised well enough herself she was only scratching the surface, indicating the tip of an iceberg. Anyway, the book came at a right time for me. As a youngster, when asked what I wanted 'to be' in life, I used to answer with some aplomb: 'foreign correspondent!' (but of what country, in what countries? – more and more in and of a country of the mind, its elements culled from countries various). As time went on, my father would say, laughing, that I was all set to turn out an 'intellectual tramp'. It's true it wasn't very obvious where I was going – I was ready to move in any direction that attracted me. But maybe 'wandering scholar' was the beginning of *some* kind of definition.

'Wandering scholars' is the English term for what were known, in their time (let's say from the fourth to the sixteenth century) and in the Low Latin that was their favourite language, as *vagantes*, a term of disapproval, at least at the beginning, even of abuse, but which they themselves raised up to be the name of something like an order, on a par with Benedictines, Cistercians, Franciscans and all the rest: the *ordo vagorum*. These were erratic scholars and itchy-footed monks (*fugitivi clerici et peregrini, monachi vagi*), who abandoned stable positions and moved about the world (*qui circumeunt mundum*), from country to country (*per diversas provincias*) and from place to place (*loca commutantes*). One church council after another, from that of Nicea, AD 325 on (*quod non oporteat ex civitate in civitatem migrare*), fulminated against their independent instability, their transgressive travelling and their gyrovagating genius: *ubi stabilitas, ibi religio*! they thundered, 'dig and sow!'. It's true that certain among the *vagantes* were little more than Bohemian bums, scurrilous scallywags, rakehelly rascals, rogues and ragamuffins, out for an easy kip and bite at any generous or easy-beguiled homestead, in exchange for a joke and maybe some juggling, with words and with balls, but there were others. Even the frowning councils had to admit that some among them were looking for extensions of knowledge (*solidiorem eruditionem quaerantes*). But there was more to it than that – something that church councils and later university administrations had little or no conception of.

Helen Waddell calls them 'one of the earliest disintegrating forces of the medieval church'. They clung to Latin language and learning, to pagan culture, not as to some refuge of erudition, but as to a this-wordly conception of things as against the other-worldly conception of the Christian church (*De contemptu mundi* – how many Christian texts bore that title or its equivalent!). And to say they clung to it is a bad metaphor – they flung it rather in the face of ecclesiastical authority, and let its echoes take on vernacular tones as they wandered through this or that town, this or that village, this or that countryside. They might have thought now and then that they were living a decline and fall (the decline and fall, not of a Roman Empire, for which they cared not at all, but of the pagan spirit) – but it was a decline and fall with a spring to it. In fact there was a new music in the air, and an evolution going on, much lighter and more full of light than the overheavy renaissance of the pagan culture that was to come later. It gets into the early Provençal culture, it gets into German *Minnesang*, and it reaches one of its own high moments in the *Carmina Burana*:

Nunquam erit habilis
Qui non est instabilis
Et corde iocundo
Non sit vagus mundo

You have to imagine the Archpoet (so called because he chose
to be known by no other name) plodding and sometimes skip-
ping, laughing and sometimes coughing, along the roads of
Lombardy ('Down the broad way I go, full of life and unregret-
ting'). The existence of these poet-scholars has undefined long-
itudes and latitudes, they are pilgrims on the face of the earth,
intellectual libertines at large, knowing no frontiers: '*Se nuls me
dit, "Guarniers, ou vas?" tuz li munz est miens envirun*'. The
Latin slips over easily into French, Provençal, Anglo-Norman and
German, without losing its universality. And if the metre of the
verse is Latin, other rhythms pulsate in it, and room will be given
at times not only to local speech but to non-human expression –
for example, in the *Carmina Burana*, a blackbird singing in a
lime tree:

Vidi
Viridi
Phyllidem sub tilia

This is no imperial *veni vidi vici*, no human imposition or
dictation, it is the world whistling. The lyrics of the wandering
scholars are full, in spring, of the sense of wild earth and a rain-
washed morning and open space. In autumn, they are leaves on
the wind, *folia a vento rapta* (is that Latin, or is it already Dante's
Italian?). A euphonious, euphoric Europe is in the making.

One can be sure that there was a strong Scotic (I use that word
to cover both Scottish and Irish) presence among the cohorts of
the wandering scholars in the large sense I've just evoked. But
their names have gone with the anonymous wind and their identities have drifted with the general stream. As from the sixth
century, however, there's a specifically Scotic current coming in a
steady stream from the West. Rather than Late Latin, it's post-
pagan, Celto-Christian – but Latin and Greek, with Hebrew,
come into it also. As Ernest Renan was to say, these men were to
become 'masters of grammar and literature to the whole of
Western civilisation'.

In order to define the primal energies of the movement, it's necessary to go back to the arrival of Christianity in the outlying areas of Europe, and to a complex (and fertile) cultural situation.

There was a Christian presence and influence in the lands of the West as from the third century, and we hear of Celto-Christian communities at the time of the withdrawal of the Roman armies. When the first Anglo-Saxon bully boys turned up, there were 'twelve houses of God' in the hills of Wales. Then came Ninian. After studies at the house of St Martin, at Tours, in Gaul, he set up his own monastery, *Candida Casa*, in Wigtown-shire, and from there radiated out west to Ireland and north to Orkney and Iceland. As to St Patrick, he was, as every Irish schoolboy ought to know, born near Glasgow and was taken off to Ireland by pirates. After a hard and lonely time of it, he also went to Gaul to perfect his education, crossing 'sea-deserts and forest-deserts', till he received, in a dream, a call to come back to Ireland, which he did, preaching the doctrine of the Trinity via the symbol of a clover leaf, and setting up monasteries, *muinntir*, here and there. These Celto-Christian monasteries were marked in a high degree by austerity, study, and artistic activity. If there was a strong accent on penitence (with all kinds of severe practices, such as standing for hours and days on end in the form of the cross, or singing psalms up to the neck in freezing water), there was just as strong an accent on the need to become *nobilissime instructus* (which meant, along with Gaelic, the study of Latin, Greek and Hebrew, and of religion, philosophy and poetry), and all of this lead to the production of texts and books – witness, for example, the exquisite Book of Kells. The figures that come immediately to mind are Columba, with his foundation on Iona and his poems such as '*Altus Prosator*', Malachie O'Morgair, who was always on the move, and Sillan of Bangor known as 'the great teacher of the world', *famosus mundi magister*.

Three elements, I would suggest, made for the particular fertility of the cultural humus here. First, there was the proximity of the Celtic pagan culture, making for a peculiar pagano-Christian synthesis. If God and Christ and Mary were on the horizon, Lir the old sea-god, Lug the god of Light, Ogma the god of eloquence and Brigit the goddess of wisdom and poetry were not so far away – and the Christ was often evoked as 'my druid'. More than a few *filid* (Druid poets) must have been among the converted,

bringing their knowledge and their word skills. It's not difficult
to detect pagan elements in texts such as St Patrick's hymn:

> Fast as the wind
> deep as the sea
> solid as a rock
> I go on my way

and it's a fast move one can make from pagan poems such as:

> Wind keen and cold
> the sun low
> short its course
> sea running high
>
> crimson the bracken
> it has lost its shape
> the wild goose has raised
> it's accustomed cry

to Celto-Christian lyrics like this:

> Thick wood all around
> and a blackbird singing praise
> above my lined little book
> I hear the trilling of countless birds
>
> the clear cuckoo calls, what lovely talk
> in its grey cloak from the top of the bush
> truly, and may the good God help me
> I'm writing well in this forest glade

I'd go one further, delving into deep symbolic consciousness.
We know from the old texts that Finn (Fionn mac Cumhaill) had
twelve residences ('Finn had twelve castles in the dark glen of
stones'), of which the principal was the White Fort, *an Dun Geal*.
Might not Ninian's *Candida Casa*, White House, be a reminis-
cence of it?

So, there was the pagan-Celtic influence. Then, there was an
influence from the East. In the Bangor antiphonary, the monks'
rule is described as *Vinea nera ex Aegypto transducta*, black wine
brought out of Egypt. It was this influence from the hermit lands
of the eastern Mediterranean, Egypt and Syria, that made both
for the austerity of the practices and for certain elements in the

decorative manuscript art: those red dots painted facing the Atlantic came via hands and eyes whose environment was the burning sand of the desert . . . And finally, with all this as background, the rest coming from the originality of one man's mind, there was Pelagianism. Pelagius (that was his monk's name, from the Greek – 'he of the sea') was born around 350. After his early education, he moved to Rome for further study, and from there made for North Africa and the Middle East – he died in Egypt about 430. What is extraordinary about Pelagius is that, at a time when the Pauline and Augustinian notion of original sin was spreading over the world like a cancer, Pelagius denied it altogether: Nature wasn't contaminated and to be condemned, it was the basis to work on, it was something to be cultivated. Instead of leaving the human being caught between the pincers of guilt and grace, Pelagius insists on potentiality, the possibility of extension and expansion: in place of a fantasy-ridden tunnel, he sees a broad, open reach.

Those Celto-pagan Pelagian-Christian monks were perched there on the cliffs 'at the edge of the world', and then in the sixth century, they started flying over the waters, in droves. Again, wideflung travelling was written into the tradition – it's there in the Immraim poems that speak of moving to the far limits and finding unknown islands in the sea. But now it was called peregrination and 'white martyrdom'. Every monk worth his salt was out 'to peregrinate for the Christ' (*pro Christo peregrinari*) ready to go 'right to the limits' (*ad limina*). You have to imagine hordes of apostolic vagabonds, wild enough looking characters some of them, with their long hair shaved in a half-moon at the front, a sturdy pilgrim staff in their hands, a bell dangling at their belt, and on their backs a bag full of books, or at least bits of books. Eric of Auxerre wrote about 'all those Scotic philosophers landing on our shores', saying that 'the more intelligent and learned they are, the more they want to travel'. Brandan, born in Kerry, founds a monastery at Clonfert, and then when a certain Barintus tells of a trip he made to visit a disciple of his on a distant island, embarks for the Hebrides, Iceland, Brittany, and maybe farther. St Malo, St Pol, St Renan settle in Brittany. Others come to Reims, Cambrai, Soissons. There were so many of them at Péronne the place was called Perrona Scottorum. Malcallan crosses the Ardennes. Others trek along the misty waters of

the Meuse, tramp the sleety roads of northern France. Colomba-
nus arrives, in 575, on the Breton coast not far from where I'm
writing this text, crosses Armorica, treks over the whole of Gaul,
founding missionary station after missionary station, and great
monasteries at Luxeuil, and at Bobbio in Italy, while one of his
disciples sets up St Gall in Switzerland. Sedulius Scotus teaches at
Liège, studies texts ranging from those of the Church Fathers to
those of Porphyry, and writes poems, for example, about bees at
work on an early spring day:

> *Nunc vaga puniceis apium plebs laeta labore*
> *Floribus instrepitans pollite melle legit*

– as though the bees were *vagantes* if not *peregrini*. And then
there's the wandering scholar and peregrine who perhaps interests
me most, Johannes Scotus Erigena, called to France by Charles the
Bald to translate texts from the Greek, and who worked princi-
pally at Laon, where there were *scriptoria* (manuscript-making
ateliers) galore, as at nearby Flavigny. 'One of the most solitary
thinkers in the West', as a recent (American) study defines him,
Erigena is the man who said: *sunt lumina* (there are lights) and
who worked out a whole new vocabulary that was to keep minds
thinking for centuries. The Church authorities dismissed him as
'pantheistic'. And he is followed closely, still in the same erratic-
ecstatic line, by Duns Scotus, whom Hopkins, not the least of
English poets, called 'of realty the rarest-veined unraveller'.
Travellers and unravellers all . . .

   The intellectual and ecclesiastical authorities, all the humdrum
minds in power and those who hung around them, did not like
at all those wandering scholars and peregrine spirits. Their
existence was extravagant, their encyclopaedic knowledge was
overwhelming, their intellectual acuity was disquieting and
unorthodox, and their ideas were incomprehensible, but definitely heretical. 'Who do they think they are', cried a bishop
somewhere, 'those Scots who have the gall to disagree with
everybody?!' Especially when they began to put in question
certain of the Church's main tenets: Clement, from the Hebrides,
was not so sure that celibacy was a good idea and spoke his
thoughts out loud; Samson had doubts about baptism . . . The
towns were settling down, looked over by fat bishoprics. The
Scotic movement took place rather 'in the desert', and tended to

create a nomadic network outside the congested context of civilisation. But every effort was made to curtail it and rope in the wild spirits, or condemn them to exhaustion in the void. History finally won: the Scotic movement as a whole was absorbed into the established orders. But traces of the spirit remained, maintaining a whiter, faster current in the muddy waters of a thickening culture. When Belgian abbeys on the Scarpe and the Escaut began to draw up 'charts of liberty', the inspiration can be traced back to Scotic influence. And it would be possible to trace the influence right up into the twentieth century. An open field, despite everything, is still extant.

3. The Nomadic Intellect: Evolution Lines

Up to now, I've tried to give a general idea of the 'Scot abroad' via what I called 'the exportation of energy and intelligence' (an exportation that resulted often in subsequent importation of new knowledge, new ideas), tracing a line from the earliest times of the nation till the late fourteenth century and beyond. I've also tried to draw the map of a field of culture, in the opening of which Scots played an active part, and which for me still provides an interesting basis. What I want to do now is enter the complex, complicated modern period. The plot thickens, history gets heavier, the contradictions increase in frequency. If the logic of development corresponded with the course of history, general perspectives would be more inspiring than they usually are – but that is very rarely the case: few are the human communities that know a steady state of evolution. The question is always how, against the mechanics of history, to maintain some dynamic that transcends history, keeping open an alternative space that counteracts history. That is the work of individuals. Individual and society can meet, but they do not always meet, which means that the culture is rarely what it might be.

Scotland's contacts with the Continent, and, as we shall see, with France in particular, were to continue at full force at the time of the Renaissance, and the anthropological type of the Continental Scot was still foremost. Even after Scotland started up its own university system in 1410 at St Andrews, largely on the French model (its founder, Henry Wardlaw, was a graduate of Paris), Scottish students still tended to go to the Continent whenever they could: you find their names (Walter de Scotia, Simon de Scotia, Jacobus de Scotia, Alexander de Scotia . . .) in the archives of Paris, Orleans, Avignon, Louvain, Cologne, Bologna and Padua, very often with the word *pauper* after it, indicating that, being without sufficient resources, they were to be relieved of the payment of fees. In France, during the Renaissance, if you were looking for a teacher, a philosopher or a poet, it was often a Scotsman you would find. The number of Scots teaching and writing all kinds of books in France during those times is amazing: George Buchanan in Paris and Bordeaux; Michael Scott in Paris; Robert Pittiloch in Gascony; William Elphinstone in Paris; James Beaton (called by Mary Stuart 'Monsieur de Glasco') in Paris; James Kidd in Toulouse; James Crichton (the Admirable) in Paris and Bordeaux; John Cameron in Bordeaux, Adam Abernethy in Montpellier, John Gordon at Avignon . . .

The Reformation was to do a great deal to sever the contact with France, which now appeared to many as first and foremost a Roman Catholic country. And the French Revolution, which tried to get rid of religion altogether, was, again for many, to make the severance more severe. Take David Irving, in his *Lives of the Scottish Poets* (1810). If, at one point in his book, he speaks approvingly of France as 'a favourite spot for Scottish wanderers', when he comes to Robert Burns' enthusiasm for revolutionary France, he does all he can to scotch it. Not only does he not care for 'the levity of the national character', but the volatility of French politics is anathema to him: 'Of all civilized countries, France is the least calculated for realizing any scheme of rational liberty . . . They who still persist in contemplating France as the future parent of European freedom must certainly have approached the brink of insanity'. You see what I meant when I referred above to contradictions (Burns himself was not free of them) and, incidentally, clodhopping heaviness.

As from 1603, and more so as from 1707, Scotland was caught in a cleft stick. On the one hand, she was going to be hyper-English (I mean by that: subordinated to the English super-structure that now, at times, called itself British), and on the other, super-Scottish, in an antiquarian, romantic folksy or narrowly nationalist kind of way. The watershed is the Darien Scheme of 1695. There you have the Scottish economy in a disastrous state, and a company of bold minds, 'The Company of Scotland', getting together to try and remedy things by founding a trading station in the Panama area that would work with Africa and the Indies. The English East India Company wants none of it, England puts pressure on the merchants of Hamburg so they won't subscribe, and Parliament comes up with the Alien Act. The scheme falls through lamentably, Scotland loses her last chance of overseas connections, the whole pattern of culture changes: as Seafield said, it was 'the end o' an auld sang'.

The result for Scotland of this loss of continentality, and intercontinentality, was provincialisation and an ingrowing discontent, that could come across in any of many ways: contortions of the psyche; aggressive identity-ideology; the couthy complacency of localism . . . Add to that locally fabricated ingredients such as hard-bitten Calvinism (leading to æsthetic malnutrition and moral *rigor mortis*), as well as whole regiments of rubber-brained pedagogicals, parochial patterers, evangelical haverers, not to speak of bonnie prince Charlies, and you have all the enemies of large, cogent and coherent Scottishness. Of course, there were compensations, there always are. The 'lad o' pairts' could always develop – partially. Success could be obtained in a system of education that was out to eradicate the old intellectual type entirely. As Shairp, Principal of St Andrews, put it in 1856: 'For one genius lost by a public school training, a hundred clever lads were improved by having conceit or eccentricity knocked out of them'. That's the type that, with the real autochthonous genius ironed out of them, wear kilts, learn Gaelic, adopt a 'more nationalist-than-thou' attitude and write novels in Lallans about the rise and fall of Auchtermuchty. You could also make a lyrical and drunken last stand, like Burns, or churn out more or less corny historical novels, like Scott. Other developments on the self-same or parallel lines would follow, relentlessly: the rut deepened, and since it was labelled 'Identity', there was little move to get out of it.

There were, however, in the thickening context of post-Union Scotland, and I salute them in the bygoing, attempts to maintain an interest in broad issues, to keep open what Irving called a sense of 'enlarged investigation', get out of what George Davie (in *The Democratic Intellect*, Edinburgh University Press, 1961) called the 'commonplace intrigues of narrow-minded provincialism', by working along the continental lines still extant, though more and more threatened, in Scottish education (if the English trend was imperial and empirical, you might say the Scottish was continental and intellectual). Unfortunately, the basis Davie took for his study, and which was in fact the main reference of the nineteenth century figures he chose to examine, was the Common Sense philosophy of Thomas Reid. Not only was Davie himself apparently convinced of the intrinsic merits of Reid's philosophy, he felt confirmed in his conviction by the fact that it had been adopted in France. I for my part am less convinced than Davie of the merits of Reid's 'common sense', and do not think that the French intellectuals who adopted it represented the vanguard of French intelligence – on the contrary. Add to that the fact that, in the Scottish context, the debate around it turns into a ding-dong battle between a commonsensical squad on the one hand and an evangelical clan on the other. That said, there are, looked at closely, various brands and blends in this Common Sense philosophy, and it's worthwhile examining the interflow, especially since, as always in polemics, every now and then you can pick up echoes and asides that come from an area larger than the issues of the debate.

Here's John Stuart Blackie, Professor of Greek in Edinburgh, speaking, in a book called *The Advancement of Learning* (1852):

> My cry is for learning in the widest and most comprehensive sense of the word; not for Greek and Latin learning only, but for Icelandic also and Sanscrit; for the history of the beautiful forms of art and of great social revolutions, as well as of Greek particles and Latin pronouns. What Scotland wants, and what Scotland, I feel assured, will at no distant period produce, is not new editions of trite Greek plays already edited so often, and tortured so critically . . ., on the contrary, we demand a scholarship with a large human soul and a pregnant social significance, which shall not seek with a studious feebleness to avoid, but rather with generous vigour to find contact with, all the great intellectual and social movements of the age.

To this, Robert Flint, Professor of Divinity in Edinburgh, replied appreciatively:

I thank with all my heart Professor Blackie for his exertions in favour of learning – learning in its genuine and catholic sense – in Scotland. May God speed the movement he represents! Look what comes of the want of this learning. I lay it down as a fact, well known by all who are acquainted with our Universities, that the highest result of peculiarly Scottish discipline is to be found in those who have imbibed most thoroughly the mental philosophy and theology taught in them. What is the result, then, as seen in those men? They are strong-minded, logical, sharp men – without a doubt. Attack them on their own ground and in the ordinary ways, and you will not find them flinch or fail. But they are rigid and one-sided. Their ground is narrow, their thoughts all run in beaten tracks. They are the last men in the world you would expect to find forming a speculation as to the philosophy of history or venturing on the independent solution of a difficult problem either in social life or social science.

But the Evangelicals also had their word to say. Here's the Rev. John Cairns, in an 1851 article in the *North British Review* coming into the attack:

The ethical chairs in our Universities obtained a kind of licence to propagate and diffuse a refined paganism, unbound by any living influence of Christianity. Hutcheson and Smith propounded their kindred systems from the chair in Glasgow. Reid consented to sink the theologian in the philosopher in the same University. From the high post of honour in Edinburgh, Ferguson, Stewart and Brown continued for half a century to dilate in their different styles on the beauties of virtue and the authority of conscience, without a single recognition of the Divine influence, which can alone charm virtue into existence and restore into the hands of conscience its fallen sceptre.

While the pious, more or less pietistic, of Edinburgh, were hitting out at the pagans, more or less refined, of Glasgow, and vice versa, J. F. Ferrier, who eventually went to St Andrews to work out his *Institutes of Metaphysic* from a lonely tower, felt obliged to display his identity papers, saying, in *Scottish Philosophy, the*

Old and the New, that he was as Scottish as the next man, though he didn't agree with Thomas Reid, and that he was talking sense even though it maybe wasn't Common Sense:

> My philosophy is Scottish to the very core; it is national in every fibre and articulation of its frame. It is a natural growth of old Scotland's soil, and has drunk in no nourishment from any other land. Are we to judge of the productions of Scotland by looking merely to what Scotland has hitherto produced? May not a philosopher be, heart and soul, a Scotsman – may he not be a Scotsman in all his intellectual movements, even although he should have the misfortune to differ in certain respects, from Dr Reid and Sir William Hamilton? To expatriate a man on such grounds would be rather a severe sentence, and one which the country, I take it, would be very slow to confirm.

And I'll leave the last word in my summative little colloquy concerning the Common Sense philosophy, to David Masson, writing in the *North British Review* (May–August 1852), since at the very least he gets his feet back on the ground, and to a congenial landscape-mindscape:

> A Scotchman, when he thinks, cannot so easily and comfortably as the Englishman repose on an upper level of propositions co-ordinated for him by tradition, sweet feeling, and pleasant circumstance . . . It amazes Scotchmen at the present day to see on what proximate propositions even Englishmen who are celebrated as thinkers can rest in their speculations . . . Quietism; mysticism; that soft, meditative disposition which takes things for granted in the co-ordination established by mere life and usage, pouring into the confusion thus externally given, the rich oil of an abounding inner joy, interpenetrating all and harmonizing all – these are, for the most part, alien to the Scotchman. No, his walk, as a thinker, is not by the meadows and wheatfields, and the green lanes, and the ivy-clad parish churches, where all is gentle and antique and fertile, but by the bleak sea-shore which parts the certain from the limitless, where there is doubt in the sea-mews' shriek, and where it is well if, in the advancing tide, he can find a footing on a rock.

What I find lacking in all this debate is that 'quickening
process' which Ferrier wanted from philosophy, and I have some
sympathy with Edward Caird of Glasgow (he held the Chair of
Moral Philosophy there around 1865) who

> most rarely referred to the philosophical views which were
> current in Scotland in his time, whether as conscious
> doctrines or as unconscious assumptions implicit in the
> traditional morality and religion. Session after session
> passed and no allusion, near or remote, was made to the
> Scottish school of Common Sense. No Scottish name later
> than David Hume passed his lips. (Jones and Muirhead *Life
> of Caird*, cited in Davie, op. cit.).

I think the last great general moment in Scottish culture came
when the ideas of Montesquieu and Buffon came ashore in
Scotland where they were picked up by Hume, William Robertson, Adam Smith, Lord Kames, Adam Ferguson, Lord Mon-
tboddo, Dugald Stewart, giving rise to what has been called the
Scottish Enlightenment. And to the philosophy, sceptical and
investigatory, that resulted, I would add the geology of James
Hutton, who, in his *Theory of the Earth*, was the first to introduce into geology the notion of evolution in time and who
worked out a cycle of the rocks going from formation to
decomposition to sedimentation to metamorphosis to resurfa-
cing. I would add that cosmography was part integral of the early
Scottish education (witness George Buchanan and John Bellen-
den). It's something like that I would like to see now, along with
a renewal of Scotland's contact with the Continent. Perhaps that
could happen at this end of the twentieth century.

Here we come to the theme of Europe – *Eoruip*, as it's written
in the oldest collection we have of Gaelic poetry in Scotland, the
sixteenth-century *Book of the Dean of Lismore*.

Europe, the new Europe: what you might call USE (United
States of Europe) will be some time in the making. The units
involved may not be the states as we know them, nor even
nations – I like to think in terms of bioregions and AMPs (areas of
manageable proportion). Nations tend to move between the
imposition or imitation of foreign models (colonialism) and
the enclosure in local identity (nationalism). I'd propose a change
from the idea of 'native' (which is genealogical) to the notion of

inhabitant (which is geopoetical). Everyone will inhabit a part of the earth-world, 'earth-world' being the ultimate concept. Just as there will soon be a single monetary system, the euro (I can't help thinking of the first general monetary system in America: the *peso fuerte*, or *duro*), we can envisage perhaps a new general cultural system – always moving towards world-economy, world-culture.

That, I submit, is the programme of the 'Scot abroad' as I see him. I've tried to show signs of it, pre-figurations of it, over the centuries. There, in any case, is the tradition, or let's just say the tendency, I have been following, in my own way. There is the field I work in.

9

The Franco-Scottish Connection

As every professional or assiduously amateur lecturer knows, the thing, when you're asked for a lecture months before you're actually going to be on the job, and when your head may be turned in a different if not totally opposite direction, is to provide a title that will cover the theme while at the same time leaving you a good deal of navigational leeway.

That was my problem when Edinburgh University got in touch with me about the celebration of the fiftieth anniversary of the French Institute in Scotland.

With the kind of considerations I've just evoked in mind, I thought of a dozen possible titles for this talk, which I will spare you, before hitting on one that seemed simple, strong and open: 'The French Connection'. I was all in all quite pleased with this when Marie-Claude, my French wife, who is forever putting argumentative spokes into the wheel of my cosmic complacency, remarked that this was the title of a French (or Franco-American?) film about a drug network and that Edinburgh University might not care to have such a title placarded under its name all over Scotland. I protested, as I always do – to begin with. After all, if we followed this logic, the book by the Japanese poet-novelist, *The Snow Country*, might be interpreted as the under-cover invitation to a cocaine party. But the more I weighed the pros and cons, the more I came to feel Marie-Claude was maybe right. So I thought up some more titles, each more extravagant than the other, which, again, I will spare you. Till I came round to this variation on my original one. 'The Franco-Scottish Connection'. While, I realise, this in its turn could be interpreted as simply a Caledonian extension of the French connection, like a hallucinogenic hopping-up of the Auld Alliance, I decided to risk it. Given the context, and without context language hasn't a chance (the thing is always to discover the most *enlivening* context), I think everyone sees what I'm going to be dealing with, not to say *in*, and that Edinburgh University has no need to worry, at least about connotations.

As to content, what we're concerned with, in general terms, is the socio-political, intellectual and cultural relationship between France and Scotland.

The theme is huge. So much so that if I went about it historically, we would be here till midnight and beyond. While that wouldn't bother me a bit (once I'm started, I can go on forever), I realise some of my listeners may have other engagements. Which is why I'll try and look at it all from higher up, from a sceptical, phenomenological point of view – an attitude which, in addition, seems appropriate for a talk delivered in the David Hume Tower.

If our general theme is the relationship between France and Scotland, our *particular* theme is the presence, the influence of French thought and practice in Scotland. I've spoken quite frequently, both in France and in Scotland, about Scottish presence in France. To speak about French presence and influence in and on Scotland is a trickier, more thistle-prickly proposition, because Scotland has often had a kind of schizophrenic attitude to France.

Take, to begin with, the national bard, Robert Burns. On the one hand, Burns, who liked to think of himself at times as Robert Ruisseau (next door to Rousseau), sends cannonades to the French revolutionary government; on the other, he takes up a very localist, *generally* anti-French attitude, wiping out any useful distinction that might be made between, say, feudal Versailles and the Republican project, when he makes fun, for example, of dances 'brent ower frae France'.

In his *Lives of the Scottish Poets* (1810), David Irving at one point lauds France as 'a favourite spot for Scottish wanderers', and at another strikes out at what he calls 'the levity of the national character' and what he thinks of as the madness of French politics.

Then consider Carlyle. If, for the prophet of Craigenputtock, in his lectures on modern revolutions (London 1839), the French Revolution is 'the principal politico-historical phenomenon of modern times', it is also 'a great catastrophe'. Luther, says Carlyle, who sees the Revolution as the culmination of Protestantism (in a large sense of the word), had protested against false priesthood, Cromwell had protested against false priesthood and kingship, the French Revolution protested against false priesthood, king-ship and the nobility. So far, so good. It was a struggle against a delusion, and, since, as Carlyle says in a wide-ranging discourse that mingles economy with eschatology, it was a delusion that had no cash at its disposal, the struggle against it was successful. It was there, according to Carlyle, that the trouble began. For instead of giving a constitution the time to grow organically, the French, in Carlyle's estimation, set about making one, on the spot, practi-cally on the Champ-de-Mars, with minds that were a mixture of ruthless logic and humanitarian sentimentality.

With regard to individual figures, if Carlyle is unequivocal about Robespierre: 'a screech-owl fanatic', he has at least some respect for the 'gigantic heathen', Mirabeau. As to those indivi-duals who philosophically prepared the way to the Revolution, Carlyle dismissed Voltaire, for example (who always had a good word to say for Scotland, declaring that if you were after a skilful man, in any field, from philosophy to gardening, it was to Scotland you should go), as 'a Frenchman all over'. It took in fact, I find it hard to admit, but there it is, an Englishman, Leigh Hunt, to come to Voltaire's rescue and save him from being totally mauled by the dyspeptic monster from Ecclefechan. Hunt recognised that Voltaire was indeed 'French all over', that is, more than slightly un-English, but urged extenuating circum-stances and pleaded for a more charitable judgment: 'A French-man, with all his faults, has infinite social virtues, and is no small constituent part of the great human family'. With this pro-French plea that will strike many of us as not only very reasonable, but downright minimal, Carlyle must, I trust, have grunted a grum-bling, grudging consent. But France obviously bothered him. When Ralph Waldo Emerson was in England, in 1847–8, he of course called on Carlyle, then living at Cheyne Row in Chelsea, with whom he had corresponded for years, and together they went on an excursion to Stonehenge. On the way, Carlyle complained that Americans, put off by the coldness, insularity and snobbishness of the English, instead of 'manfully staying in London', usually 'run away to France and enjoy themselves'. To enjoy oneself is something Carlyle did not approve of – unless it was by wielding a polemical blunderbuss, and writing biblical diatribes that make Spengler's *Decline of the West* sound like *The People's Friend*. There's a lot I like in Carlyle, but there is also a lot I loathe. He can be one awful drone – like a bagpipe with no possibility at all of grace notes.

Within the Scottish people as a whole a kind of ambiguity persists. If there is general goodwill towards French folk, tied in with fond recollections of the Auld Alliance, there is also a deep-seated feeling, first, that the French can be a bit high-handed, which goes back to memories of domineering Norman castles and marauding military bands: second, that they can leave you in the lurch, which recalls the conspicuous absence of the French at the rising of 1745. The fact that Robert the Bruce himself was of Norman-French descent will be forgotten, or neglected. There is also the feeling, on the part of Protestants, that France is a bastion of Roman Catholicism – Protestants who will momentarily forget that France was also the birthplace of Calvin, from whose *Institutions* a good deal of their own thinking and practice stems. Add to that the feeling that the French are over-fastidious, over-emotive, over-intellectual, over-talkative, over-polite, over-discursive, in general over the top, and you complete, though it still remains blurred, a vaguely pervasive psycho-sociological portrait.

Let's leave sociology aside and do a little biography, taking a particular example of Franco-Scottish connections. As one born in the context I've just described, I opted at one point resolutely for France. Why?

Consider a twelve-year-old school pupil in Ayrshire, just beginning to learn French. His teacher at Largs Higher Grade has got it into her head that she's going to give all her pupils French names beginning with the first letter of their Scottish names. So in class this Kenneth gets addressed as Clément. He doesn't like that, the name seems to him too soft (only later will he learn that Clément was the name of one of those Hebridean monks of the early Middle Ages who founded centres of learning in France . . .), but he's interested. He's still at the level of *la plume de ma tante*, or *le chapeau de mon oncle*, but he's interested, and it's as if his brain was trying out unknown muscles, his tongue too. At home, he twiddles the knob of the radio till he gets a French channel, and imitates what he hears, from the tone of General de Gaulle to that of a *chansonnier*. By the age of fifteen, reading for his own pleasure in a Nelson's Classics edition Victor Hugo's *Travailleurs de la mer*, mostly on a shaggy rock overlooking the north end of Fairlie, he's not only interested, he's fascinated. He reads some sentences again and again, till he knows them almost by heart: *L'Atlantique ronge nos côtes. La pression du courant du pôle déforme notre falaise ouest.* (The Atlantic gnaws at our coast. The pressure of the polar current deforms our western cliffs); *Le matin de cette Christmas, la route qui longe la mer de Saint-Pierre-Port au Valle était toute blanche. Il avait neigé de minuit jusqu'à l'aube* (On the morning of that Christmas, the sea-road from St Peter Port to the Valle was all white. Snow had been falling from midnight till dawn). He loved that character Gilliatt, who 'saw nature in a strange kind of way', and how many chapter titles (A Word on the Secret Collaborations of the Elements), how many phrases ('No super-naturalism, but the latent continuation of infinite nature') seemed to add new dimensions to his mind. A couple of years later and he's reading Gide's *Nourritures terrestres*, that 'manual of escape and deliverance', as Gide, a Protestant protesting against Protestantism, called it: *Je vous ai vus, grands champs, baignés de la blancheur de l'aube* (I've seen you, great fields, bathed in dawn-whiteness). Then there was Rimbaud, striding along the roads of northern France and Belgium, talking about '*l'aube exaltée ainsi qu'un peuple de colombes*' ('dawn uprising like a nation of doves').

At eighteen, having by this time added German to his repertoire, our student decides to study French and German at Glasgow University, with philosophy on the side. It's the German and the philosophy that lead him to Nietzsche, into whose works he is going to plunge for three ecstatic years, including one in frozen solitude at Munich. The infidelity to French is only apparent, since there is no European author more francophile than Friedrich Nietzsche. It was he who said the only review he could read was the *Journal des Débats*, that the mere existence of a Frenchman such as Montaigne increased tenfold the pleasure of living on earth, and that only in the case of France was it possible to pronounce in one sentence the words 'nation' and 'culture' without committing a flagrant contradiction in terms.

At the end of his study course at Glasgow, armed with a postgraduate scholarship, our *Scotus vagans* knows that it's not Oxford or Cambridge he now has to make for, but Paris. Certainly in Britain there were poetic figures here and there, valued mostly for their picturesqueness and local colour, and, dotted over the heavily domesticated environment, intellectuals (a dirty word in English) making vague signs when they weren't engaged in biting their toenails with introverted intensity, but things had been happening in France: surrealism, existentialism . . ., that Britain had never heard of, or, when it had heard of them, had only translated into its own domestic terms. And in France, whatever the versatile confusion at times, whatever the versaillistic pomposity at others, at least the *general* cultural question was always posed.

Our gallivanting Glaswegian, our erratic scholar, spends four years in Paris working on a thesis about poetry and politics in the context of surrealism (which meant among much else copying out long out-of-print texts and pamphlets in the Bibliothèque Nationale, the Bibliothèque Sainte-Geneviève and various other recondite spots), but mainly wandering all over Paris, up and down streets, in and out of various types of establishment from Montparnasse to Pigalle, from boulevard St Michel to the Porte des Lilas, picking up material for a manuscript that grew into gargantuan proportions and for which it was going to take him years again to find an adequate shape, finally, after much elimination and concentration, calling it *Incandescent Limbo*. He was also writing poems, mainly set in Scotland (Glasgow and the West Coast), which, preceded by a text in which he laid out the first elements of his artistic credo, were to constitute his first book, published in Paris.

After four years in Paris, interrupted by stays at an old farmhouse in the Ardèche, down in the Cévennes country (where he wrote a book at lightning speed, *Letters from Gourgounel*), he decided to come back to Scotland, to teach French literature at the University, but, more fundamentally, to see whether, both inside and outside the University, he could open up a new energy-field according to the ideas he had got together in the outland. It was at this time also that he started to publish in English – from London, since there were no Scottish publishers other than those who did Waverley novels, Trossachs tours and cookery books. He did not care much for London, where litera-ture was turning more and more into a sub-section of the entertainment industry, situated somewhere between lurid so-ciology and inturned fantasia, but one English critic did say that his books stood outside the 'muddy eddy' of contemporary production and portended something entirely different. The issue became clear when he presented his fourth manuscript, *Incan-descent Limbo*, to his London publishers. He was advised to keep it in the fridge for later on, and in the meantime write a nice little novel. Our adamant author, already thinking France-wards again, said that he would get his incandescent manuscript published over the water. 'Ah, but France is *a literary country*', he was told.

It was in France, in fact, that our Scottish-born intellectual nomad was to publish his books over the next few decades. From the French, or from the original English manuscripts, they were translated into other languages, but did not appear in the English-language countries, with which he felt, intellectually, poetically and culturally, less and less contact.

It was only in the late 1980s that contact was renewed. And when our Franco-Scot returned, it was with the same general idea of opening up a new energy-field, new cultural space, and with, as one of the contributing areas, the notion of renewing the Franco-Scottish connection that had been part of Scotland's and Europe's liveliest times.

That's why he's here, that's why I'm here, today.

Now for a little chronological anthology.

I submit that the first Franco-Scottish cultural collaboration took place on Iona, around the year 479. That's when a wander-ing pilgrim from Gaul got marooned on the island and became friends with Adomnan, the then abbot. Arculf, for that was his name, told Adomnan about his travels and about the places he had visited: Jerusalem, Jericho, the Dead Sea region, Nazareth, the Sea of Galilee, the source of the Jordan, Damascus, Joppa,

Alexandria, Crete, Constantinople, Rome, Sicily, the Lipari
Isles . . . Adomnan was all ears. Could Arculf draw him the
townplan of Alexandria, and would he mind describing those
Sicilian volcanoes again? He scraped quick notes on wax tablets
and later wrote it all down on vellum, calling the manuscript *De
locis sanctis*, 'on the holy places'. I love that Adomnan. Not only
does he give us vivid details about the life of Columba and the life
on the island, he tells us also of a crane that arrived on Iona in a
bad state and that they nursed back into good condition, without
even trying to convert it. Don't let's forget too, in the context of
our Franco-Scottish connections, that a lot of the inspiration (not
all of it, but a lot) came from Martin of Tours via Ninian. And
figures following that line were going to be in France again and
again. I'm thinking of Erigena and Duns Scot. Everybody knows
the little dinner dialogue between Erigena and Charles the Bald,
king of France. Trying to get Erigena's goat, Charles came away
with this: *Quod distat inter sottum et Scotum*? (What is there
between a sot and a Scot?) The answer came back like a shot:
Mensa tantum (just a table). We have to draw the conclusion that
Charles the Bald of France had a sense of humour, otherwise
Erigena would not have lived as long as he did.

Moving further up the Middle Ages, there are French texts that
not only speak of the mainland coast, the mountain country, the
whole topography of Scotland, but speak of them well. If one
can't forget that in the *Roman de la Rose*, looking for the origin
of Hunger, Jean de Meun situates her in 'a stony, icy field' (*un
champ pierreux et glacé*) in Scotland, I'm thinking more of
certain craggy, frost-bristling pages you can find in Froissart
concerning our *forests et froidures*, or the evocation in Brantôme
of *ceste belle et grande forest de Calidoyne*.

At the time of the Renaissance, the French considered Scotland
as a land of philosophers and artists (Étienne Perlin, sixteenth century: *Les Escossois qui se mettent à estudier deviennent volontiers
bons philosophes et bons artiens*) and the intellectual traffic
between the two countries was intense, with people like Buchanan
or Ronsard carrying the connection on their backs. It was in
Scotland, as a page at Mary Stuart's court, that Ronsard learned
the rudiments of lyrical writing. And it was in France that
Buchanan plunged into the opening field of the New Knowledge,
writing the best Latin poems of the age in Paris and in Bordeaux,

and in the bygoing teaching Montaigne. Buchanan had a hard time of it in Scotland, conditions in Paris were far from idyllic, as he made clear in his poem *Quam misera sit conditio docentium litteras humaniores Lutetiae* ('On the wretched life of literature teachers in Paris'), but he was ever active, that is, rarely mopingly introspective, and I think he probably lived, on the inside and on the outside, the happiest moments of his life in Bordeaux.

With the Enlightenment, French ideas (those of Buffon, Montesquieu, etc.) were arriving pêle-mêle on Scottish shores, being picked up and developed in interesting, idiomatic ways on the spot, by Adam Fergusson (*An Essay on the History of Civil Society*), William Robertson and Dugald Stuart, and with Dunbar, professor of philosophy at Aberdeen, providing one of the early syntheses, *Essays on the History of Mankind in Rude and Cultivated Ages* (1788), trying to get a 'common sense' out of all the researches, cogitations and hypotheses. During this time, of course, David Hume was navigating regularly between Edinburgh and Paris, disturbing dogmatic somnolence and intellectual comfort whenever he came across it.

In the nineteenth century, again there's a notable two-way traffic between France and Scotland, with Charles Nodier's *Scottish Sketches* (1820) at the beginning, and Robert Louis Stevenson's French sketches at the end. It's the *desertic* nature of Scotland that impresses Nodier. He says he knows well the pleasure of looking at civilized and cultivated landscapes, but that the 'terrible solemnity' of those mountains and moors, if it can be oppressive and despairing at first, can make human society and culture seem like a paltry caricature of what life can be: *Ce que l'on ne conçoit pas sans l'avoir vu, c'est ce qu'il y a de solennel et de terrible dans l'aspect d'un désert où rien n'existe que des forces de la création.* Nodier's mind is still theological, but he approaches there some aspects of the geopoetical. As to Stevenson, his essays on French literature, *Men and Books*, were the first I ever read. Of the nine studies in *Men and Books*, two are Scots-related, two American, one English, one Japanese – and three French. Those French essays are devoted to Victor Hugo, Charles of Orleans and François Villon. Stevenson demonstrates how much finer and more complete Hugo is than Scott, with his 'greater self-conscious art' and his 'more powerful epical value', making for greater *enfranchisement* of the mind. In the Charles of Orleans essay, he points out that in the year 1415 Henry V of England had two prisoners in the Tower of London, one Scottish, James I, the other French, Charles of Orleans, and that both the Scotsman and the Frenchman, no doubt to Henry's total incomprehension, spent their time writing poems. Charles of Orleans may not be a great poet, says Stevenson, but he appreciates the man's ability to 'speak small and clear'. He has more poetic consideration, and perhaps some existential envy, for Fraŋois Villon, whose work he describes, in a beautiful phrase, as 'sharp as an etching, written with a shuddering soul'.

But if I spoke of 'sketches' at the beginning of this section of my talk, I was thinking mainly of those two little books that I read with delight in my skylight room at Allanton Park Terrace in Fairlie when I was about fifteen years old: *An Inland Voyage* and *Travels with a Donkey in the Cevennes*. For Stevenson, France meant a certain grace of living, able to 'make ordinary moments ornamental', but mainly a release from constraint, a 'spirit of independence'. This is the sensation we have as we travel with him along the Oise, and through the Gévaudan and the Vivarais. Here there's a coincidence worth perhaps evoking. Earlier on in this talk, I mentioned in passing the place where I wrote my own first prose-book, *Letters from Gourgounel* – a farmhouse in the Ardèche. It was an appropriate place for a young writer in more ways than one – the poet Stéphane Mallarmé, who taught English down there at the start of his career, said that it summed up his situation perfectly: *l'art et la dèche* (art and poverty). But to come to the coincidence. At one point, Marie-Claude and I used to frequent a monastery up in the Lozère, where we'd buy some bottles of the wine the monks made, *Fleur des Neiges*. The name of the monastery was *Notre-Dame des Neiges*. It was years before I realised it was the very monastery where Stevenson had stayed that autumn of 1878.

It was in the spring of 1877 and the summer of 1878 that Patrick Geddes was working at the Marine Biology Station at Roscoff in Brittany, just a stone's throw from where I now live, where he had been sent by T. H. Huxley. Geddes had not liked London, but he was in his element in France. After Roscoff, he followed the professor of biology Lacaze-Duthiers to Paris, where he wrote a paper on animal chlorophyl and the physiology of green planarians while studying with Lacaze-Duthiers at the

Sorbonne and with Wurtz and Gautier at the École de Médecine. Geddes delighted in the Parisian context. He found, as he wrote later in an essay ('Student days in Paris'), both the university and the city richer in impressions than anything he had known before. If he'd been impressed by the energy and the intellectual generosity of Lacaze, he found the same and more in people like Pasteur and Chevreul, director of the Jardin des Plantes. He attended many a lecture, notably one by Ernest Renan, and was enthralled. France for Geddes meant intellectual vivacity, critical acumen, an ethos of hard-working action, and moral freedom – in fact, he was to say, in a phrase that to many may seem a bit provocative, if not perverse, that every Scot should go to Paris, not only for an intellectual, but for a moral education.

It was in Paris that Geddes encountered the work of the sociologist Frederic Le Play, from whom he was to derive his famous trilogy: Work, Place, Folk. And throughout his life he worked to strengthen and expand the Franco-Scottish connection, inviting people like the geographer Elisée Reclus to give lectures at his Outlook Tower in Edinburgh. In 1900, in the aftermath of the Exposition Universelle in Paris, he got together an international assembly that included Pasteur and Renan, with the idea of reviving the old Scots College, an idea that never left him. A quarter of a century later, he was able to buy a big house just outside Montpellier and set up his new Scots College there, connected, in his mind, with the meteorology station on the Aigoual in the Cévennes and the marine biology station at Sète, the aim being to create 'a crossroads, a strategic point of learning and culture'.

Continuing still further along our Franco-Scottish line, we come to Hugh MacDiarmid. Contrary to what some might expect, who would see MacDiarmid only with Karl Marx on his left hand, Duncan ban MacIntyre on his right, and a lallans dictionary on his back, French references abound in MacDiarmid. The French intellectual he was closest to personally was of course Denis Saurat, referred to in that most ill-composed autobiography in all the history of literature, *Lucky Poet*, as 'my friend Professor Denis Saurat'. If I judge from the two pages devoted to him in that book, Denis Saurat seemed to stew in the same kind of metaphysics ('supernatural rationalism', he says in a 1934 review of Saurat's *Histoire des religions*) as MacDiarmid

himself did in 'A Drunk Man Looks at the Thistle'. Leaving all
this alone, I prefer to stick to the strict facts. Denis Saurat was
among the first, if not *the* first, to talk (in the *Revue anglo-
américaine*, in 1924) about 'the Scottish Renaissance group',
giving definition to what up to then was known vaguely and
offhandedly as 'the Northern Numbers movement', and he did
translations of MacDiarmid's poems for *The Scottish Chapbook*
and *The Scottish Nation*. For more interesting French references
in MacDiarmid, it's to *In Memoriam James Joyce* one must turn,
and there they abound. We go from Paul Hazard (*La crise de la
conscience européenne*) to Carco ('the Toulouse-Lautrec of
speech') to Proust writing on the style of Flaubert, and from
there to Jean Paulhan (*Les Fleurs de Tarbes*), Brice Parrain
(*Traité sur la nature et la fonction du langage*), Jean-Paul Sartre
(*Recherches sur le langage*), Francis Ponge (*Le Parti-pris des
choses*), Mallarmé (*Le Coup de dés*), not forgetting the Occitan
poet Raimbaut de Vaqueiras and Anquetil Du Perron, the
translator of the Upanishads into French from the Persian. It's
probably Paul Valéry, though, that is referred to most, whether it
be to his essays, such as *Poésie et pensée abstraite* or his
philosophical narrative, *Monsieur Teste*. If MacDiarmid is sometimes annoyed at Valéry's excessive use of the word 'pure', he is
fascinated by the extreme experience Valéry went through as a
young man in Genoa concerning 'language and the point of
consciousness'.

Another Scottish intellectual very much in touch with what
was going on in science and thought in France was D'Arcy
Thompson. In his morphological study *On Growth and Form*,
D'Arcy was concerned with the search for 'community of principles' or 'essential similitudes' between the phenomena of organic
and inorganic, animate and inanimate things, saying that this
research has been undertaken by few, whereas the search for
differences, distinctions, contrasts has been frequent. If D'Arcy
Thomson can adduce French examples: Carnot, Perrin, Vicq
d'Azyr . . . among the searchers for analogy and similitude, it's a
French thinker (Dunan, *Le problème de la vie*) he quotes as an
example of the search for difference. And I think the hypothesis
might be advanced that the 'British' mind will *tend* to a sense
of wholeness, the French mind will *tend* to make distinctions.
Both, I suggest, are necessary for intellectual evolution. Perpetual

analysis can be a wearing business, and if you spend all your time cutting hairs in four, as the saying goes, you're going to move from detail to detail to detail, *ad infinitum*. On the other hand, if one is too easily content with 'a sense of wholeness' (the 'it's all one, man' kind of thing), then holism can turn rapidly into the most holy or unholy kind of hotch-potch. I'd go one further, and suggest the same for language. English tends to be looser, more relaxed than French, but is often content with haziness, repetition, a floozy kind of vagueness. French will be clear, precise, but will tend to rigidity, over-perfection. By bringing French and English together, you give suppleness to your French, and clear precision to your English. Or you can at least work with that idea in mind. Wordsworth once declared that no Scotsman could write English. I wouldn't lose any sleep over such a statement, but if we admit for a minute it's true, or at least valid as a working hypothesis, if we can't write English, maybe we can learn to write in Scoto-French, which may be a linguistic and intellectual proposition a whole lot more interesting.

While we're on morphology, and still thinking of French presence in Scotland, French studies on Scotland, I'd like to mention two geographical texts among the documents I've gathered in over the years and that are now part integral of my Atlantic library. I have particular affection for a little text, *Les Montagnes d'Écosse*, by Marcel Bertrand, *professeur à l'École des Mines* (1892), in which he states that for anyone interested in mountains, Scotland is a privileged place and that '*la chaîne calédonienne est une des plus anciennes, sinon la plus ancienne que nous puissions reconstituer*' – there, he says, we find ourselves on primary ground, worthy of a 'geological pilgrimage'. Then there's Alain Godard's *Recherches de géomorphologie en Écosse du Nord-Ouest* (University of Strasburg, 1965), one of the best studies of the structural geomorphology of Scotland that I know of, rich in descriptions of erosion processes and in the results of the *perturbations originaires de l'Atlantique*.

Having outlined the Franco-Scottish connection as I conceive of it and try to practise it, it remains for me to say a few specific words about the Institut Français d'Écosse itself. Since a booklet by Alan Steele and Stéphane Crouzat concerning its history and

its place among the many Franco-Scottish groups that have preceded it and accompany it has been, or is about to be, published
by the Institut to mark this fiftieth anniversary, I can allow
myself to be completely personal, which is after all what is
expected of me in this context.

Of the co-initiators of the Institut Français d'Écosse, I knew
only one, Alan Boase, who was my professor and later colleague
at Glasgow University. Alan Boase once called me 'a most difficult person'. I think I can return the compliment. But in fact we
got on quite well together, maybe as animals of the same or
similar *irritabile genus*, and I salute his memory.

As to the Institute, that little France in Scotland to which
Marie-Claude had already repaired as a regular teacher, I actually worked there for a while – on a very part-time basis, it's true.
That was the year 1966–7, when I commuted between the little
Haymarket station in Edinburgh and the ever-loving Glasgow
Central. I gave a class in French poetry, and participated in the
'morning conversations' in return for which I was allotted a back
room looking over the beautiful Dean valley. I enjoyed that year,
and it was in that room I wrote the long poem *Walking the Coast*.

So, long live the Institut Français d'Écosse!

And long live the Franco-Scottish connection, which is a kind
of prefiguration if not model of the kind of Europe we would like
to see.

10

Looking Out:
From Neotechnics to Geopoetics

If you cross the Luxembourg Gardens, in Paris, from Montparnasse to the Latin Quarter, along the main thoroughfare, just before the pond and the lawn that fronts the Senate House, you come across a statue raised in 1906 by the Société d'Économie sociale (the Society of Social Economics) to commemorate the birth centenary of Pierre Guillaume Frédéric Le Play. On one face of the pedestal, you have the social functions performed by Le Play (for example, Commissioner at various times of Universal Exhibitions, Senator of the Republic), on the other, a list of some of his books: *Les Ouvriers Européens*, (The Workers of Europe), *La Réforme sociale* (Social Reform), *La Constitution essentielle de l'humanité* (The Essential Constitution of Humanity) . . .

If I've stopped at Le Play's statue (indeed I say hello to him every time I pass through the Gardens), which few, very few people do, it's because this was the man who had such a great influence on the thought and practice of one of the largest and most far-seeing minds to have ever come out of Scotland: Patrick Geddes.

Before picking up on Geddes' thought, in order to see where it took off from Le Play, it will be useful to look into the Frenchman's life, work and thought.

1. The Le Play Method

Frédéric Le Play was born on 11 April 1806, in a little town, Rivière Saint-Sauveur, near Honfleur, in Normandy. A brilliant pupil at Le Havre, he was finally considered good material for

129

the prestigious École Polytechnique in Paris. It was there, after intensive studies in mathematics, chemistry and geology, that he graduated as a mining engineer and it was as a mining engineer that he was going to travel all over Europe: Belgium, Germany, Denmark, Sweden, Norway, Switzerland, Italy, the Danube Provinces, Hungary, Britain, Spain, Russia . . ., taking notes, not only technical, but also social and economic. Whenever and wherever possible, he made those trips on foot. While still a polytechnic student during his first big trip, in Germany, mainly in the Harz, he covered 6,800 kilometres, doing 80 kilometres a day at the rate of 8 minutes 30 seconds to the kilometre (he kept precise accounts), which, as anybody who's done any real walking knows, is pretty good going. And he was always ready for difficult situations. In 1833, coming back from Spain on a ship with a mad captain and a drunken crew, he took over control, fixed the position, directed operations and brought the ship safely into harbour. In Russia, examining a carboniferous area between the Caspian and the Sea of Azof, he suggested technical improvements in the local coal-mining industry, and while he was at it, prospected silver, copper and iron mines in the Urals. When the first Universal Exhibition was held in London, at the Crystal Palace, in 1851, he was a member of the jury for steel tools. Again, while he was at it, he wrote a social and economic report on an English working-class family that was later included in his book, *Les Ouvriers européens* (The Workers of Europe, 1855). When the second World Exhibition was held in Paris, at the Palais de l'Industrie on the Champs-Elysées, Le Play was General Commissioner. At the third, in London again, in 1862, he was head of the French section.

In 1867, at the fourth World Exhibition, he was the main organiser, and he worked out an ingenious scheme for providing a global view of world production, using a system of radial paths and concentric circles. Along the radial paths, you could see all the products of any one country; round the concentric circles, you could compare any particular product from any one country with its equivalent in another. That exhibition was held on the banks of the Seine, between the Pont Royal and the Pont d'Iéna. To convey visitors easily from one point to another, Le Play had the idea of boats – that was the origin of the *bateaux-mouches* that still ply along the river. While organising these exhibitions (for which he became a State Councillor and a Senator), while travelling from place to place taking his innumerable notes, Le Play taught metallurgy at the School of Mining in Paris, later occupying a Chair of Political Economy at the Collège de France. He lived latterly at 6 Place Saint-Sulpice, getting up at 6 a.m. every day and working twelve hours (ten on less good days) in a big room (kept at an even temperature between 14 and 15 degrees centigrade), looking out over the square.

What with gothic or romantic images of bloody and noisy revolution, and tinsel conceptions of 'Gay Paree', it's often forgotten that Paris has always been a place of social, political and economic experimentation. As a young man, Le Play attended the meetings of a Saint-Simonist phalanstery up on Montmartre, a practice for which he was condemned by the Haute Cour, risking the guillotine. Pardoned, he was, instead, sent to America. He used his American exile to study social, industrial and economic conditions in the US, sending back detailed reports to the *Journal des Débats*. A great believer in intercontinental communication (though he foresaw the disturbing effect which American industry would initially have on Europe), he advocated canals in Panama and Nicaragua. This is may be the place to mention too that Le Play was the first to suggest a tunnel under the Channel . . .

Le Play's was a free and wide-ranging mind. Socio-politically, if at one time he had been attracted to Utopian thinking, he was finally going to give up the idea of Utopia, as well as that of revolution, with no nostalgia for any *ancien régime*, and no fixation on the *status quo*. So what remained? First-hand study, down-to-earth method, experimental sociology, applied social art.

In 1856, Le Play founded the *Société d'économie et de sciences sociales* (the Society for Social Science and Economy), which turned in a very short time into the *Société internationale des études pratiques d'économie sociale* (the International Society for Practical Studies in Social Economy). This international society had a whole network of local organisms, known as *Unions internationales pour la paix sociale* (Unions for Social Peace). Le Play conceived the whole organisation as a school of social progress. What you might call its motto was the triad: *Lieu, Travail, Famille* (Place, Work, Family). Where Auguste Comte worked on the historical classification of societies, where

Durckheim tended to stress social and institutional behaviour, Le Play concentrated on the individual. But the individual, he says, belongs to a group. There are various types of group: workshop, association, county, province, State, but the basic unity is the family. Leplaysian sociology studies the family, and in particular the working-class family, as representing the bottom line. Now a family, he says, belongs to one of three types: the *famille patriarchale*, gathered under the patriarch, the *famille-souche*, the stem-family, with sons and daughters leaving and returning, and the *famille instable*, the instable family, with no coherence, no consistent inheritance. As to method, wary of theoretical systematisation and of statistics, anxious to avoid hasty generalisations, Le Play relies on the monography. Based on direct observation and on questions concerning environment, belief, life-ideal, moral, habits, employment, occupations, budget, means of expression, etc., the Leplaysian monography tries to make as many soundings as possible. It has its limitations, but for the age it was a new and exciting field.

Some of Le Play's disciples were going to develop his conceptions and his method. Butel, with a monography on the Vallée d'Ossau, was going to criticise Le Play's notion of the Pyrenean family as a 'stem-family'. Working on an idea still latent in Le Play's *Les Ouvriers européens*, Henri de Tourville was to develop the idea of the 'particularist family formation', which sons and daughters leave in order to find their own ways. In this formation, stress is laid on individual initiative. Picking up from Le Play and de Tourville, Edmond Demolins was to distinguish between the communitarian formation (dependence on the collectivity, passive waiting for authority and the State) and the particularist formation (where the group is secondary to the individual, and where the accent is on self-reliance), taking pains to stress that this particularist formation does not imply ruthless individualism, since the particularist may well decide to found an association – but an association based on individual dynamics. In order to foster particularism, Demolins founded the École des Roches in 1899. As a geographer too, Demolins tended to stress the influence of geographical environment (without turning this into any absolute geographical determinism). Following this line, studies were to be written concerning less family types than regional types – witness, a study by Paul Bureau on *Le Paysan des fjords* (The Peasant of the Fjords). Then there were further studies in economy, foretelling the rise of an economy that would be neither individualist nor collectivist, but fiscal.

Out of Le Play's 'Work, Place, Family', and via his multiple monographic method, studies, then, were being made bringing together social structure, geographical environment and systems of economy.

This is where Patrick Geddes comes in.

2. Geddes: Field 1

Patrick Geddes (1854–1932) bears all the marks of a certain type of Scot who, for various reasons, has often, if not always, had a hard time of it in modern Scotland. In an address delivered at the University College of Dundee in 1890, he said that, while being 'no less enthusiastic a Scotsman as any here', he was not going to indulge in 'the usual cheap flatteries about our being the best educated and the most advanced people in the world'. If, out of Scotland, at all periods, had emerged some of the finest minds in the world ('world-famous scholars, writers and men of action'), the country itself, in its 'popular and cultural movements', in its concepts and arguments, was always two or three generations late: '. . . while the Scotsman has often led the age, Scotland has no less often lagged behind in it'. Lest this be thought of as special pleading, and be reduced to the status of a disgruntled expression of frustration by a man who, despite brilliance in his field, had been refused (in 1888) the Regius Chair of Botany at Edinburgh, and some of whose books were practically boycotted (I'm thinking notably of *The Evolution of Sex*), here's a statement by Colin Denovan (in a series of essays, *For a Celtic Future*, published by the Celtic League: Dublin, 1983):

> Scotland has produced many people who do not appear to have achieved the public recognition at home which their talents and their achievements would seem to merit. Often, it is the case that they are better appreciated abroad. Meanwhile, others of small or even apocryphal achievement loom larger in the public consciousness.

During his life-time, in the field of sociology and town-planning, Geddes was to have more recognition and impact in India than in

Scotland, and, so far as his general educational and cultural project goes, it was finally to have its main base in France, a country to which Geddes was attracted from early on. But there sems to be a renewed interest in Geddes' work today in Scotland, and that could be one of the signs of a new general opening.

As a youth, Geddes was fired by the example of Scottish personalities such as the Admirable Crichton, and over the years he came to see himself as a modern avatar of the wandering Scot, a particularly errant and erratic example of the medieval wandering scholar, nailing his theses up on any convenient wall, and ready to take on all-comers. Not, as we shall see, that Geddes' project was anything like a neat bundle of cut-and-dried theses – it had more scope, wider reference and larger aims. Geddes belongs to that scattered band of extravagant Scots that includes, say, to take some recent examples, Ruskin and Carlyle (in a different way, MacDiarmid). When he lived in London, he haunted Cheyne Row, and in an essay, 'Homes and haunts of famous authors', tells of seeing Carlyle and a friend in the street and thinking of 'ancient peripatetic philosophers'. He was for a while, too, in correspondence with Ruskin. Geddes himself was endowed with an extraordinary initiatory and inspiring energy, knowing, as he wrote in one of his multitudinous and multifarious notes that 'Etho-polity [it's one of his many neologisms] occurs when some initiator emerges from his retreat'.

It's customary, in presenting Geddes, to make out a list of his many activities: botanist, sociologist, urbanist, educator, literary man . . . and then classify him as an 'all-rounder', more or less vaguely implying eclectic amateurism and versatile, confusionistic enthusiasm. I am no enemy of classification (seen as temporary model, movement towards coherence – not as an intellectually respectable way of getting rid of worrying phenomena), but I submit that 'all-rounder' is insufficient, and all too vague. What some call eclecticism can be the initial move towards a larger coherence, what some see as extravagant displacement can be the drift towards some new unidentified centre. The various *aspects* of a mind like that of Geddes only take on coherence and cogency when you see their *prospect*. That's what I want to do in the central part of this essay. Geddes called himself 'a synthesizing generalist'. That's certainly a better definition than 'all-rounder'. In his general introduction to Geddes' work, *The Worlds of*

Patrick Geddes (Routledge and Kegan Paul, 1978), Philip Board-
man calls him, in passing, 'at heart a poet'. In the context, this
does not mean a great deal (it refers to some emotional repression
due to a Presbyterian upbringing and to an occasional shot at
verse). But I'll use the word in a larger sense – as Geddes himself
used it at times. And I think that poetics, as the expression of
synthetic study, multi-streamed thought and a world-vision, was
a problem for Ruskin, Carlyle and MacDiarmid. Near the end of
his life, in 1931, Geddes spoke of 'the Teufelsdröckhian bags of
papers' he felt he had to unravel. Throughout his studies and
cogitations, experiences and meditations, he piled up masses of
notes and fragments ('idea-middens', he called them), which only
rarely got to the state of coherent *opus*. The image I have in my
mind's eye of Patrick Geddes is of him sitting in 'The Edinburgh
Room' at the Tower Planning Exhibition in London, 1910,
surrounded by a congeries of diagrams, postcards, newspaper
clippings, woodcuts . . . and talking his head off to anyone who
cared to listen.

3. Geddes: Field 2

Originally intending to study botany, Geddes went up to Edinburgh University, decided he didn't like the teaching methods
('conning inventories of plant-mummies') and went back home
after a week. It was only some time later he got the chance to study
biology under T. H. Huxley in London. That was his real start.

Huxley was exactly what Geddes was after. This was the man
who delivered public lectures with provoking titles such as 'Man
and the Other Animals', in which he made fun of the funda-
mentalists and Bible-thumpers, and who wrote wide-ranging
books such as *Man's Place in Nature* (1863). He was also a real
teacher: Geddes liked both his methods and his general outlook.
In an essay on 'Huxley as Teacher', he described Huxley's
lectures as 'broadly biological', saying that they 'early opened
to us in its colours and perspectives' the 'larger physiology of
Nature-ecology'. What particularly interested Geddes was the
border-line between plant and animal life, as revealed, for
example, in the 'yellow cells' of radiolarians. The work went
on well, but if Geddes liked Huxley, he liked London less, and
he'd early made it clear that when the time came he'd be keen to

continue his studies at Continental centres of research rather than at any institution to be found in England, or Scotland. Probably anxious to keep him, Huxley got his very promising pupil a job as demonstrator in practical physiology at University College, London, but, seeing that Geddes was chafing, finally sent him in the spring of 1877 to Roscoff in Brittany, where Professor Lacaze-Duthiers of the Sorbonne had founded a marine biology station. That was Geddes' introduction to France, and he loved it. He was back at Roscoff in the summer of 1878, continuing his studies of a certain primitive flatworm found on the beaches of Brittany. Thereafter, he followed Lacaze-Duthiers to Paris, where he published, in French, his paper: '*Sur la chlorophylle animale et la physiologie des planaires verts*' (on animal cholrophyl and the physiology of green planarians), while studying with Lacaze-Duthiers at the Sorbonne, and with Wurtz and Gautier at the École de Médecine.

Geddes delighted in the Parisian context. In a typescript 'student days in Paris', he evoked those times and expressed his love of France:

> The University and the City were each richer in impressions, experiences and impulses than all I had known before . . . Here, the energy and helpfulness of Lacaze and the other teachers. There the superman-like intensity of Pasteur, beyond all men I have ever seen. The patriarcal Chevreul (at ninety he was still director of the Jardin des Plantes) I remember with particular distinctness and no little gratitude . . . And what vivid conversation everywhere! When I read Anatole France I hear his old master and mine – Pierre Lafitte – talking. And even the single lecture of Renan's I went to was enough to give me an enduring idea of that subtly mingled mind. It was indeed a time of renewal.

Again and again, in letters and in lectures (I'm thinking of his 1910 lecture in Chicago: 'The Real France'), in conversations and in texts, Geddes came back on his appreciation of the territory 'over the water'. The elements he insisted on were moral freedom (France freed Geddes from the Wee Free Kirk and from Victorianism), intellectual vivacity, the search for truth ('*To see the thing as it is*, that is the perpetual quest, the essential atmosphere of French criticism') and the ethos of action:

What else does one learn in Paris? How its world-surpass-
ing clearness of thought and excellence of workmanship
have developed simply by following the one main road to
these fundamental human moralities of truth and action:
that of doing a day's work. For here is the hardest working
of all great cities.

Given this appreciation, it's no surprise to see Geddes, from
that moment on, striving, beyond all Auld Alliance havering and
romantic Jacobitism, to strengthen the contact between Scotland
and France. In 1900, in the aftermath of the Exposition Universelle in Paris, he got together an 'international assembly',
which included eminent figures such as Pasteur and Renan, with
the idea of reviving the old Scots College (it dates back to 1325)
in the Rue du Cardinal Lemoine. During the latter part of his life,
say from 1924 on, this idea of a renewed Scots College became an
obsession with him. As to place, his attention focused on
Montpellier, in Southern France. With money received as compensation for the loss of his Cities Exhibition (it had sunk on its
way to India during the 1914–18 War), he was able to buy a
place just a few miles from Montpellier, at Assas, spelling out its
address with pleasure as: Collège des Écossais, Garrigue des
Brusses, Montpellier, Hérault, France. He saw this Scots College
as, geographically, situated between the meteorological station
on the Aigoual, in the Cévennes, and the marine biology station
at Sète, on the Mediterranian coast, while being in intellectuel
contact with centres of learning in Arles, Nîmes, Avignon,
Tarascon, Béziers, Narbonne, etc. Closely related to the Scots
College, which would house, not a coterie, not a party, but 'an
evolutionary group', were, to Geddes' eyes, the School of
Archaelogy at Les Eyzies and the School of Regional Survey at
Domme in the Dordogne, run by Paul Reclus, the son of an old
friend of his, Elie Reclus, the ethnologist brother of Elisée Reclus
the geographer. Around the Scots College, he envisaged a College
of Americans, a College of Indians, in fact a College of every
nation, region and group under the sun. Gathered there in 'the
incomparable region of Languedoc', they would create the
equivalent of the old Oc culture, able to make of the area 'a
cross-roads, a strategic point of learning and culture'.
Lewis Mumford, disciple of Patrick Geddes, author of *The*

Culture of Cities (Secker and Warburg, 1938) called this project 'a white elephant'. Well, long live white elephants! The world would be poorer without them.

But to come back to Geddes' life-line.

It's often asked why, in the latter years of the 1870s, there was a break in that line, with Geddes abandoning what promised to be a succesful career in biology for . . . something else, that was a lot more undefinable. The first thing to be said is that there was never any real 'break'. Geddes never abandoned biology (he brought out *Life: Outlines of General Biology* in the last year of his life); he never abandoned anything, be it country or discipline, he extended them into a wider context, he radiated them out into a larger field. But around 1878, 1879, a sea-change, a modification of vision, rather than anything like a catastrophe (even in the mathematical sense) took place.

Two reasons can be adduced for it: one technical, the other intellectual. The technical reason is the one that is usually highlighted, since it is more graphic. The intellectual one is often played down, but it is, to my mind, more significant. In any case, they are connected.

Bad eyesight ran in Geddes' family and he had strained his eyes with months of intense microscopic work. Add to that the glaring light of the Mexican plateau, and it will come as no great surprise that in the course of a scientific expedition to Mexico in 1879, during which he was to pursue research in geology, botany and zoology, Geddes went temporarily blind, spending ten weeks' convalescence in total darkness. Microscopic research was over for him – but, as often happens in creative careers, this negative event had a positive result: it was while feeling with his hands the frame and bars of a window that Geddes got the idea of his 'thinking machines', that is, those graphs, grids, schemata that he worked out in order to co-ordinate and interrelate thought, comparing them to Mercator lines or the logarithms of Napier. Beginning with a nine-square frame inspired by the window ('transplanted' onto folded paper), Geddes finally worked out one of 144 squares. By way of illustration, I'll stick to the nine-square grid. Putting PLACE in the first square, WORK in the fifth and FOLK in the ninth, you can work out combinations of PLACE-WORK, PLACE-FOLK; WORK-PLACE, WORK-FOLK; FOLK-PLACE, FOLK-WORK, and see them interacting. The same goes with, for example,

SENSE, EXPERIENCE, FEELING; EMOTION, IDEATION, IMAGERY; ETHO-
POLITY, SYNERGY, ACHIEVEMENT. What you get out of the grid
depends, obviously enough, on what you feed into it – which is
to say that if the graph is to be more than a trivial game, it requires
intellectual preparation. This brings us to the second, in my
estimation, more fundamental reason for Geddes' sea-change.

One day in Paris, walking along the Rue Jacob, Geddes' eye
was caught by a poster advertising lectures by one Edmond
Demolins on something called '*La nouvelle science sociale*'
('the new social science'). Intrigued, he attended the lecture –
and it was a revelation. If this introduction by one of the disciples
of Le Play to Le Play's thought struck Geddes so powerfully, it
was because his mental terrain was at least partly prepared for it.
While studying, assiduously, under Huxley, Geddes had also
been following his own idiosyncratic course of reading. Among
the authors that interested him most (Huxley approved of neither
of them) were Herbert Spencer and Auguste Comte. Over against
the hardcore Darwinists (among them, Huxley) who saw in
natural evolution only blood-and-claw competition and a ruthless survival of the fittest, Spencer, while hardly denying those
other elements, saw also signs of co-operation. Geddes was interested. As to Comte, the Frenchman's ideas were in the English air
ever since 1865, when John Stuart Mill published his *Auguste
Comte and Positivism*. Geddes had read that book, as well as
some of Comte's works, and he had got in touch with the English
Positivists headed by Richard Congreve. What attracted Geddes
to Comtian social science was its attempt at overall coherence
and its project, Comte's motto being: *Induire pour déduire afin
de construire* ('induce before you deduce in order to construct').
Geddes was also intellectually fascinated by Comte's classification of human social history: from the theological-military
society to the State-and-individual society and from there to
the industrial-scientific society, as well as by its idea that mathematics, physics, chemistry and biology should all be seen as pre-
liminaries, prolegomena, to a new science.

As to Le Play, who, as we have seen, considered Comte too
systematic and abstract, his work might at least have been
accepted as a complement, but it was almost totally unknown.
The Edinburgh Review, which in its best days had an eye to
France, makes no mention of it between 1855 and 1860, though

Le Play's *Workers of Europe* had appeared in 1855 and the International Society for Practical Studies in Social Economy was founded in 1856. *The Westminster Gazette* made a brief mention in 1858. And that was it. Le Play's work had no influence either in concepts or in field techniques till Geddes discovered it and took it over. Certainly, he took what he wanted, what he could use. He dropped the study of family budgets, the distribution of power within the family group, the mode of succession, and concentrated on the triad Place-Work-Family, which he immediately translated into Place-Work-Folk, using for his third factor a term at once less precise, but also less restricted that that of Le Play. Again, the terrain was prepared, in that this sociological triad was parallel to the triad of environment, function, organism he was familiar with in biology. What Le Play inspired in Geddes was the idea of the regional monograph, which in turn lead to his famous Valley Section diagram: a river-profile from its source in the mountains to its entry into the sea, with hunter, miner and shepherd in the hills, farmer and woodsman in the middle reaches, fisherman and trader at the stream-mouth. But while monographing, Geddes never lost sight of the general scheme, provided by Comte. Indeed, he came to see his action in the field of sociology as a combination of Comte and Le Play, as he wrote in *The Sociological Review* (X, 1918):

> The science of sociology was born when Auguste Comte [. . .] saw the long record of human history as a conflict and co-operation of the four social types: People, Chiefs, Intellectuals and Emotionals. At the same time Frédéric Le Play [. . .] was revealing the importance of rustic types for geography and economics. Long overdue is the problem of uniting these two standpoints [. . .] That is the purpose of the Regional Survey, at once rustic and civic.

The vocabulary here is slightly quaint (Geddes often oscillates between quaintness and neologism), and to interpret Le Play's work purely in terms of 'rustic types' is more than a bit reductive, but the general tendency is there, and that tendency was to deepen as time went by.

By 1890, Geddes was teaching sociology in Edinburgh. In 1903, with Victor Branford and others, he founded, in London, the Sociological Society, that had started off as a study group trying to apply the work of Comte and Le Play. In 1908 came *The Sociological Review*. Very little of Le Play's work appeared in its pages: in 1912, there was a translation of a monography that was part of *The Workers of Europe*: 'Domestic Life and the Consumption of Wealth. The Economic Method of Le Play', and in 1920 appeared a short biography. An at least partial translation of *The Workers of Europe* only came in 1936, with Zimmerman's *Family and Society*. Attention seemed to be directed rather to Le Play's disciples: de Tourville, de Rousiers, Demolins, since it was felt that the master himself stuck too close to family studies, and that more openings, more enlightenment, could be expected from the Place, Work, Folk triad. This comes across in a review by Victor Branford of a study 'Life in a Highland Glen' (*The Sociological Review*, XIX, 1927): 'This paper illustrates the Le Play method at a phase in its development where the details of family life tended to obscure the dramatic interplay between Place, Work and Folk'. One of the work-groups of the Sociological Society, the 'Social Science' group, spent two years translating Demolin's *Comment la route crée le type social* (how roads create social types). And *The Sociological Review* published studies along these lines: 'Norwegian studies' (1924), 'The Brenner Region' (1927), 'Rome, Past, Present and Possible' (1927), by Patrick Geddes and Victor Branford (1927).

But Le Play remained the source inspiration. When the Sociological Society acquired new premises in 1920, the place was called *Le Play House*. When the Le Play Society, which had begun its existence in the Department of Geography, University College, London, started up in 1930 (merging later with the Regional Association and the Civil Educational League to form the Institute of Sociology), the reference was again explicit and the Le Play method (laid out in R. E. Dickinson's *The Le Play Method in Regional Surveying* – London, the Le Play Society, 1934) was considered the best way of studying, in interaction, landscape, social settlement and human types. Relevant papers appeared in quick succession: *Luxembourg Studies* (1933), *Les Eyzies and District* (1934), *Polish Studies* (1934), *Eastern Carpathian Studies* (1936), *Scandinavian Studies* (1938).

It was Patrick Geddes who was behind all this movement. But by the time it was in full swing, he was already elsewhere. What can you do with a sociologist who writes (as Geddes did in his

The Evergreen Review, 1895), about 'the Sociology of Autumn'?
Try and follow him into yet another field.

4. Geddes: Field 3

In that strange and attractive essay 'The Sociology of Autumn',
Geddes restates the main thesis of human evolution he got from
Le Play: that surroundings – soil and climate – determine all the
primary forms of labour, that this labour in its turn determines
the nature of the family, that the nature of the family leads into
the structure of society, and that the given social structure
influences the individual in his life and thought. But from now
on, Geddes will be insisting on *possibility*. It happens, he says,
that, at some moment or another, an individual will look out
through his or her 'narrow window', momentarily aware of latent
possibilities in life, science and art, only to be dragged away from
it to workshop or 'bed and table'. Of those who remain obstinately looking out from their window, most will devote themselves to 'the unnumbered descriptive specialisms' of this or that
discipline, be it on the physical, organic or social plane. There
exists however now the possibility of creating, beyond all the
narrow windows, an Open Tower, allowing 'a larger view of
nature and Life', a synthetic experience, bringing together again
art and science, physics and æsthetics, economics and ethics, as
at the time of the Renaissance with, say, Leonardo da Vinci. Both
materialism and spiritualism, the two results of mechanical
dualism, have had their day, and the way lies open to a great
'single discipline', which is 'complex indeed, but no more a mere
maze than a mere chaos' and which leads to 'a single presentment
of the world', 'a growing Cosmos, a literal Uni-verse'.

As against all short-sighted action and reaction, as against all
short-term views coming forward in the name of realism, Geddes
advocates, not imagination (which is compensation rather than
live thought), not Utopian projection, but reality-vision, a conception more complex than realism. He insists on a basis in
science, not requiring specialist knowledge, only, say, in mathematics, some acquaintance with simple algebraic equations,
elementary geometry, and, in physics and physiology, some
awareness of the preservation and dissipation of energy, the
permanence of matter through transformation, and the functions

of a living organism. Such preliminary scientific knowledge is pushed out into sociology and economics, and these in their turn extend into æsthetics: 'We have thus reached the new paradox that the sphere of practical physical economics is to discuss the ways and means of increasing not so much bread, as Art' ('An analysis of the principles of economics', 1884).

Socio-economically, Geddes had been Demonstrator in Botany, then Assistant in Practical Botany, at Edinburgh University, till the philanthropist Martin White, interested in experimental education, created for him a Chair at Dundee, the big advantage of which was that Geddes could pack all his teaching into three months (April to June), free the rest of the time to move about. And move about he did, his intensive and extensive mind going in all directions.

A lot of the time, he had his Cities Exhibition on his back. This was one of his contributions to 'active sociology', which he saw as an alternative to party politics, as well as to nationalism and Marxism (as early as 1886, in a series of lectures, 'Conditions of the Capitalist and of the Labourer', he said he'd like to look at it all 'in a quiet, natural-history sort of way'). The Cities Exhibition was an attempt to analyse cities, see what could be done to make dead or dying ones livable, and create institutions, study-groups, associations to foster that high living called culture. From Edinburgh to Bombay, 'active sociology' meant also what he called 'conservative surgery' and the improvement of slum areas. To the Carnegie Trust in Dunfermline he presented 'A study of Parks, Gardens and Culture-Institutes'. He created a botanic garden at Dundee, landscape-gardening (what he called 'garden-writing') being an old love of his. In 1914, he was invited to undertake town planning reform in Ireland, and took the opportunity, since war was in the air, to voice his ideas about 'dynamic Peace'. In India, where he was finally to occupy a Chair of Sociology at Bombay, he introduced the physicist J. C. Bose to the poet Rabindranath Tagore, and tried to persuade Gandhi to bring about 'a further reorganisation of the evolutionary sciences'.

In addition to presenting his exhibitions, Geddes decided to start publishing live books, outside the confused mass of 'literature'. To do this, he set up his own house, Patrick Geddes and Colleagues, with W. H. White, of the Edinburgh Riverside Press, as distributor. In addition to his magazine, *The Evergreen Review,* he had three lists: an 'Evolution Series', with books like *The Armenian Question* by Victor Branford and himself, and *The Biology of Colour* by Marion Newbigin; an 'Ethic Art' series, with, for example, a book on *St Genevieve of Paris* by Puvis de Chavannes; and a 'Celtic Library', publishing old Celtic poems (*Lyra Celtica*), Breton tales (*The Shadow of Arvor*) and 'mountain songs and island runes' (*From the Hills of Dream*) by Fiona Macleod. With these latter books, Geddes hoped to provide the basis for a 'Scots Renascence', an idea that was going to be picked up later. Geddes well knew it was only the beginning of a beginning: 'Our recent and current writers have but touched a fringe of their possibilities' (preface to the autumn volume of *The Evergreen Review*). As to *The Evergreen Review*, which took its name from the writings of the eighteenth-century poet Allan Ramsay, it was based on the general idea of a 'return to Nature', a slogan seen as 'a rallying call which each age must answer in its own way'. The nineteenth century had written its answer large in Science, Industry, Literature and Art – 'yet many solutions are still lacking'. Geddes was feeling his way out into a larger field. If he was and is mainly known as a town-planner, a city-surveyor, he was also looking to a new exodus into 'the outside world', that of the other animals, of plants and rocks.

There was the city, there was the university (which I take here to stand for all culture-institutions) – there was also the universe.

It was to city, university and universe, to this universalist conception of things, that Geddes consecrated his Outlook Tower, considered by him as the acme and symbol of his work, the concrete embodiment of that 'open tower' he evoked in his essay 'The Sociology of Autumn'. The place, reputed to have been the town mansion of the Laird of Cockpen, later known as Short's Observatory (Short being an optician who had installed a periscope at its summit) was a high house situated near the castle in Edinburgh. Discovering that it was available on lease, Geddes, with his flair for locations, saw immediately that he could use it, not only as a kind of cosmorama, conducive to concentric and expanding vision, but also as a place to concentrate all his plans, projects and work-in-progress, and which would be in close contact with similar institutions all over the world. Furthermore, since 1892, Geddes had been inviting to give talks in Edinburgh all the liveliest minds he had come in contact with or had heard of: Elisée and Paul Reclus, Kropotkin, Haeckel, Paul Desjardins, Edmond Demolins, William James – psychologists, anthropologists, sociologists, geographers, ethnologists, philosophers . . . He now invited them to the Outlook Tower, which, in his ever-developing conception of things, was to contain also an 'inlook tower' (a bare-walled room for solitary meditation), and which, again, was seen by him only as a beginning. In 1902, with the idea of supplementing, if not actually incorporating, the Royal Geographical Society, he worked out with the geographer Bartholomew plans for a new National Institute of Geography that to his mind would be 'a *super* outlook tower'. And in a letter he referred to Outlook Tower as a kind of prototype for 'that great citadel of culture I have so often dreamt of but must leave others to build'.

During all this time, to come back to more intellectual matters, Geddes was trying out a whole constellation of terms in order to express his cosmic vision and define that global 'single discipline' he had in mind.

To prevent, or at least circumvent, any facile dismissal of his project as 'Utopian', Geddes stressed that he was concerned, not with *utopia* (etymologically: no place) but with *eu-topia* (good place). If we refer back to Comte's analysis of the stages of human history: theological and militaristic; State-controlled and individualistic; scientific and industrialist, it can be said that Geddes felt the time was ripe to try and move in to another stage, which he sometimes called etho-polity, sometimes ethicosm, based on psychorganic, eu-psychic, biosophical living, the process towards this stage being what he sometimes called eu-polito-genics (the science of good cities). None of this is very satisfactory, but it is not difficult to see what Geddes was trying to get at. Within this global nebula, an inner circle of more technical vocabulary is at once more precise and more pleasing to the ear of the mind: paleotechnics, neotechnics (or eutechnics), biotechnics and geotechnics. Paleotechnics meant waste of natural resources, blighted landscapes, pandemoniac cities full of factories, offices, slums and stunted human lives. Neotechnics meant the use of non-polluting energy and the attempt to reunite utility with beauty, city with landscape. Biotechnics would promote new life-thinking, leading to more developed human lives, more expanded psyches. As to geotechnics, it was the means for human beings to learn how to really and fully inhabit the earth. In his book *From Geography to Geotechnics* (University of Illinois Press, 1968), Benton MacKaye of the Tennessee Valley Authority said that he had wanted to use this Geddesian concept as early as 1928 (in his book *The New Exploration*, Harcourt Brace) but had been dissuaded to do so by Lewis Mumford (who later regretted his advice), accepting an orthodox, uninspired 'regional planning'. It had taken him, he said, thirty years to come out into the open.

'Coming out into the open' – that is exactly what Geddes proposed, in a letter of 1917, that he and Victor Branford should do. What did he mean by that? He meant, again, without abandoning them, but integrating them into a higher and more open unity, coming out from behind town planning, the work of the Sociological Society, Valley Section diagramming and even the Outlook Tower. If the Valley Section presented a river from the sociological point of view, what Geddes proposed now was a plunge into the 'cosmic life-stream', which, with its 'extraordinary magnitude and extensiveness' would provide 'more of a world-vision' and hence complete 'our otherwise too microcosmal and local ones'. Already, in notes of 1902, he was talking about 'carrying things farther and deeper' and about possible extensions of the Outlook Tower beyond geography and civics into 'actual autogenetic process'. He's moving out, via what he called in the book *Life*, published in 1932, 'bio-psychosis' or 'psycho-biosis' (a transcending of subject-object dialectics, the mainstay of modernity), and beyond the Place-Work-Folk triad, into higher and higher individuation. This kind of *opening* actually happened to Geddes now and then throughout his life, and it was then that he broke into poetry, sounding at times like a breathless Whitman. One of those moments took place at Simla, in the foothills of the Himalaya, in 1922. Before coming to this last experience, he recalls other critical and creative occasions:

Best of all is Convalescence! This I tell
With Knowledge of what I'm saying, since once, again and
    now:
Vivid experience! Thus, long ago – student in London –
    illness –
Then, six weeks at Roscoff! There – after years concentrated
On Huxley's (Cuvier's) analyses, comparisons of form –

I woke anew, fuller than ever, to the living world.
Initiated now to Bio-drama-life of Sea! Thence researches
     afresh;
Impelling years of work later, through life essential
. . .
Earlier, later – but come to last month's. After near year on
     plains,
And that's burning plain – Penjab, April May June – to hottest,
Town-planning Patiala, and other towns; contriving to renew
The last great Moghal Garden, terraced, streamed but greatly
     lapsed,
Much now ev'n forest, jungle; then roasted at Amritsar's Temple
     Golden –
Barefoot, days long, on sun-hot marble pavements by its sacred
     Tanks
I got fresh fever, so came to this hilltop
Of chilly mists and rains torrential . . .

   On occasions such as those, Geddes hardly knew what had hit
him. At times he deprecates it all as 'bardic yells'. At other times
he treads warily around it, talking about 'the life of feeling' and
its expression as a necessary 'basement or catacomb' to 'the
tower of thought and action'. At other times again, he sees
practical energy, scientific intellect and poetic emotion coming
together into a higher unity – 'like the three colours that make up
white light'. It's interesting, too, to see him not stopping at
emotion in his conception of poetry. He sees Goethe's essay
on morphology 'not only as a culmination of his scientific work,
but as perhaps the very greatest of his poems'.
   If all I've been laying out in this essay constitutes a theoretical
and practical lead-up to geopoetics, with this outer circle of
Geddes' work, we are actually touching on the new field.

11

Scotland, History and the Writer

The field is the world. (David Hume)

I'd like to begin by thanking the University of Grenoble, and in particular the group for Scottish Studies, for inviting me as 'guest speaker' at their congress. I think it should be remarked at least in passing that this was rather a bold gesture on their part, liable to cause some irritation, certainly not in any enlightened company, but let's say, in adjacent and dimmer precincts.

After all, at the present moment, I have spent almost half of my life *outside* Scotland. Not only that, but at one moment in my life-line, I broke entirely with English-language publishing, and *a fortiori* with the Scottish literary scene, going into a nine-year silence from which I emerged to publish books in French, but not in English, the language in which most of the manuscripts were written. So much for my personal history, making for the kind of paradox that some minds find hard to swallow. Add to that, on the intellectual level, that, in the present historico-cultural context, I can conceive of 'national culture' at most only as a half-way house (I have always been a partisan and protagonist of what Goethe, away back at the beginning of the nineteenth century, called *Weltliteratur*, world literature) and that I radically put in question, both from a socio-political point of view and from that of the psychology of creativity, the ideology of identity – I think and work rather in terms of a play of energy. I have never made any secret of these premises, indeed, on occasion, I have shouted them over the rooftops. Which is why, for example, a few years ago, at a symposium on

148

Scottish literature, after a paper had been delivered on my work, one irate gentleman jumped up and came out with the triumphant expostulation: was I a Scottish writer at all, did I even talk Lallans?! As is swiftly evident to any listener, I do not talk Lallans, I talk English with a Glasgow and West Coast accent – as Carlyle talked English with an Annandale accent, Burns with an Ayrshire accent, and MacDiarmid with a Border accent. Nobody in contemporary Scotland talks consistent Lallans – that is part of our historical linguistic situation. What we speak is English with local accents and intonations, and sprinkled with elements of Lallans, and indeed of Gaelic, which have come down to us. I see in this no great cause for lamentation, and certainly no justification for trying to write systematically in Lallans, as some literati have done and are still doing. This practice goes back to certain romantic theories of language that found their fullest expression in Johann Friedrich Herder. Picked up by MacDiarmid, they were practised and promoted by him, though he himself abandoned them when he went into his most interesting work. It's one of the signs of the inadequacy of a nationalist context that these most interesting aspects of Mac-Diarmid's work are by and large neglected in favour of the more obviously *Scottish* aspects, with the result that, instead of anything like the 'great music' or the 'diamond body', to evoke two of MacDiarmid's titles, you have a spawn of undoubtedly *Scottish* poetry that, on any demanding scale, is more or less insignificant.

This little excursion into the language question was just a fast answer to the man who chose that angle in order to express his visceral irritation at my presence and practice. To go into the questions of national culture, world literature and the problematics of identity would take more time. I've gone into them pretty thoroughly elsewhere, but will no doubt touch on them at least tangentially while moving about in the sphere of the theme I wish to explore now: historicity.

The way I intend to proceed is as follows: in the first place, I'll focus on Scotland, which was my initial context and is still one of my principal references. Thereafter, I'll try and open up some world perspectives, and, against this historical background, I'll finally come to laying out the contours of the work-field as I see it.

1. A Scottish Beginning

That Scotland has been much marked by history, that its psyche
has been bombarded and obsessed by history, is a proposition that
few, I think, would deny – but for long it was difficult to find any
significant historical study concerning the place. When I was an
adolescent in Ayrshire, the book that was generally put forward as
an authoritative history read to me even at that early age (I'd
received it as a school prize around 1950, when I was fourteen) as
if it had been written for mentally retarded four-year olds. This
was P. Hume Brown's *A Short History of Scotland*:

> The land we now call Scotland was not always known by
> that name, and the people who lived in it were not always
> called Scots. There was, indeed, a time when neither the
> land nor its people had a name to themselves. For Scotland,
> like all other countries, was once inhabited by people who
> were not civilised, but were merely savages or barbarians.
> As these people did not write books, how do we know that
> they once lived in Scotland?

This is not only bad, it is pathetic, but let me just remind you that
Hume Brown was no mere country dominie bending over back-
wards to be pedagogical, he was Professor of Ancient Scottish
History and Paleography at the University of Edinburgh and
Historiographer-Royal for Scotland. Before leaving him where
he belongs, let me just quote his conclusion:

> Scotland, like other countries in Europe, has still many
> difficulties to overcome after two great wars within one
> generation; but one of the lessons of the past is to inspire us
> with hope for the future. Thus at the close of the seven-
> teenth century, Scotland, owing to the failure of the Darien
> scheme, was at its lowest ebb. Yet the grit and courage of its
> people brought them to the great prosperity in industry and
> commerce of the eighteenth and nineteenth centuries. Nor
> should we forget that 'a thousand years in thy sight are but
> as yesterday when it is past'. Our story began with the cave-
> dwellers in the Bay of Oban and ends with the Scotland
> which we see at the present day. What would the Oban
> cave-dweller think could he look out on the Bay and see the
> steamers bringing travellers from all over the world to

admire the beautiful scenery where, with his few tools and weapons, he with difficulty gained a livelihood for himself and those who belonged to him? It has taken thousands of years to bring about this wonderful change, and we may be sure that as wonderful changes must happen in the days to come. At some future time the Scotland of to-day will no doubt appear as strange to the men then living as the Scotland of the cave-dwellers appears to us.

Having resuscitated, momentarily, this historical stillbirth, I hasten to say that things have changed considerably for the better in this field within recent years. It is now possible to obtain a survey of Scottish history without the lenifying drivel, the musty mythology, the theological twaddle and the infantile style that marked so much of it in the past. This is the case notably with the New History of Scotland, with its volumes ranging from Smyth's *Warlords and Holy Men* (AD 80–1000) to Harvie's *No Gods and Precious Few Heroes* (1914–80), passing through Barrow's *Kingship and Unity* (1000–1306), Grant's *Independence and Nationhood* (1306–1469), Wormald's *Court, Kirk and Community* (1470–1625), Mitchison's *Lordship to Patronage* (1603–1745), Lenman's *Integration, Enlightenment and Industrialization* (1746–1832), and the Checklands' *Industry and Ethos* (1832–1914).

But in fact, at the early period of my life I'm recalling, as a caveman myself ('the cavemen' – that's how the boys of the borough of Largs designated us villagers from Fairlie), I was much less concerned with an entity called 'Scotland' than with a few square miles on the coast of Ayrshire, bringing in the Kilbirnie hills, the Fairlie moors, the shoreline between Ardrossan and Skelmorlie and the islands of Arran and the Cumbraes, the Big Cumbrae and the Wee Cumbrae, concerning which a minister is supposed to have said: 'O Lord, bless and be gracious to the Greater and the Lesser Cumbraes and in thy mercy do not forget the adjacent islands of Great Britain and Ireland'.

At one point, I was working up to an essay on Ayrshire for a competition organised by the Edinburgh-Ayrshire Archaeological Society. That meant delving into parish records, looking up titles in the local library and buying for a shilling or two's pocket money old volumes in the secondhand bookstalls of Largs and

Glasgow. The text itself, the first 'public' text I ever wrote, won a prize and was deposited in the county library at Ayr, but what counted lastingly was the work leading up to it and the 'lines' I got from the books I read. One of these was Donald Mackenzie's *Scotland, the Ancient Kingdom* (1930):

> The story of the gradual colonization of Scotland by peoples who can be traced to different parts of the Continent takes us back to the Pleistocene Age, when the hills and valleys of the Highlands and Lowlands were assuming their final aspect under the alternating influences of masses of sculpturing ice and devastating floods, and the coast-line was still being moulded by the advancing and retreating seas. Early man in Scotland experienced sharp oscillations of climate and was the eyewitness of great geographical changes . . .

Another was Simpson's *The Celtic Church in Scotland* (1935):

> It is astonishing how little systematic work has yet been done towards identifying and plotting out what may be described as the penetration lines of Christianity in Scotland. The history of Christian origins in the land then known as Alba has too long been presented merely as an unrelated series of pretty legends . . .

The two notions of primal space and penetration lines (Simpson spoke also of 'track charts' and followed in particular the tracks of Ninian out from his *candida casa* at Whithorn) that emerge from these text awoke areas in my mind and outlined fields of work that were to occupy me for years.

But there were also more strictly literary works. For example, Irving's *Lives of the Scottish Poets* (1810). It was there I first heard of Richard of St Victor, of Duns Scot ('*Scotia me genuit, Anglia suscepit, Gallia edocuit, Germania tenet*'), of John Mair, 'a celebrated Doctor of the Sorbonne', of John Cameron ('. . . at the age of about twenty years, he was appointed Professor of Greek in the University of Glasgow [. . .] being seized with the desire of visiting foreign countries, he soon relinquished his situation; and, in the year 1600, passed over to France, the favourite region of Scottish wanderers . . .'), and of that fantastical writer, Urquhart of Cromarty who, in *The Jewel*, also brings up the French connection:

... to so high a pitch did the glory of the Scottish nation attain over all the parts of France, and for so long time together continue in that obtained height, by vertue of an ascendant the French conceived the Scots to have above all nations in matter of their subtlety in philosophical disceptations, that there hath not been till of late, for these several ages together, any lord, gentleman, or other in that country, who being desirous to have his son instructed in the principles of philosophy, would intrust him to the discipline of any other than a Scottish master.

With references such as these, I was gradually filling in my own Scottish intellectual map where, for example, neolithic beachcombers (Azilian, Maglemosian, Cro-Magnon) rubbed shoulders with men versed in the subtleties of logic and philosophy. It was completely outside, among other aspects of Scottish psychopolitical pathology, the Anglo-Scotic schizophrenia that had set in after 1707.

You can see that schizophrenia even in a steady-headed bloke like Sir Walter Scott. Here's a note in his *Journal* for February 1826: 'It is difficult to steer betwixt the natural impulse of one's national feelings setting in one direction, and the prudent regard to the interests of the empire and its internal peace and quiet . . .' Scott's *Tales of a Grandfather* ('stories *taken from* Scottish history' – my italics) were written certainly with that national consciousness in mind, but also with the idea of propagating a neo-feudal sense of things in the face of French revolutionary radicalism: Scott's history is to a large extent a Tory story, and Abbotsford was more an antiquarian fastness than in any sense a hive of live history. Scott even goes so far as to make an apology for superficial literature. 'Better a superficial book', he says of his *Life of Napoleon* in a *Journal* note for December 1825,

which brings well and strikingly together the known and acknowledged facts, than a dull boring narrative . . . Nothing is so tiresome as walking through some beautiful scene with a *minute philosopher*, a botanist, or pebble-gatherer, who is eternally calling your attention away from the grand features of the natural scenery to look at grasses and chucky-stones.

Without at all aspiring to be boring, one may well think that a certain minuteness may unearth truth beyond the 'known and acknowledged', just as, while admiring the large landscape, one may still have an eye for grasses and chucky-stones.

As a youngster, I moved from Sir Walter Scott to that 'literary vagrant', as he called himself, Robert Louis Stevenson. Stevenson could be accurate if need be (he tried seriously for the Chair of Constitutional Law at Edinburgh), and he was interested enough in history to project the composition of a *History of the Highlands* (he had his father send out books to him in Davos around 1880), but when he came to write *Kidnapped*, which is in some respects a spin-off from his research into the Appin murder and other events having taken place in the region of Ballachulish and the Isle of Mull, he threw accuracy to the winds: 'This is no furniture for the scholar's library, but a book for the winter evening schoolroom'. That's what makes for Stevenson's charm, and maybe his limitation. I don't think R. L. Stevenson ever wrote the book(s) he might have written, but I loved his vagrancy, as well as that rhythm of writing he evokes in a letter:

> I have not, I believe, remained so long in any one place as here at Davos. That tells on my old gipsy nature; like a violin hung up, I begin to lose what music there was in me; and with the music, I do not know what else besides, or do not know what to call it, but something radically part of life, a rhythm, perhaps.

Then there was Carlyle. I must have been about seventeen when *Sartor Resartus* and *Heroes and Hero-Worship* came my way, the former delighting me, the latter leaving me with more mixed feelings. That human beings superior in strength, courage or intelligence can be raised to the status of divine hero is a fact of the history of religions (Hume remarks on it in his essay on polytheism), that personal force is a significant factor, not only of political history but in cultural activity, can hardly be denied, but that history was only extended biography is a notion I could not accept, no more than the idea, derived from Fichte, that it was a kind of 'inarticulate Bible' in which the hero was the incarnation of some Divine Idea. There were misgivings and reservations, then. But the project of offering 'some glimpses into the very marrow of the world's history' excited my mind, as well as the creation of a new 'literature of power' that would combine and transcend the forces of church, university and parliament. In fact, what Carlyle was ultimately talking about in his wide arc from Odin to Robert Burns was the new figure of the intellectual, whom he called the man of letters:

> A very singular phenomenon . . . He is new, I say; he has hardly lasted above a century in the world yet. Never, till about a hundred years ago, was there seen any figure of a Great Soul living apart in that anomalous manner; endeavouring to speak forth the inspiration that was in him by Printed Books, and find place and subsistence by what the world would please to give him for doing that.

Carlyle even goes so far as to declare that this man of letters is 'our most important modern person', but if the full-throated transcendentalism is a little hard to take (it comes across more quietly in Emerson's *Representative Men*), Carlyle also had some humour, and it's a humorous, sympathetic portrait of this same man of letters and intellectual that he gives when he presents Teufelsdröckh, Professor of 'all kinds of sciences' in the University of God-knows-where.

It was with images such as those I've just recollected in mind, and with this outline of a programme (of life and study) that I went up to the University of Glasgow.

2. World Perspectives

In Glasgow, and in Paris, then in Glasgow again, I plunged into a pretty deep and extensive reading of world (that is, more-than-Scottish) history – that was between the years 1954, when I first went up to Glasgow University and 1967, when I handed in my resignation of the post I occupied at that same University as lecturer in modern French literature, where my main theme had been: 'After Rimbaud – what?'

When I think of the Glasgow of those years, I have an image of big clocks looming over a cancerous townscape and the book that immediately rises to the surface of my mind is Spengler's *Decline of the West*, that 'sketch of a morphology of universal history'. Even if only a sketch, it's a bulky and chaotic book, its chapter headings strung out in a ragged line as follows: The Sense of Numbers, The Problem of Universal History, The Macro-cosm, Musicality and Plasticity, Mental Image and Vital Feeling, Faustian Science and Apollonian Science, Origin and Landscape, Cities and Peoples, The Problems of Arab Culture, The State, The Formal World of Economic Life. I read it in a chilly room in Scotstoun, and, whatever my later judgment of Spengler, and especially of the later Spengler, this book fascinated me at that time. Way beyond any simple story, and outside all specialist historical scholarship, it was like a great and craggy symbol of I knew not what, but the places and dates mentioned at the end of the two Prefaces: 'Munich, December 1917', 'Blankenburg in the Harz, December 1922', seemed written in letters of black fire. Spengler put it forward as the first Philosophy of Destiny, the main destiny in question being that of Western Europeo-Amer-ican culture. For Spengler, that culture had spent its forces and was now entering its final state of civilization: it was dying, as other cultures – Indian, Babylonian, Chinese, Egyptian, Arabian, Mexican – had lived and died. The possibilities of great art were exhausted. Some minds might continue to believe naïvely in some notion of linear progress, some artists would go on expressing themselves as if nothing had happened, every nation, great or small, would continue trying to convince itself it had a national culture, but the aim of Spengler's book, from a practical point of view, was to blast those naïve hopes, annihilate those cherished illusions: better go into some technical job rather than try to write poetry, better join the navy than try to be a painter, better go into politics than try to work out a new philosophy. In the meantime, from a non-practical point of view, there was the possibility of composing the great prose-poem of universal his-tory, with its periodic structure and its organic logic. This would be accomplished by a combination of research and what Spengler calls the rare gift of 'psychic transhumance'. But there was also the figure of the intellectual nomad, wandering about from location to location in the 'stony desert' of the city . . .

I was wandering about in Glasgow, wondering what there was, fundamentally, to be done. Long before Spengler talked about it, the poet Rimbaud had made up his mind to leave poetic activity altogether and become absolutely practical. Pound's *Cantos* were an illustration of the great prose-poem, while Eliot's *Wasteland* read like a lyrical version of the *Decline*. I was left with that figure of the 'intellectual nomad'. In Spengler, he is totally divorced from the environment outside the city walls. But might there not be the possibility of a renewed contact with the landscape, and maybe the elaboration of a new mindscape? That's what I had in mind when I used to cross the Clyde by the Whiteinch ferry and walk, as I frequently did, the thirty-odd miles down to the coast at Fairlie.

And I continued my readings in history.

In his *History of Europe*, Fisher had said he saw no logic in history, only wave after wave of emergences. It was these waves of world-history, the evidence of the twenty-one civilizations the world had known, with the main accent on 'the Western civilizations', that Toynbee perused in his *A Study of History*. It is an enterprise similar to Spengler's, both of these performances reminding one of that Photius (820–91) whose library (*viulio thiki*) or 'host of books' (*myriovivlon*) concerning Hellenic literature was the wonder of the age – Toynbee speaks of 'culture-heroes' (shades of Carlyle . . .) who have 'performed prodigies single-handed'. But if there are similarities between the two studies, there are great differences: Toynbee's book is less sombre, less fatalistic. So far as the future of 'the Western civilization' is concerned, for him it is still an open question – there is a possibility that it may still be in its growth phase, signs of a post-modern period (something more than the trivial extension of modernity qualified as 'contemporary') having appeared at the end of the nineteenth century.

If Toynbee sees the possibility of prolongation and opening, it's not with any facile kind of optimism. Writing around 1950 in his Volume 9, having seen Nazi Germany resort to a zoological-technical militarism and attempt to trample under brutal SS boots all that the best minds in the West had stood for, he evokes that 'keen-eyed castaway', Valéry, whose *Crise de l'esprit* (first published, in English translation, in *The Athenæum*, 1919) had sounded an elegy for civilization, 'peering down into the depths of Western Man's Subconscious Pyche from a revealing observation-post on the flotsam from a spiritual shipwreck.' So much for the workings of the mind. Politically, if the Western world, ever since the Industrial Revolution, had been moving towards some kind of unity on the economic plane, it continued on the political plane to be 'partitioned among a litter of still, and

indeed perhaps now more than ever, fanatically worshipped parochial sovereign states', the only alternative proposed to this
situation being world-wide communist collectivism. For Toynbee, the issue between a liberal West and a communist Russia (or
China) was not well exposed or understood: it was not merely an
economic debate, or struggle, between socialism and private
enterprise, it was between man's collective power and personal
freedom. Compared with the immense forge of communism,
loaded with an ethic of self-sacrifice and aura'd by an apocalyptic
vision, the liberal side had a very poor image: a small-minded
egoism, the right of the privileged to exploit others. But what was
ultimately at stake was this idea of personal liberty, the right to
think for one's self, and that, said Toynbee, ultimately went back
to Christianity, the ultimate issue for Toynbee being religious.

I had a certain attraction to communism. My own family
background was proletarian and socialist, but socialism seemed
to me rather a check on the worst excesses of liberalism than a
project, and it was communism that had that project. In Glasgow, I read Plekhanov's *Essay on the Development of the Monist
Conception of History*, and later on in Paris I read one after the
other of the Marxist and communist texts put out by the Moscow
Editions, but more and more out of a sense of duty and solidarity
than with any real conviction (the philosophical judgments of the
communist dictionaries and encyclopaedias were abominably
simplistic) – it was only after May 1968 that I abandoned this
line entirely.

Toynbee had said the ultimate issue was religious, and that if
the West were to survive, it would mean a move from economics
to religion. I'd come too far out of religion, with Hume and the
French radicals as well as the tendency of my own nature, to
accept that word. Certainly, Toynbee never used it in any
orthodox sense: the orthodox ecclesiastical tradition (to which
T. S. Eliot had turned) was one of those pillars of Hercules (the
other being communism) that the 'Western navigator' would
have to pass through in order to reach possible '*open waters
beyond*' (my italics). Toynbee's own religious solution lay in the
vicinity of St Francis of Assisi, but, although I liked a modern
Franciscan like Joseph Delteil, that could not be my way: too
much naïvety, too much facile lyricism. I kept to the situation of
the intellectual nomad as I conceived him, lucid, searching, trying

out one step after another. That we were living a breakdown was evident, that signs of a spiritual wilderness and of what Plato in the *Republic* called 'the commonwealth of swine' were to be seen on all hands was just as evident, and they have multiplied, but, as Ronald Laing (psychiatrist in Glasgow) was going to say, breakdown can also mean breakthrough. Before he had begun proposing specific solutions at all, Toynbee had said: 'Success would mean either finding some hitherto untravelled way for a civilisation to go on living . . . or else creating a mutation that would generate a new species of society'. That was my point of departure, and I kept coming back to it, ready to start out trying again, knowing well that untravelled ways are hard to find, and that mutation takes time.

Of the solutions for 'a renewal of Western Man's spiritual life' that Toynbee in his book passed, rather rapidly, under review, the first was the kind of thing put forward by Nora Chadwick (co-author, with Myles Dillon, of *The Celtic Realms*) in *Poetry and Prophecy* (Weidenfeld and Nicolson, 1967), speaking of the 'essential things' left behind in the 'pre-scientific limbo' after the scientific-rationalist revolution: 'In the Unconscious, they await the day of resurrection, ready to break through whenever the spiritual quest is undertaken anew, clothed perhaps in strange archaic garb, and whispering their primordial longing to our dreaming minds'. This was what was going to break out, notably in the States, from the 1950s on, and if I could sympathise with it to some extent, I was not fundamentally interested. I remember a lecturer at Glasgow University stopping me on the stairs of the Modern Languages Department one day, saying that there were at least some contemporaries I must feel some allegiance with, and handing me an article on the Beat Generation. I read it, but saw in it little more than what Spengler had called 'the second religiosity', that is, a populist syncretism with no development of an idea, no consequential activity. The same goes for so much of the 'spiritualist renaissance' we have heard about and witnessed since. Certainly, there was criticism to be done of 'the unconscious structure of the scientific ego', as Norman Brown put it in his book *Life against Death* (Routledge and Kegan Paul, 1959), which brought together history, psychoanalysis and anthropology, certainly there was much to be said for a 'resurrection of the body' and erotic exuberance as against models of anal-sadistic domination, but that didn't necessarily mean the kind of stereotyped carnaval that is only the other side of slavery.

Another solution presented by Toynbee and present among the 'new prophets', but rarely in any consequential way, was Mahayana Buddhism, which was going to occupy me for many years when, after a first exposure to it around the age of fifteen in the village of Fairlie (thanks to the library of an old naturalist and transcendentalist who lived there), I was to come across it again (thanks to Suzuki) in Munich, in the winter of 1957. Then there was the naturalistic conception of Chinese Taoism which, as Baynes says in *Mythology of the Soul* (quoted by Toynbee), 'reduces the terrors of the moral conflict, in which the soul swings between salvation and perdition, to the play of natural forces – Yang and Yin'. But Toynbee seems unable to hear the voice of Taoism at all. No sooner has he quoted Baynes that he speaks of 'salvation' coming from a new 'Yang-movement' that will take us from 'extraverted physical science' to 'the divine Dweller in the Innermost'. Wherever we are there, we're far away from the play of natural forces. If Toynbee is so deaf, it's because for him, nature is entirely ruled out, 'subjugated by technology' – religion is an affair between God and Man, with no place any more for what he calls the Magna Mater. I had no sympathy for the mythology of 'the great Mother', but I could not accept the idea that nature was ruled out: I had too deep an experience of the Fairlie shores and moors for that.

Which brings me to H. G. Wells' *Outline of History* (1920) and what I take to be its prolongation, *The Outlook for Homo Sapiens* (1942). The *Outline* is only what it was meant to be, a useful survey of world history for the general reader, and we can skip over fast the homiletic optimism of its concluding pages, but in the *Outlook*, written twenty or so years later, Wells is making the interesting statement that it is *time for history to turn into ecology*. I won't develop the question here, but I emphasise that phrase, while discouraging anyone from using the word ecology, especially in its superfical usage, as a label for my work. I am only indicating a general tendency.

Before turning now to the actual work-field as I see it, and as I try to practise it, I'd like to refer to one more book on history, read a little later than the ones evoked, but which belongs to this context, to the movement up to that work-field. I'm thinking of Charles Olson's *The Special View of History*, a seminar run at Black Mountain College, North Carolina, in 1956.

Olson's point of departure is the statement by the pre-Socratic, that is, pre-discoursive, philosopher Heraclitus: 'Man is estranged from that with which he is most familiar'. The history of the past two and a half millenia, whether seen as a march of events, the working out of some law, fate, destiny, or as 'making it' (the noise of the latest disturbance on the news), has been the history of that estrangement, and the question is, how to get beyond it, out of it. Primal steps towards an exit have been present for some time: dialectic as 'the study of things in their own being and movement' (Hegel), new notions of space-time, matter-energy, new knowledge of language. But, out of habit, out of inertia, the old discourse, the old modes continue: 'I don't know that any one of us is caught up and going at the speed or at the depth of the knowledge of reality we new possess'. A *new* history, an *essential* history would mean a new energy, a new dynamic, the conception of history as 'the function of any one of us', the intensity of the life process, as well as a recovery of the old Herodotean sense of history (*'istorin*): finding out for one's self. The project here is to re-place Man in his field, thus restoring to him forwardness, direction, value within an actionable context that is larger than the individual, all of which involves a new æsthetics: an æsthetics that is more and other than the refinement of discourse. For the individual actively engaged in this process, the complete undertaking will mean not only the relinquishing of certainties, as in some sceptical stance, but a projection of one's self into unknown territories, and a following out of multiple paths: 'Where shall we go, what whall we do?'

3. The Work-field

I've arrived now at the third concept in my sub-title: writer. It's a word I don't like much, as having little definition, little demand. In his *Journal*, under the date 4 December 1825, Scott evokes the numbers of writers in Scotland 'scribbling nonsense for twopence a page all day, and laying out twice their earnings at night in whisky-punch'. He's referring to the apprentices in 'writers' offices', but it's easy enough to extrapolate. Rimbaud also has an arresting phrase: 'So many writers, few authors'. Knowing his Latin, the man with the wind at his heels knew that an author, etymologically (*augere, auctum*), is 'a man who augments'. Who augments what? Let's say the sense of life. That's one gauge. But it's still not enough. There are no real activating words for the scope and the sharpness involved in the work as I see it. The word 'poet' is too much of a hold-all to be of any cogent and coherent use. Well, let's forget the labels, the thing is, to get into the work-field, the *whole* work-field.

Obviously, what I'll be presenting here is the merest outline. And I wouldn't feel the need even for this outline – I'd just say, after leading up to them through my reading of history, 'the rest is in my books' – were it not for the fact that, owing to historico-cultural contingency, so few of these books are at present available in English.

When, for poetic, intellectual and cultural reasons, I left Scotland in 1967, it was not to take the suddron road, that 'high road to London', which so many Scottish intellectuals have taken even since the times of James I and VI, it was to cross over the water to France, which was renewing a much older tradition, that of Duns Scot, that of Michael Scot, that of George Buchanan, among so many others.

By the time I settled in the Atlantic Pyrenees, where I was to live for seventeen years before I flitted to Brittany in 1983, I had published a first book in Paris (*En toute candeur*) and three in London (*Letters from Gourgounel, The Cold Wind of Dawn, The Most Difficult Area*). Once there in the Pyrenees, for nine years, holed up like Bodhidharma in his cave, I published nothing – but a lot of work was going on in the silence. By 1975, I had about five full manuscripts ready, and they began to appear, from Paris, as from 1976: *Incandescent Limbo, Travels in the Drifting Dawn, Walking the Coast* . . . I'm giving the English titles here, but these manuscripts, written in English, were appearing in French translation. And this practice was to continue for years, with books appearing also in other languages, translated from the French or from the original English manuscript, but not in English. At present, about twenty-five books are available in French, in the field of narrative, the essay and poetry. But only a fraction of this work is available in English. I renewed contact with English-language publishing only in 1989. Since then, the Edinburgh house of Mainstream has made a good start into making the work available to English-language readers. A collected longer poems exists: *The Bird Path*, a collected shorter poems: *Handbook for the Diamond Country*, and two narrative books, *Travels in the Drifting Dawn* and *The Blue Road*. As yet, none of the essay-books such as *The Outward Movement, A Quiet Apocalypse, The Nomad Mind* have appeared, only a few separate essays in magazines.

In these essays, I try to draw up a new mental cartography. As for the prose-books, which I call way-books (they may have faraway ancestors in the Middle English *Weye of Paradys*, the Middle French *Voie de Paradis* – but are devoid of allegory), they follow roads and paths through territories within that general map: *Travels in the Drifting Dawn* moves through Europe, from Ireland to North Africa, from Holland to Spain; *The Blue Road* follows the North Bank of the St Lawrence up into Labrador; *The Face of the East Wind* moves through South-East Asia . . . And the poems, whether they be diamond-type poems or longer peregrine poems, present moments and movements of greater density along those itineraries, within those territories. I've likened this triple writing activity to the parts of an arrow: the essays are the feathers, giving direction; the way-books are the shaft, ongoing movement; and the poems are the arrow-head. And of course, to continue the image, an arrow aims at a target. Schopenhauer says that good work hits a target everybody sees and knows, whereas fundamental work aims at a target most people are not yet aware of. The ambition, here, is fundamental: founding and grounding.

It remains, perhaps, to come back to the question raised at the beginning of this talk: to what extent am I a *Scottish* writer? I think myself it must be obvious to anyone with half an eye, half an ear that, while working largely outside Scotland (like so many Scots in the past), while trying to break up frameworks that have in my estimation curtailed art and thought in Scotland but which many Scots cling to as to an identity, while insisting on the universal rather than the Scottish, I have always carried a great deal of Scotland with me and have never ceased to study the country and its culture. It was MacDiarmid, arch-nationalist though he was, who said that what is important is not a Scottish moment, but a universal moment. I go with that. But a universal moment can also, of course, be a Scottish moment. That, however, depends as much on Scotland as on me.

We shall see.

12

The High Field

When the pamphlet *Metaphysics and Poetry* appeared in 1975 (Lothlorian Publications), all the logical empiricists and linguistic positivists among us could only see it as an enormous naïvety, a harking back to an obsolete mental landscape. For myself, whatever my reservations vis-à-vis the word 'metaphysics', it was an invitation to re-open a territory that has tended lately to disappear from the literary maps and now requires some illumination. Hence this essay, as a contribution to that conversation between Hugh MacDiarmid and Walter Perrie, as well as, in the bygoing, a friendly dialogue between myself and some other Scottish writers.

1.

Thought and poetry (*dichten* and *denken*, *pensée* and *poésie* – they're phonologically closer in other languages) are twins. Related, though each with its own specificity, both are concerned with opening, a sense of totality and the language-of-a-world. The more thinking a poet is, the better, though there may be temporary problems of adjustment between the two activities (one need only think of Coleridge). What is certain is that when they are absolutely divorced, thought becomes desiccated (an academic game), and poetry becomes 'personal' (etc. etc., all the stuff a demanding mind can do without). That said, the thinking poet, the poetic thinker, will tend to avoid the arena of 'philosophy'. Who, to put it more precisely, wouldn't want to move in a field (area, territory) where such heavyweights of the mind as 'spiritualism' and 'materialism' are definitely out of place? It is not that these terms are completely meaningless, it is that they are clumsy mechanisms, and the squabble between them a tedious cacophany. For thinking to be adequate to the universe (an open, moving universe such as we now sense) it has to take in all the energies implied in 'spiritualism', 'realism', 'materialism', 'idealism', and move at speed (poetry is, among other things, *fast thinking*), going beyond their lumbering classroom manoeuvrings. If we accept for this kind of thinking, which is definitely a prerequisite for 'the kind of poetry I want', the term 'metaphysics', it is obvious enough that over the past few years, on the cultural scene and in the mental landscape, it has been conspicuous by its absence.

2.

A few years back, D. Emmet wrote in *The Nature of Metaphysical Thinking* (Macmillan, 1967):

> Possibly a reason why metaphysics in the grand style is out of favour at the moment is not only due to the preoccupation of philosophers with problems of method and analysis, but is also due to the lack of relating ideas in terms of which some co-ordination of thought and experience might be achieved. This may be due to a lack of philosophers with sufficient breadth of intellectual vision and intuitive penetration. It may also be due to the actual situation both of our intellectual world and of our historical circumstances.

Now it is unlikely, as I've suggested, that we want a return to 'metaphysics in the grand style', but a co-ordination (which in poetry would be a fusion at white heat) of thought and experience – high thought and immediate experience – seems much to be desired.

It is in this context that we must see the work of MacDiarmid. His concern has been just this kind of co-ordination (as it was Pound's).

In the light of the above remarks concerning the need to go beyond the compartmentalisation of the -isms, it will come as no surprise to hear MacDiarmid (*coincidentia oppositorum* in person!) defining himself in the pamphlet *Metaphysics and Poetry* as a spiritual materialist, a transcendental Marxist: 'contradictions are inevitable for anyone who has a certain depth of intellectual perception'. But before going into MacDiarmid's own ground, it will be as well, if only to clear the decks, to hear what he has to say about the socio-cultural scene in general. He makes no bones about it, and if articles continue to be written and anthologies to be produced, MacDiarmid says quite bluntly: 'There's no English poetry of course, we're ruling that out entirely – it doesn't exist'. And asked why this should be so, he answers: 'The whole framework of English society has been against it. Their schooling system kills the imagination – their whole system is opposed to the emergence of æsthetic values'.

Without wanting to claim that English poetry *does* exist at the present moment, we can put down to MacDiarmid's notorious Anglophobia the fact that he should single out the *English* system of education. Does *any* system of national education set out to foster the development of æsthetic values? Unfortunately, no. So much so that the term national education might seem pretty close to a contradiction in terms . . . The question, tactfully perhaps, is not put to MacDiarmid in the pamphlet whether he thinks the Scottish situation is better, or whether there is a *Scottish* poetry. Pushed to it, he would probably have come to admit, with a chuckle, that it isn't and there isn't. But he would immediately have added, at least if it was one of his public platform optimistic days, that a revolutionary nationalism could bring it about. I personally think that it takes, and will take, a great deal more than nationalism, even of the revolutionary brand, to bring about a live culture, and would say in fact that cultural nationalism can be as big a blinker as there is. Because not all nationalists are as internationalist and as universalist as MacDiarmid is himself, whose ideology and 'faith', especially when translated by epigeons, is very far from corresponding to the farthest reaches of his work. Many have followed this ideology and the result has been a spawn of '*Scottish* poetry' with which MacDiarmid could feel little affinity other than sentimental, and with which I feel no affinity whatsoever. In a word, for me the field lies way outside the nationalist belt. This does *not* mean, far from it, neglect of Scoto-Celtic culture in its higher instances, it simply prevents narrow definition and self-satisfied parochial production. As William Carlos Williams, who suffered long enough from an American hang-up, finally came to say: 'When I say new world, I do not mean American'; or again, 'The local is not an object of art, it is merely a variant serving to locate the acme point of white penetration'. It's that 'white penetration' we want.

3.

MacDiarmid is perfectly explicit: most poetry, of whatever provenance, is damnably trivial (the real thing being so damned difficult). Which is why he was concerned largely with what we might call meta-poetry, meaning by that the introduction into his texts of 'nonpoetic' elements: those great whacks of information-loaded prose destined to lift the mind into the sphere in which the ultimate poetic (*noetic*) act might be possible.

I tend to see MacDiarmid the way Nietzsche saw Carlyle: desperately trying (Ecclefechan Gongorism . . .) to introduce some scope and height of thought into the all-pervading '*echt-britische Beschränkheit*' (D. H. Lawrence called it 'pettyfogging narrowness'). The poetic future may not be the multifarious gigantism that MacDiarmid, spiritual realist, transcendental materialist, uncommon communist, poet *at large*, throwing up all his work-notes on the page, represents, it may be rather, to quote Williams again, 'penetrant and simple'. But that gigantism, that whole craggy, contradictory, volcanic landscape must be seen as a necessary stage in the process, and at the very least a source of exaltation. All in all, a move towards what MacDiarmid calls, in the 'Lament for the Great Music':

That land I have dreamt of where the supreme values
which the people recognizes are states of mind
their ruling passion the attainment of higher consciousness

– but can that land be a nation, or is it not rather what the Chinese text calls 'the land that is nowhere'?

4.

It was because I could not believe that the 'land' MacDiarmid refers to was conceivable in national terms, and because I was utterly bored with a context in which the intellectual buggy all too rarely gets out of the parallel ruts of prim academicism and beer-mug populism, that I broke at one point with the idea of the nation, with the prevalent stultifying notions of 'Scottish identity', and even, momentarily, with the country itself (though, without waving any banners, I took a lot of Scotland with me).

Which (this meta-national position) is why a Scottish critic (David Black, writing in *Akros*, August, 1975), while appreciating the work (what he could know of it) I have been doing over the past few years (most of it has appeared first in France, in French) could say of me that 'he kept out of Scotland much of the time and did little to take advantage of his "Scottishness"', and of certain poems of mine: 'I do find myself wondering if they are quite from his centre: they have slightly the air of being written in a foreign accent, Californian I shouldn't be surprised, or sometimes French'. Now this is both perceptive, and curious. To take the curious aspect first: this notion of centre and the pushing forward of the national qualification (even with the critical distance implied by the inverted commas). From the point of view of the psychology of creativity, the notion of 'centre' begs a lot of questions. I'd say that a really creative mind works rather in a field (of tension, of contradiction) which is productive of ideas and hence provokes a perpetual renewal of identity, the whole process being vastly different from the orbiting around some hypothetical centre. And didn't MacDiarmid himself, in *Scottish Eccentrics* (Routledge, 1936), say that the Scottish mind is essentially *centrifugal*? This 'central' reference is too limited and stems from a stunted psycho-cultural landscape.

When the work of Mallarmé came on the French scene, did any critic bother to say that he wasn't working from his 'French centre', though his work certainly looked alien enough? Nobody said Baudelaire wasn't French either, though Sainte-Beuve experienced his mental landscape as a Kamchatka. The fact was that the French cultural scene had intellectual reach enough to be able to take in a Kamchatka, not being restricted to Ménilmontant or Fouilly-les-Oies. Could it be that the Scottish scene lacks such reaches? It pretty obviously does. Which is why, without trying to turn myself into a Frenchman, I moved to France. It was, be it recalled, a way taken by many a Scot before Scotland became obsessed by its national identity – think, for example, of Richard of St Victor in medieval Paris. So much for the French side of my 'strangeness'.

As to the American side, it's true that I was attracted to American literature from the start. That is, I think, because the metaphysical thrust is so much stronger in that literature than in, say, English literature, which so often stays hog-tied to socio-personal environment. Whitman's 'the poets of the cosmos advance to first principles'; Melville's 'strike through the mask; Williams' 'the thrust must go through to the white' – all that is my language. American literature opens out on to metaphysical space. It cannot be forgotten that it had its beginnings in the transcendentalist movement, with the whole of German metaphysics, filtered largely through Carlyle (his correspondence with Emerson) behind it. Carlyle is the bridge between Scotland and America, and the kind of thing I was looking for I tended to find in 'transplanted' Scots like Melville or Jeffers. These, and others like them, I see as *extravagant* (in the etymological sense) Scots, engaged in what Melville called 'ontological heroics'.

5.

There is, then, a certain France as well as a certain America in my mental field, though, I repeat, my aim was never to take out new cultural identity papers and become either American or French. It was an undefined becoming that interested me, all I knew about it was that it didn't fit in with existing structures. Aware of his far-outness, Valéry, mediterranean Frenchman, referred to himself humorously as 'the last Atlantean' (*le dernier Atlante*). In a similar way, with the same kind of humour, I came to refer to myself as a Hyperborean. For this term, two initial references.
First, Melville:

In those Hyperborean regions, to which enthusiastic truth, and earnestness, and independence, will invariably lead a mind fitted by nature for profound and fearless thought, all objects are seen in a dubious, uncertain and refracting light.

Further, of Melville, Lewis Mumford writes that he

had faced the colourless, unintegrated, primal world that underlies and antedates that which we know through our senses, our feelings, our experiences: he had touched the bare, unkind beginning of things, that chaos which existed

when darkness reigned over the waters, and only Moby
Dick stirred in the deep. He had beheld the white unre-
fracted truth which exists before it passes through man's
being and is broken up into the colours of art and thought
and custom and ritual and organized society.

Second reference, Nietzsche:

We are Hyperboreans. We are very well aware in what
remoteness we live. Pindar knew of us: 'Neither by land nor
by sea will you find the way to the Hyperboreans'. Beyond
the North, beyond the ice, beyond death itself, lies our life,
our happiness. We have found the way out of centuries of
labyrinth. Who else found it? Modern man perhaps? I don't
know whether I'm coming or going – that's the theme song
of modern man. It's that modernity we were sick of. Rather
live out in the ice-fields than amid that modern mess.

6.

So much for the origin of the word in my vocabulary. As to the
mental territory it designates, I expressed my first entry into it in
the poem-book *The Cold Wind of Dawn* (there is a Nietzschean
title for you!), but things really became acute with the book that
came after it: *The Most Difficult Area*, the last book I was to
publish in Britain for quite some time.

To take only one critical reaction to this book, and an
intelligent one, though to my mind it doesn't go far enough,
because it approaches these poems, less with a readiness to
penetrate into the situation in which they were written than
with an established notion about what poetry 'should be', that is,
it is only *literary* criticism, whereas what was wanted, if the
criticism was really to approach the work, was a criticism going
thoroughly into intellectual grounds *that put literature itself in
question* – I'm referring to Robin Fulton's pages on my work in
Contemporary Scottish Poetry (Macdonald, 1974). Quoting
from the poem 'At the limits of saying'

> At the limits of saying
> in the eros-silence
> alone with the alone

at the limits of saying
the brain empty and quiet
like shell and like stone

at the limits of saying
the soul flies to the mouth
and the poem is born

Fulton comments: 'But *what* poem? Is the poem written in words on that particular page a mere preliminary jotting for that other greater poem whose existence we must take on trust?' The immediate answer to Fulton's question is, of course, that this text is in the nature of an *ars poetica*, indicating the kind of state of being involved in the creation of a poem as I understood it. It is *programme*, not realisation, and was not meant to be. Robin Fulton might retort that a good proportion of the book is programme, rather than the creation of poems. I'd take that. The book is largely the description of a situation. I'd say simply that the situation as described is a lot more interesting and worth exploration than so much 'poetry'. The problem is not, as Fulton says on a non-paradoxical reading of the poem, how to conceive of poetry as 'something which takes over when words leave off' (though it might be said, in a larger context, that the essential is indeed there) but how to utter an apprehension which normal discourse, normal poetry, never approaches. *That* is the problem (and Fulton sees it himself, but leaves it hanging in the air as if it were strictly for the birds). The book is called, let it be remembered, 'the most difficult *area*', not 'Twenty-seven poems' or whatever. Fulton does find poems that seem to him a solution of the problem (he quotes 'Extraordinary Moment' and 'Sesshu'): 'there are a few short poems which do seem to indicate a possibility. These have clearly learned from oriental models'. But again, with the notion of 'literary model' the problem, the issue is avoided. The *work* as I saw it involved much more than the imitation of models – with that we're still inside literary space. I was much more concerned with *way* than *model*, and with the entry into an unedited space, which I was to call 'white world'. More on that later. For the moment I'd like to give some idea of what I take to be a more adequate analysis of *The Most Difficult Area*, something coming closer to the *point* of the book.

7.

Fulton says that the conception of poetry which comes across in the *Area* is narrow. True enough. But if you go into experience far enough (experience both existential and intellectual) there are times when the path *is* narrow – somebody referred to it once as a razor's edge. You can, of course, write reams of poetry, and be quite happy about it, without coming anywhere near that path. It's for somebody that is not only suspicious of language which, through its tendency to generalisation, confuses the issues, obscures the mindscape, and fixes what is essentially volatile (Thoreau: 'The volatile truth of our words should continually betray the inadequacy of the residual statement') but is also asking themselves radical questions as to personal identity, agreeing with Valéry that 'we know ourselves only by hearsay', that is, according to a phraseology which is alien. This kind of problem, by the way, is incomparably more interesting than the use or non-use of Lallans . . .

The prolegomena to the *Area* talks of a bird (a rare bird that is becoming rarer), the Rosy Gull, that 'goes north when other birds go south'. That 'north' is the point of the book. Valéry again: 'Nobody goes right to the limit, to the extreme north of man'; and the same writes: 'There's not much sense in writing if it's not to get to the very summit of being'. What Fulton in his essay calls 'substance', the absence of which he points out in the *Area*, was for me old stock, to be *consumed*. The unit of the book is not a person with substance, it is an I (undefined) with a desire.

Desire, *eros*. For Plotinus (discreetly present in the very poem Fulton quotes, 'alone with the alone') *eros* is what pushes to purification, what tends towards liberation of the mind, what drives you towards your real self (*intuitus ad seipsum* – Ficino translating Plotinus), what leads to a direct contact with light, to a spiritual density (that light and density being figured in the *Area* by rosy quartz). What we are concerned with, then, in the *Area* is the itinerary of a self towards its summit, the movement comprising both *eros* and *logos* ('*eros* and *logos* here conjoined') within a landscape that is chaos-cosmos.

It is a *difficult* area. MacDiarmid talked about it and certainly knew it. He knew about Valéry's night in Genoa of October 1892. He speaks of Hölderlin's later poetry with 'silence supervening at

poetry's height', and of Mallarmé's 'embodied silences'. And he
quotes Hindemith questioning the relevance of even sound itself
to music: 'Sound shrinks to nothingness and musical composition
becomes an abstract philosophical activity'. There's a passage in
the *In Memoriam James Joyce* (Maclellan, 1955), where all the
above references occur and that might almost stand as an
epigraph to the *Area*:

> Even so, Conscience calls the self of Dasein
> Out of the state in which it is lost
> In the 'one like many'. The caller
> Is unfamiliar to 'oneself' in its everydayness
> And speaks in the uncanny mode of silence
> To call the self back into the silence
> Of the 'existent' potentiality of being.

MacDiarmid is probably quoting here, as he so often does, and
the language is more than a bit jargonesque, but the phrases refer
to something real, and it was that something I was going through
in *The Most Difficult Area*.

In view of what I've been trying to get down here, rapidly,
anyone who finds Robin Fulton's last sentence concerning the
Area – 'A poet who limits his conception of poetry in this way
and whose engrossing interest seems to be in experience beyond
language could quite logically stop writing' – may be tempted to
translate it so: 'Only a poet who, at one point or another, limits
his conception of poetry in this way, and whose engrossing
interest lies in experience beyond language, is liable to produce
writing that is something more than an obsolete branch of the
entertainment industry'. I didn't stop writing. Far from it. I just
stopped publishing in Britain.

The genus of the *Area* is not literary but theoretical (Valéry:
the theory of one's self). It is less concerned with literature than
with what Valéry calls 'psychic culture'. It is, also, the book of a
separation, a disjunction.

The situation of *The Most Difficult Area* with regard to
literary (let's say *merely* literary) criticism I see in the terms
William Carlos Williams used to describe the critical situation of
Joyce's work: 'They do not see Joyce blossoming white above
their heads . . . they are *literary* critics'. Not that I would claim
anything like 'a blossoming' for the *Area*. No, the aim of the

book is at once less ambitious and more radical than that. It is concerned with the difficult beginnings of a ground on which, perhaps, 'a blossoming' might occur.

That was the object of the work I was undertaking, had undertaken from the *Cold Wind* on. It was just that with the *Area* I'd come across the first real difficulties. Looking back on it now, I see myself vis-à-vis literary criticism in the position that Antonin Artaud found himself in with regard to Jacques Rivière: involved in a brokenness, difficulties of articulation, a vacuum both fascinating and annihilating. Metaphysical ground, rather than literary ground, I'd say, involved in the breakdown of a certain Western metaphysics (e.g. idea of a permanent, continuous self made in the image of a God itself made in the image of that ideal self) and engaged in the beginnings of *something else*.

8.

Since the time of the 'most difficult area', I have been occupied, in various ways, with that 'something else': let's say, a larger space of being, to which the *Area* was in some sense a gate. The penetration of that space has meant the kind of *intensive* work I've just gone into, but it has concurrently involved the *extensive* exploration of apparently exotic and heterogeneous mental landscapes.

In the introduction to his anthology *The Golden Treasury of Scottish Poetry* (Macmillan, 1948), à propos of the 'little white rose of Scotland', Hugh MacDiarmid wrote:

> If I have been concerned with the little white rose of Scotland, I have also been concerned to ensure that its roots are given their proper scope. Those who have tried to root up one of the dwarf bushes of our white rose . . . know how astonishingly far these run. So it is with our poetry too. It cannot be confined to a little Anglo-Scottish margin . . . Towards the end of his life Mr Yeats returned to the Upanishads and recommended them to the attention of our younger poets. That movement back to the ancient Gaelic classics and then North to Iceland and then East to Persia and India is the course the refluence of Gaelic genius must take.

It's one of the paradoxes of MacDiarmid's position in Scotland that, while recommending work of a certain scope and height, he brings together, as in this anthology, work that is obviously enough Scottish, but shows no sign of what he is recommending. In a similar way, when, in his preface to *The Ten Principal Upanishads*, Yeats looks to 'a neighbourhood where some new Upanishad, some half-asiatic masterpiece, may start up amid our averted eyes', and then when we see in what direction he is looking – Day Lewis, MacNeice, Auden, Laura Riding – we can only think that the time was yet to come, that another area of attention had to be opened and defined.

To come back to Scotland, it has remained, despite MacDiarmid's injunctions (and the high reaches of his poetry), at the sign of the thistle rather than at that of the white rose. It is only now, perhaps, within the Isles as a whole, that signs of the desire for something larger are beginning to appear. Which is one of the reasons why I am writing this essay.

As I've suggested elsewhere, in other studies, the move North that MacDiarmid speaks of has to mean more than Iceland and the Scandinavian sagas, just as the move East has to mean more than Persia and India. I'd speak rather of the whole of *Eurasia septentrionalis*. But with the general tenor of MacDiarmid's remarks I'm in complete agreement, and when he writes, in *In Memoriam James Joyce*,

> Unlike you Joyce, I am more concerned
> With the East than with the West and the poetry I seek
> Must be the work of one who has always known
> That the Tarim Valley is of more importance
> Than Jordan or the Rhine in world history.

he's talking about the work that has absorbed me for the last twenty years.

9.

There can be no question here of anything like an exposition of the 'Eastern field', but since MacDiarmid mentions the Tarim Basin, we can take that for a start, and for an analogy.

It would indeed be difficult to overestimate the importance of the Tarim Basin for world culture. This desertic region, now the

Sinkiang Uighur Autonomous Region of the Chinese People's
Republic, is practically closed in by mountains: to the West, the
Pamirs; to the north, the Tienshan; to the south, the Kunlun –
only to the east does it have an opening, on to the Chinese
province of Kansu. It is, geographically, a place of concentration. It was to become so culturally. The caravan route known as
the Silk Road, the main passageway between East and West,
began its eastern section after crossing the Pamirs. There, two
ways were possible over the Tarim desert land: north by the
Tienshan foothills, south by the Kunlun, but both roads met
some 1,200 miles further on at Tunhwang in Kansu. Tunhwang
itself was, and still is, one of the richest cultural hoards in the
world, but the whole of this vast desert, all 50,000 square miles
of it, was scattered with oases (Kucha, Tulfan . . .) and these
were destined to become lively religious centres. There, Hellenic,
Iranian, Indian and Chinese culture, all the elements that came
along the Silk Road, met and fused, the essence of the fusion
being Buddhism, in its various forms (Hinayana, Mahayana,
Vajrayana).

Reflecting on the Road, on the desert, and on the centres, I
have always had in mind less the merchants and the soldiers than
the pilgrims: that Fa-hsien, for example, who left Ch'ang-an
(itself a city to my liking, with Buddhist priests rubbing
shoulders with Nestorian monks, and Taoist geomancers walking the same street as silk-dealers from Foochow!) for India, in
search of Buddhist manuscripts; or that Hsüan-tsang who, also
starting out from Ch'ang-an, went to Tulfan, then followed the
northern route to Kucha, from there trekked to Tashkent and
Samarkand, finally arriving in India through the Gandhâra
country. These special cases apart, I have been attracted to
the figure of the pilgrim in general as depicted in so many
Buddhist paintings: straw hat, knotted staff in hand, back
weighed down with a bundle of sutra scrolls. An eighth-century
poem by T'ao Han says something of what went on in the
pilgrim's mind:

Pines and cypresses hide the mountain gorge
But to the West I see a narrow path.
The sky opens, a peak reveals itself
And, as though risen from emptiness, a monastery appears.

Night comes, monkeys and birds fall silent.
I gaze at the blue mountains and the moon in the lake
Till my soul goes beyond these visible things
At one and the same time errant and captive . . .

A desert, pilgrimage, a difficult road, manuscripts . . . In
describing the Tarim Basin I have been describing the territory
I have been living in and working in these last few years. To go
now further into the root of the matter.

10.

The root of the matter is the question of identity: the state of
consciousness. When one is tired of personal poetry, not too
interested in more or less frantic attempts to get out of one's
'self', and unattracted by technicalities that aim at eliminating
the subject altogether, where does one go?

Discussing the concept of self in the context of Buddhism,
Suzuki (in *Zen Buddhism and Psychoanalysis*, Allen and Unwin,
1960) speaks of a 'metaphysical self' as opposed to the psychological, moral self that belongs to the limited world. With reference
to the Vedanta, René Guénon speaks of the liberation (*lysis*) from
the limited self in terms of metaphysics, positing a sphere that is
'universal', 'transcendent'. It is by dissolution of the 'little self' that
the larger self (*mahâtman* in Sanskrit, *ta wo* in Chinese) can come
into being. The Chinese text, the *Pi Yen Lu* (Blue Cliff Records)
describes the universal self as like 'white waves breaking in the
sky'. This 'universal self' is not *absolutely* transcendental, not
purely metaphysical, rather, shall we say for a start, it is immanent-
transcendent, physical-metaphysical. Speaking within the Christian context, Meister Eckhart, so close to Buddhism, distinguishes
four stages in the itinerary of the self: first stage, separation from
God; second stage, similarity with God; third stage, identification
with God; fourth stage, beyond God – in what Eckhart calls a
desert, what Buddhism calls emptiness, what I call white world. It
is white world that lies at the end of the Hyperborean path.

I have purposely aligned these phrases quickly, knowing that
the phrases in themselves cannot impart knowledge, but can only
indicate a territory. The penetration of that territory is a question
of *work*. Poetic work, as I understand it.

11.

The 'white world' is where poetry and metaphysics meet.

This white world is not a place of glacial dread or of terrifying blankness – as with the traumatised Poe, or Melville at times, or Mallarmé whom I would call a *frozen* Buddhist – though it may seem so at first (see certain poems in *The Most Difficult Area*). It is not inhuman either or superhuman – though it may be outside humanism as we know it.

In his book on the Tarahumaras, Artaud called for a 'life in metaphysics', saying that the Renaissance, which brought us humanism, far from being a rebirth, meant a curtailment, in that it limited mind to the human sphere, whereas for him the field was infinitely wider, and called for a different way of being in the world.

Whether metaphysical is to be retained as an epithet for it is merely a question of usage. When this way becomes more 'natural', it will be possible to drop the transcendental epithet. But in the meantime the word will be useful as that: the indication of a possible transcendence (of the humanist definitions). Without such a transcendence, culture, as Nietzsche foresaw, would go to the dogs, that is, to what he called the 'last men', hideously productive, but creatively nil.

I realise that all this may sound excessively complicated. But the practice itself, once one is into it, is not complicated.

A Chinese writer (Liu Kia-Hway, the translator into French of Chuang-tzu) puts it this way:

> Let us give ourselves up to an immediate perception of the reality around us. This flash of sun, this blade of grass . . . These immediately reveal the presence of ontological being, an obscure, indivisible presence in which everything is gathered in and nothing excluded. It is a full and sovereign presence, a presence which makes for the joy of a man deeply integrated with his ontological sources.

And what I have been trying to get at can come across in the simplest of haiku.

It's thinking of the white world, and of my last visit to MacDiarmid, that I'll quote this haiku in conclusion:

They spoke no word
the host, the guest
and the white chrysanthemum.

13

Talking Transformation

The pre-text, the point of departure, of this essay is the event organised around the linguistic philosophy of Noam Chomsky by the Free University and the review *Scottish Child* in Glasgow in January 1990. Its aim will be to move through the field of generative (transformational) grammar as well as the philosophy of common sense, a theme also raised on this occasion, into . . . something else. So that, if the initial subtitle of the essay might have been: Scotland, Chomsky and Common Sense, its actual subtitle could be: The crisis of reason, radical research and the new field of creativity.

1. Common-sense Scotland

Scotland has for long prided itself on its reasonableness, and has for just as long been caricatured for its tendency to verbose ratiocination. That there is argumentative capacity in the Scottish mind, as well as a keen sense of logic (think, say, of Richard of St Victor or of David Hume), is something I willingly accept, and highly appreciate. But that the specific philosophy of 'Common Sense' is something worth disinterring and distributing I very much doubt. In fact, I'd see it as just another deviation preventing any real advance in thought, in expression and in culture.

We owe the 'Common Sense school' in philosophy to the Reverend Thomas Reid, who was born at Strachan, in Kincardine-shire, in 1710. By 1726, Reid had completed his studies at the University of Aberdeen, but he stayed on another ten years as librarian. Then, in 1734, he became a minister (like his father) at Newmacher, near Aberdeen. Sixteen years later, he obtained the

Chair of Philosophy at King's College, Aberdeen, where, with others (Beattie, etc.) he founded the Aberdeen Philosophical Society, known familiarly as the Wise Club. In 1764, the Reverend Reid succeeded to Adam Smith as Professor of Moral Philosophy at Glasgow, and it was in that year he published his *Enquiry into the Human Mind on the Principles of Common Sense.*

What was it all about?

Seen from a distance, without getting fankled in all the details, it was a reaction against Hume's scepticism. Reid considered (and how right he was) that Hume's thought was subversive of religion and morality (at least *Reid's* morality). Not only was it contrary to the 'experience' of Dr Reid (minister at Newmachar, near Aberdeen . . .), it was contrary to 'common sense'. This 'common sense' contained truth (indeed Truth), absolutely un-attackable by sceptical philosophy, because ultimately founded on the rock of the Divinity itself.

The British mediocracy (I prefer such existential and cultural categories to merely political ones) heaved a sigh of relief, because Hume (the man who hob-nobbed with all those French intellectuals) had had them ruffled for a while.

The French mediocracy was worried too by all those Diderots, d'Alemberts and Rousseaus Hume consorted with, and it's a little-known episode in European culture-history that when Napoleon's France was looking for a humdrum philosophy (not too obviously reactionary, just flat-footed) that would calm things down in those post-revolutionary days, it found exactly what it wanted in the 'Scottish school' as edified by Thomas Reid.

The story goes like this.

The mediocratic State imagined by Napoleon would have two main bulwarks: the university and the church. Roederer was quite plain about it when he addressed the *Corps législatif* on 14 May 1802: 'Legislators, the institution which the government proposes is not purely moral, it is political. Public instruction and religion are and must be two different institutions leading to the same goal, each with its specific methods, these being far from being mutually exclusive'. Napoleon sent his intellectuals out on the hunt for a philosophy (with religious connotations) that would shut the mouths of all the sceptics, materialists and sensualists in the land. The task rested finally on the shoulders of Royer-Collard, who was nominated Professor of Philosophy in 1811. One morning of that year, he was walking along the banks of the Seine, engrossed in thought. He'd just been reading Condillac, and if he taught what Condillac said, he'd be telling young people that our faculties are no more than transformed sensations, that general ideas are only counters in an empty game, and that a completed science is nothing more than a well-made language. All this was repugnant to the fervent Christian, the austere moralist, the man of authority that Royer-Collard was (and where would it lead the kids!), but he had nothing solid to put in its place. Then, stopping at one of those bookstalls that line the Seine, between a cook-book and a farmer's almanac, he saw, *hallelujah*, a book entitled *Enquiry into the Human Mind on the Principles of Common Sense* by a man called Thomas Reid. He picked it up, flipped through the pages. 'How much?' 'Thirty sous.'

Royer-Collard had just purchased the ideological grounds of the mediocratic university in France, that was to last right through the nineteenth century and well into the twentieth.

When I was 'invited to leave' that University in May 1968 as a 'subversive foreigner' (anarchist agitator, etc., etc.), I had fun pointing out in a Parthian shot article that it was the philosophy of a foreigner, one of my compatriots to boot, that had provided the very principles that University was based on . . .

2. The Crisis of Reason

I'd like to turn away now from Thomas Reid and others of that ilk, and move for a while in the company of a thinker with a lot more scope, a tougher thrust, and a sharper eye, Edmund Husserl.

In May 1935, Husserl gave a lecture at the *Kulturbund* in Vienna. It was entitled: 'Philosophy in the crisis of European humanity'. This lecture was part of the great mass of cogitation and writing that was to become to a large extent Husserl's testament, and which has been published under the title: *The Crisis in European Science and Transcendental Phenomenology.*

Put briefly, Husserl's aim was to jettison superficial rationalism such as that of the eighteenth century, without abandoning reason as such, that is, without wallowing in the farrago of irrationality that was already very much a sign of the times. But it's worth going into the argument in some detail, or rather, worth following the path of thought step by step, because we're concerned with the discovery of a whole work-field (that of transcendental phenomenology), out of which might arise a new livable world, rather with any mere 'debate' between reason and unreason.

For Husserl, that rational process of thought called philosophy had its one and only origin in the Greece of the seventh and sixth centuries BC. There you had the rise of a 'new type of cultural figure', the philosopher, i.e. a man who, beyond the familial and familiar context of day-to-day cares and obligations, beyond the consolations and constrictions of mythology and religion, devotes his time and his life to *theoria*: contemplation of the universe. The unaccustomed stance and activity of these 'intellectuals' drew the attention of non-philosophers, who recognized its rectifying (archontic) function in society, so that, gradually, the whole community was transformed. This new rationality, the philosophical form of existence, allied to sunlit geometries, meant not only universal vision as against local tradition and personal prejudice, but an all-encompassing science and an enlightened way of living. The theorem of Pythagoras, that beautiful example, among others, of ideal objectivity, was the same in every language . . .

A few lines above, I used the word 'intellectual', anachronistically of course (it only came into currency in the nineteenth century), but intentionally, because it is the pivot on which we turn from that bright moment of Athens to the modern cognitive and existential situation which, even when it tries, is not 'intellectual' at all in any strong sense of the word, but, when not bordering on total mindlessness, is merely *intellectualistic*. What happened in the modern age was that rationality turned into rationalism, which means, among other things, a loss of the sense of world, a culture that rings more and more hollow (hardly helped by periodical attempts to give it substance via naturalism, social realism or oniric fantasia), and a proliferation of narrow specialties. How that move from 'full world' and knowledge of whole being to 'objective world', unilateral conceptions and endless series of sterile research came about is the history of Western philosophy, to which Husserl devoted a great deal of his thinking and teaching. But beyond history and criticism, his aim was radical analysis of the critical situation that had arisen and the creation of means to get out of it into a new work-field.

The means Husserl gradually came to evolve was transcendental phenomenology, and he found the basis of it in not only one of the first, but one of the most radical of modern thinkers, René Descartes.

If Descartes was largely responsible for the establishment of the modern context of objectivist rationalism, one can also find in his 'meditations on primary philosophy', even though he himself was not aware of it (eager as he was to set up modern scientific theory while doing some geometrical theology on the side), the 'transcendental motive' that Husserl himself was to develop. What Descartes did, for a start, was to put the whole of the ideological universe in question, until all that remains is the subjective thinking self (*ego* and *cogito*). That is the 'transcendental' act. What happens thereafter, however, is that this subjective leap relapses into subjectivism (with its corollary, objectivism), while the transcendentalism degenerates into psychologism. In other words, Descartes did not go right to the end of his own radicality, did not prolong (project) the transcendental leap into a space that would have rediscovered the space of original Greek philosophy (primal space), he only founded the secondary context of modernity. If this modernity has known triumphs, it has now reached a stage where, for example, scientists are no longer philosophers, but mere laboratory artisans (hence a science with very little living sense to say to people), where philosophy has degenerated into the mere history of philosophy as a succession of 'schools' one plods through ponderously before giving it all up to become a logical positivist, and where psychological distress, based ultimately on the loss of world, is rife and rampant.

Transcendental phenomenology takes over where Descartes swerved into his deviation. Like Descartes at his beginning, Husserl starts off by excluding from his mind all presuppositions, and then proceeds to try and see (feel, think) with the utmost possible clarity the data (the phenomena) of the world as they come to his *attention*, as he goes towards them (*intention*). We move from reasoning (on a confused basis) to perception and kinæsthetics, we move out from theoretical discourse into the phenomenological field, from formal logic into transcendental logic. Doing so, we are able to provide radical clarification of confused and confusing terms such as community, culture, nature,

world. We give science a new and superior form. We invent a new
ontology which includes 'all regional forms of existence'.

Such was the ambiance and the ambition of transcendental
phenomenology when Husserl was putting the final touches to
his unitary scheme in 1936, just three years before the outbreak
of a war that was to mean wholesale regression on all sides, and
from which Europe has still not recovered, not by far.

The 'human sciences', which were very much a feature of the
post-war period, have piled up masses of secondary discourse
which has little radical value. When it was interesting at all, it
was based on the linguistics of Saussure. So, for any move
forward, it's as well to look at language first.

3. From Linguistics to Poetics

Within modernity, Descartes' attempt had been the proto-foun-
dation of a live and intelligent world. Husserl had been out for an
ultimate, radical foundation. In his turn, Chomsky is looking for
a similar foundation. Just as phenomenology goes from superficiality to depth via successive layers, so Chomsky, in his study
of language, goes from surface phenomena to what he calls 'deep
structures'. And the similarity, the connection, is not only one of
procedure, it is one of reference. Like Husserl, Chomsky looks, in
the first instance, to Descartes.

A couple of times already in this essay, I've made reference to
political contexts: the adaptation of Scottish common-sense philosophy under Napoleon, and the outbreak of the 1939–45 war
that marginalised such thinking as that of Husserl. One is
inevitably confronted by socio-political situations (the thing is,
not to become enmeshed in them). And Chomsky is no exception.
Indeed he is probably better known by most for his political
stance: criticism of policy, analysis of ideology, than for his work
on grammar. The question is often put to him whether there is
any connection between these two activities. He answers, no –
that the political criticism and the ideological analysis could just
as well have been done by somebody else. Inded, he says that any
citizen could do it. All it needs is 'good sense', that *bon sens*
Descartes spoke of, and which he says is 'something shared by
everybody'. If Chomsky is certainly right in wanting to pull
discourse away from the technocratic 'expert' in politics and

social affairs and put it back in the vicinity of the 'man of common sense' (who, as Wittgenstein points out, is *not* the 'philosopher of common sense'), he may be a bit too optimistic about the prevalence of this 'good sense'. All kinds of media are in action today to deviate it, obfuscate it, benumb it. And there is something much more insidious than ideology, it is that 'atmosphere' another American linguist, Sapir, refers to in his essay *Culture, genuine and spurious*: 'the flat and tedious sameness of spiritual outlook, the anemic make-believe, the smug intolerance of the challenging, that so imprison our souls'. In that kind of context, 'common sense' and 'ordinariness' (which, given knowledge, are active principles) themselves turn into ideology. I'm pretty sure Chomsky must have felt 'common sense' ideology pretty thick in the air in Glasgow, as well as the advocacy of a realism that is already a limitation of any radical 'good sense'. As Wittgenstein points out again, common sense (in the *radical* sense) is neither realistic nor idealistic – it evolves outside those stuffy compartments.

Leaving platform polemics, which never get very far, let's look at grammar, and maybe at the possibilities of a new grammar of existence, a new poetics of experience.

When Chomsky came on the scene, the linguistic field was occupied by two principal schools of thought: structuralism, stemming from Saussure and developed by the linguistic circle of Prague (Jakobson, Troubetskoy); and formalism (allied to behavioural conditioned reflex psychology), represented mainly by Bloomfield. Chomskian primal reaction to these two schools is, one, that everything in language (and semiotics in general) is not reflex action based on apprenticeship, and, two, that formal structure is not enough. That some elements at least are innate in the mind would be evidenced by the fact that, at the age of three or four days, infants can distinguish between sounds like P, T and K, which form a pretty close acoustic continuum. As to structure, if you say something like: 'Colourless green ideas sleep furiously', you've got a structure that answers to all the strict rules of grammar – but you've got no sense (only, at best, an example of very limited Lewis-Carroll-type 'poetry'). In other words, sense comes from something deeper than structure.

Let's try and go deeper.

If the original principles and perspectives of generative grammar were, by that theory, innate in Chomsky's mind, they found corroboration in what has for long been called 'philosophical grammar' and which Chomsky calls 'cartesian linguistics', since it goes back to the cogitations of Descartes as applied in the *Grammar of Port-Royal*. With regard to normal linguistic practice, which consists in the accumulation of facts and the application of methodologies, Chomsky is an anarchist in that he leaves ordinary form, structure, method in a search for *order*, a much more interesting, more difficult, more fertile concept. The anarchist looks for a finer sense of order than mere arrangement, searches out deeper principles, more general processes. With Chomsky, you see a mind moving, you see a conceptual imagination in action, a brain at work with a sense not only of the instrumentality of language, but of its creativity. Humboldt (*On the Structural Diversity of Human Languages*, 1830), saw language as *energeia* (act, action) rather than as mere *ergon* (fact, artefact). Chomsky is 'humboldtian' in this sense.

But he differs from Humboldt in this, that he is universalist, where Humboldt is relativist. What linguistic relativism says is that no two languages show the same world, that each and every language reflects a local historical experience, a local cultural landscape. What linguistic universalism says, on the other hand, is that if such differences undoubtedly exist, the underlying structure is nevertheless the same. If each particular tongue is, as Humboldt maintained, a local selection from a random totality (relativism), the universalist will say that it also contains elements of that totality, that total conceptual field. It might be possible to see each language as the segment of a circle, this schema indicating not only the relation between one language and another, but between each language and the whole. Which is of course what makes translation possible.

Humboldt was part of that Romantic movement which saw the break-down of classicist unity and the discovery of all kinds of variety and diversity, including persons, local peoples and nations. Chomsky is active at a time which has seen the conflicts that arise when one nation asserts itself against another, as well as ineffectual attempts at *inter*nationalism. But this historical-political difference is superficial. A new universalist position is strengthened rather by depth-psychology, which puts personal identity in question, revealing deeper structures, and by physics, which has blasted the notion of simple localism. All the relativists tend to speak of particular social realities – cf. Sapir: 'No two languages are ever sufficiently similar to be considered as representing the same social reality'. The new universalist will hardly deny this, but he will say that the universal he is after lies, not at the level of sociology, nor even of anthropology, but at the level, say, of neuro-physiology and molecular biology, at the level, ultimately, where mind and cosmos, human and non-human, come together.

In other words, if we want Scottish references here, the relevant names are not Thomas (Common Sense) Reid, or James (nationalist hype) Macpherson, but, say, the physiologist Bell, with his *The Nervous System of the Human Body* (1830) or, closer to us, D'Arcy Thomson, with his sense of universal form. It's a question ultimately of how to use the nervous system with the maximum of efficiency, which doesn't mean pounding at it, but knowing how to let it deploy and employ its resources. This requires life-techniques, and finds expression in dimensions of writing (the art I happen to take to most, not excluding, far from it, others) that most criticism has never heard of. And I am not suggesting (God save the mark!) schools of 'creative writing' – the ground lies deeper than all that. That critics and most 'literary people' should be the slowest to catch on to the dynamics and the dimensions of new work may seem paradoxical, but from the point of view of the 'good sense' philosophy we've been trying to get at here via Descartes, Husserl and Chomsky, it is not surprising at all. The official (or habitual) critic is caught up in a mediary context with its norms and its models, not to say its prejudices and its preconceptions, whereas individuals with open minds have nothing to limit their brain-power, nothing to alter their sensation, nothing to blinker their eyes.

I'm thinking of a writing that would be aware of and use the extensional disciplines put forward by the logician Korzybski when he set up the Institute of Semantics in 1938 – and I'm thinking of extensions of them. I'm thinking of a writing knowing how to move through local systems and sensitive fields towards world-logic and world-sensation. I'm thinking of *kinesis* rather than that *mimesis* literature has lived on since Aristotle. I'm thinking of Minkowskian world-lines, I'm thinking of beautiful geometries such as those you find in Gauss on curves, or

Riemann on the hypotheses underlying all geometry, and I'm thinking of a grounding deeper still than geometry – what I've called geopoetics. I'm thinking of Kurt Lewin's topological psychology, of William White's notions concerning 'neoplastic' language. I'm thinking of multiplicities and complicities, of continuities and discontinuities. And I weep (almost!) when, in contrast, I see the mass of piety and pathos, thick psychology and sad sociology, that is also called 'literature'.

To come back to language (the live primal element, the original event), and to the universalist-relativist dialectic (outside the musty provincialisms that beset us), one of the most interesting relativists is the American ethno-linguist Whorf. In his famous study of the Hopi language ('An American-Indian Model of the Universe'), he insists on the particularities of Hopi and makes the claim that its structures and conceptions make it closer to the vision of the universe of modern physics than any other known language. In the course of his demonstration, he quotes the very beautiful Hopi phrase for spring: 'whiteness coming down'. Now, it may be that, as an examiner looking in from without, he is reading the Hopi expression etymologically, as one tends to do with a foreign language – Pound does it with Chinese. If we 'translated' English the same way, into Hopi, we might get, for spring, 'fresh water rising', just as we might get for 'consider', 'he talks with a star' (*cum sidere*). There, at the level of *etymon* (primary word), Hopi and English don't sound so different. It is to that primal level that universalist linguistics try to penetrate.

It is to that level, I submit, that what I would like to call, in its most general terminology, open world poetics also tries to penetrate. There may be local reference and coloration, but the thrust will always be through to that open world – beyond the expression of any closed system, of any mediary society. The greatest singularity is not the person who piles up most particulars, but the one who opens the largest perspective. This means at one and the same time a high level of abstraction and a deep sensation.

Whiteness coming down.

14

Kentigern on Atlantic Quay

As I said in an earlier chapter of this book, Kentigern is an old acquaintance of mine. I met up with him first on the stained glass window of a church in Fairlie, Ayrshire, where I was brought up: there he was, book in hand, preaching to the gulls. Under the name of St Mungo, Kentigern became the patron saint of Glasgow. But I prefer the older name: Kentigern – 'the head of the house of the moon'. In fact, Kentigern is not only an old acquaintance, he's a kind of alter ego. If somebody even wanted to go so far as to see some phonetic connection between Ken-ti-gern and Ken-neth-White, I wouldn't say he or she is totally wrong. Beyond the phonetic connection, if anyone wanted to push the similarity even farther into intellectual and cultural areas, I'd be the last to deny the possibility of such an extrapolation. It's the kind of intellectual and cultural geometry I indulge in myself. A Scot to my liking invented logarithms. I go in for logos-rhythms: eros, logos and cosmos rhythms.

We're already there in oceanic territory: the tidal rhythms of the Atlantic. As to Atlantic Quay, in Glasgow, I'm taking it as a kind of vantage point, a place of observation, a symbolic site.

But to our theme: 'Kentigern on Atlantic Quay – cultural perspectives in the late twentieth century'.

I'm going to be talking once again about history and a life-situation, and about ways of opening up a new cultural field.

'What a journey!', as Lawrence Sterne says in *Tristram Shandy*.

1. On the Tracks of Kentigern

With Kentigern and others of his kind, we're in a geographical territory situated *in occiduis Britanniae partibus*, in the western parts of Britain, as the life of St Ninian puts it, and in a religious, intellectual area that was the northern frontier of the Roman diocese of Britain. And we're concerned with the history of the Celtic church – rather the Brito-Celtic church – in Scotland, in Alba, before its integration into the Roman state-system at the Synod of Whitby in 664. Those were stormy times, marked by the clash of Christian and Pagan, and, within the Celto-British church itself, from the early fourth century on, by the Pelagian heresy. Stormy times and wild country . . . When I say 'Kentigern and his like', I'm thinking of other figures such as St Ninian, St Colomban and St Adamnan. Colomba and Iona have captured most of the attention. But if there was the Scotic community, other communities, Brito-Pictic (those of Ninian and Kentigern) were just as significant, and if there was Iona, there was also Whithorn, Lismore, Applecross – and Glasgow.

Out from those centres, apostolic wanderers, fond of *diserts* (quiet retreats for meditation), would cross the wild stretches of country, raising a cross wherever they held a preaching, founding cells and monasteries, missionary stations, on sea-girt promontories, rocky headlands.

If the Scotic church tended to look back to Bangor, the Brito-Pictic one looked back to St Martin of Tours, in France. It was from there that Ninian, a native of Galloway, had come back to Alba in 397, to found, at Whithorn, *Candida Casa*, which probably had the greatest influence of all. Up from *Candida Casa*, Ninian came to the Clyde and Glasgow, crossed the Central Plain at Stirling, moved up Strathmore via Dunnotar, went round the Mounth, reached the Great Glen, continued on up to Sutherland, founding monasteries and cells all along the way.

Kentigern was to continue this work.

The life of Kentigern by Joceline, a monk of Furness, says he founded a church in Glasgow in 573. He came, as the text says, '*ad Cathures, quae nunc Glasgu vocatur [. . .] juxta cemiterium quoddam a Sancto Niniano quandam consecratum*' (he came up to the Cathurs which is now called Glasgow [. . .] close by the cemetery erstwhile consecrated by St Ninian). Built up at a bend in the Clyde (making it a 'moon-harbour', like Bordeaux), Glasgow was a pagan stronghold, and Kentigern had a hard time there, especially at the hands of a local bully-boy called Morken Bulg. Beating a strategic retreat, Kentigern decided to let Glasgow simmer a while, and went down to Wales. He was back up in the moon-town around 574, when King Rhydderch had got the better of Gwenddolew's forces, if not of his mind – that was Kentigern's job. Settled on the banks of the Molendinar (*'ad locum nomine Mellingdenor'*, says Joceline), while his mother, St Enoch, had a sister sanctuary on what was later to become St Enoch Square, Kentigern reorganised his community and got ready for a great missionary movement North. He followed what, ever since Ninian, had become the traditional route, across the Mounth, along the valleys of the Dee and the Don, up into the lands of Mar, and from there sent emissaries further on still, to the Orkneys and Iceland. In Chapter XXX of the *Life*, Jocelyn has this:

> He went to Albania, and there with great and almost unbearable toil, often exposed to death [. . .] , he reclaimed that land from the worship of idols and from profane rites that were almost equal to idolatry, setting up the landmarks of faith, and the customs of the church, and the laws of the canons. For there he erected many churches, and dedicated them when erected, ordaining priests and clerics; and he consecrated many of his disciples bishops. He also founded many monasteries in these parts, and placed over them as fathers the disciples whom he had instructed.

Before going on, let me insist on the fact and make it quite clear, that, having placed Kentigern in his historical context, and followed his way, I was going to see him more and more with a good deal of abstraction. What I've always liked is that wayfaring over the land, and a capacious mind able to concentrate all the elements of a culture. But I am just as much attracted by the Pelagians, and I can sympathise more than a little with the pagan Pictish king Canatulachama, with whom Kentigern must have had a windy conversation up there on the East Coast of Pictland.

To talk about alter egos is not to talk about Siamese twins . . .

I can imagine, by a system of existential projection, a Kentigern interested in the relationship between Picto-Scottish art and Scythian art, in the relationship between Celtic myth and Amerindian myth, in the move between the Caucasus and the Grampians . . .

I've tried to live up to that image.

2. In Glasgow, Mid- and Late Twentieth Century

I came on to the Glasgow scene about fourteen centuries after Kentigern.

The city had changed a bit.

It had been marked by Calvinism, Victorianism, and an industrial revolution had left it bruised and numb. There was still plenty of energy around, but it tended to be inarticulate, and expressed itself in a particularly local brand of black or gallows humour. It had the reputation of a hell-hole, and tried to live up to it, often succeeding.

The landscape was cancerous, with big clocks tolling the time, and the river had lost all memory of salmon.

I wandered about that landscape, day and night. Trying to get my bearings, trying to see what there was, radically, to be done.

I also did a lot of reading.

Maybe the book that marked me most at the time was Spengler's *Decline of the West*, that 'sketch of a morphology of universal history'. For Spengler, Western, Europeo-American culture had had its day – the way other civilizations and cultures had had their day before it. Civilization might go on, in some manner or other, 'culture' would still be produced – but it could all be going on against a crumbling background. The only valid intellectual work for any lucid mind not content to produce art that was merely a reflection of the decline, unwilling to wail and howl out its frustration and despair, was to try and see the whole process of history from a Sirius point of view, write, in other words, a huge historico-cultural prose-poem. That's what Spengler had done in the *Decline*, and the enterprise fascinated me. But it didn't satisfy me. I wanted to do something more with my existence than become a kind of universalist amanuensis. I identified myself with the figure not so much of the poet-historian, as of the 'intellectual nomad', described by Spengler as wandering about from rented room to rented room in the 'stony desert' of the city. That intellectual nomad figure interested me a lot more than the writers, including poets, I heard of.

In Spengler, the intellectual nomad is totally estranged from the natural context beyond the city's boundaries. I began to wonder if there might be the possibility of renewing and deepening contact with that *outside*, working out a new mindscape after emergence in the landscape. That's what I had in mind when I'd leave the city of Glasgow by the Whiteinch Ferry and walk down to the coast and back, over the Fairlie moors, at weekends.

And I continued looking into history, trying to see ways out of what Eliot called the wasteland, and which I could see sprawling all around me.

In *A Study of History*, again one of the massive efforts of the twentieth century, Toynbee is less fatalistic than Spengler. He doesn't see the future as definitively closed, but as an open question. The prolongation, for him, if it were to exist at all, would be religious. Not the kind of religious orthodoxy to which T. S. Eliot had had recourse, but a modern version of Franciscan mysticism. This indeed was the kind of thing that was to break out, mixed in with a sentimental kind of Buddhism and other ingredients, including straight Roman Catholicism, in the US in the 1950s, and in Eastern Europe in the late 1980s. I wasn't interested. But Toynbee, while never opening them up, had also spoken of two other possible paths: that of Mahayana Buddhism and that of Chinese Taoism. I had already had, while still an adolescent, some exposure to these, thanks to the library of an old hermit-naturalist down in Fairlie. I now took them up again, with the idea that the Mahayana would help me to clean up my mind-work, and that the Tao would help me to get deeper into the natural context the 'intellectual nomad', while moving from culture to culture, was trying to get back in contact with.

In short, with these perspectives in mind, and with these means at my disposal, I was trying to start out again, begin again.

Begin again . . .

That was what Joyce had recommended in *Finnegans Wake*. But for him, that meant only going on the merry-go-round once more. Literature for him was a multilinguistic rigmarole. His version of it is hilarious, it's interesting – a lot more than most literature – but it's still a rigmarole.

I wanted to start out again, if not from scratch, from deep roots, from real beginnings.

That is more difficult.

3. Into the White World

Since I came back to Scotland, I've seen that discussion often centres on questions of identity and locality. Maybe this is a good time and place to get this problematics a bit more worked out. Some time ago, in Edinburgh, I gave a talk on the state of Scotland. In the course of this talk I had occasion to refer to what I called the ideology of identity, to which some minds, in the morass and confusion, have looked, if not for a solution, at least for a refuge. I said no really creative mind worked from identity, but from a play of energy. After the talk, a woman came up to me, and said: 'But I *like* my Scottish identity'. I said I liked mine too, but it wasn't the same one. There was, to say the least, a slight misunderstanding. Maybe I was talking too fast, and from too far away – from the end point of a thirty-year work-path. When I was an adolescent in Glasgow, the question: 'Who am I?' still had meaning. So let me try now to fill in the intermediate stages between that woman's notion of identity and my play of energy.

I've never gone in much for genealogy and the family album. But I have looked around a bit. And it looks as if I emerged from a mixture of MacGregors, Camerons and Mackenzies, with McNees, Dewars, Humes and Downies in the offing. The Whites are supposed to be of the MacGregors. If Walter Scott called the MacGregors 'the children of the mist', it was because they were landless and lawless (outside the usual feudal-tribal organisation). They had been 'broken': not only were they forbidden to carry arms, their very name was an invitation to suicide. So if you were called, say, Coinnich Ban MacGregor, you might find it was advisable, as part of survival tactics, to drop the MacGregor, at least publicly, and call yourself simply Coinnich Ban, Kenneth White – while still roaming about the Trossachs and Rannoch Moor, feeling respect for the pine (the clan badge) and liking the slogan *ard choille* (the high wood), but not waving any banners.

As to my mother, she was a Cameron. The Camerons were out at Harlaw, in 1411, under Black Donald, Lord of the Isles. They were out at Killiecrankie in 1689, they were out in the '15 and the '45. It was a Duncan Cameron who piloted *L'Elisabeth* and the *Du Teillay*, out from Brest and Nantes, in Hebridean waters. And the last man to be hanged for Jacobitism in Britain was Archibald

Cameron, who had returned from exile in France to recover the gold supposedly buried by the shores of Loch Arkaig . . .

I am, by the way, no Jacobite. I am just trying to show that I know Scottish history, including clan-history, at least as well as those who keep on harping about identity.

But the further you go back, the less defined it all gets. That's true about epistemological matters in general: the deeper you go, the less you know. Take the very body. At first sight, it looks easy: head, trunk, limbs, and in the head: nose, ears, mouth . . . Then when you look closer, it's not simple organs you have, its a nervous network. That nervous network is open to all kinds of influences and what's near may be be more intimately connected with far than with what seems near. Taliesin's poem the *Cad Goddeu* (The Battle of the Trees) has this: 'I was a raindrop in the air, a word among letters, a bridge over the estuaries and a tree in the wood' and in *Migrations* we read: 'I am a poet of nature [. . .] I was in the great galaxy [. . .] I was in Canaan [. . .] I was in Denmark before Odin was born [. . .] I don't know if my body is animal or fish [. . .] I continue to evolve among three elements'. There you have the end-word on identity.

But to come back to family relations. My father's father's name was John Hume Dewar White – it was from him I got my middle names: John Dewar. With John Dewar, I have the choice between a whisky distiller and a collector of manuscripts (I'll take both), and with Hume I like to think I maybe have a connection with one of the subtlest minds ever to have come out of Scotland, who denied the reality of the self altogether – as bad as a Buddhist!

I was holed up in Glasgow, writing long scrawling manuscripts, with characters I named Mungo Reilly, the arch-Glaswegian, Archie Pelago (the Pelagian) and Logan the Loner . . . Alter egos again – doubles. In a sense, I was writing myself out.

I was also walking the coast.

That meant at one and the same time 'getting down to the bone', and leaving the nervous system open to influences.

From that activity rose poems, and the idea of the 'white world'. I conceived this as in some sense my own transpersonal world – and a re-writing of Scotland, a new Alban experiment. That notion of *Alba*, the old name of Scotland, connected both with *alba*, white, and *alp*, heights (why not, the white heights?), was there latent, in the title of my first collected book of poems: *The Cold Wind of Dawn* (dawn, *alba*), and it's there, unobtrusively again, in the title of my very latest book, *The Plateau of the Albatros*.

I later found confirmation of the 'white world' idea in shamanism, in yoga and in Zen Buddhism. But that is not the subject of the present essay.

I was walking about Scotland the way an Australian aborigine walks about Australia. Except that he walks with the ancestors. I was walking alone – with the influences.

There's a story Caxton tells about St Edmund. He was out walking when 'sodenlie there apperyd tofore him a fayr childe in whyte clothinge which sayd: Hayle felowe that goest alone'.

I liked that when I first read it – but I didn't want any angels on my path.

At most, a laughing gull.

4. Wayfaring

Well, I'd been standing there on Atlantic Quay, asking myself who I was and what there was, radically, to be done. I didn't know if there was a key to world history, but I had managed to get some perspectives, I knew roughly where I was situated, and I'd begun to feel my way out into what I considered a livelier and more liveable context. I was standing on Atlantic Quay, out on a limb, peering out (piering out . . .) into time and space, maybe into a nothingness, but aware also of waves of possibility.

I began to want to move further out.

A lot of literature just describes the prison, or comments on it, or has somebody gripping at the bars and howling – or maybe painting the bars in pretty or lurid colours. I wanted to break the cage. To minds that don't see the context radically, only psycho-sociologically, writing of the kind I envisaged will seem extravagant, even inhuman.

There's always been an extravagant touch in the Scottish mentality and in Scottish literature. Without going back to the wandering monks I evoked earlier, and that figure of the Middle Ages, the *Scotus vagans*, think of Smollett's *Roderick Random* and *Peregrine Pickle* in the eighteenth century, and Byron's ('half a Scot by birth, by education a whole one') *Childe Harold's Pilgrimage*.

Maybe I have continued this kind of thing in the twentieth century, in a different historical context, and in a different way. I'm thinking of books such as *Travels in the Drifting Dawn*, *The Blue Road*, *Pilgrim of the Void*.

Way-books, I came to call them.

These books begin in the labyrinths of big cities and gradually move into areas of emptiness, all along the way exploring territory, individual lives and fields of culture.

5. A Place in Brittany

After moving round the world a bit, I came to settle in Brittany.

That's not far, either geographically or culturally, either in miles or in mentality, from south-west Scotland. When I was a youngster in Ayrshire, I did research for, and wrote a paper on, the archaeology and pre-history of the area – it was my first public, or semi-public, text. It was at that time I realised I was living in the territory of the Damnonii, or Dumnonii (they gave their name to Dunoon), related to the Dumnonii of Devon and Cornwall, the Fir Domnann of Ireland – and the Dumnonii of the Armorican peninsula. In other words, I'm still at home . . . The Dumnonii, by the way, inhabitants of mineral-bearing areas (around Ayr and Renfrew, in Devon and Cornwall . . .) were diggers of the earth, miners. Maybe that's why my first poem-book was called *Wild Coal*. And if a later book was called *Handbook for the Diamond Country*, it was maybe because I'd pushed the basic carboniferous energy up a few degrees . . . Strathclyde, too, was a Brythonic kingdom (talking p-Celtic rather than q-Celtic), centred round Alclut, also called Dumbarton, which is of course the fort (*dun*) of the Bretons . . . All in all, then, I'm living in an outpost of Strathclyde, a kind of twentieth-century *Candida Casa*.

I'm living in an outpost in more ways than one. I've never tied my writing, my poetic and intellectual activity, to any local context, I've never been a representative of any particular social group. That means accepting a kind of outsider destiny, with regard to the local contexts. A wide circle takes longer to travel than a small one. People too sometimes find it hard to follow because, travelling a circle, you're changing direction all the time. But it's the only way to get a radical and complete sense of

world. Add to that the fact that if you fly high, you become more
and more invisible to those whose eyes have become addicted to
short-term views and strictly local socio-personal contexts. It
takes time for them to see the relevance. Again though, this flying
high is the only way to get a global view.

Outpost, outlook . . .

I talked of a sense of world. All my work is about this theme,
which is more than a theme, maybe more like a destiny. We're
living in a world-state of total confusion. Most literature, as
I've submitted, is only description or reaction, and most of the
ad hoc political solutions get nowhere, or even to positions
worse than where they started from – at best, they patch up the
cracks, for a while. What we need is a new grounding and
founding. The Old World was a fact – and it's broken up, or
buried. The New World was a promise – not kept. The Third
World is a problem. What I've been looking out to, and in to, is
a world older than the Old World, a world beyond that trans-
plantation of so much of the Old World known naïvely as the
New World, and outside the problematics of the Third World,
geared to those others. I work and speak in terms of an Open
World. A world is, fundamentally, a relation to things and a
version of things. And since poetics is, or can be, the fundamental dynamic of the human mind, that's where it starts. But
it can develop from there, via an interplay of *eros*, *logos* and
cosmos, via new, live concepts, via new lines of thinking and
research. What I've called Open World is a possibility. It has
something to say to the Old World, renewing its energies,
something to say to the New World, providing lost substance,
and something to say to the Third World which will not seem
imperialistic, based as it is not on any universalist ideology but
on planetary consciousness.

That's what I've been working at, here in my outpost – and
will continue to work at. After the poem-books, after the way-
books, I began to write map-books: *The Outward Movement, A
Quiet Apocalypse, The Nomad Mind, The Plateau of the Albatros* . . . That triple writing I've likened to an arrow: feather,
giving direction – the essay; shaft, presenting itineraries – way-
books; the head of the arrow – poems. An arrow needs a bow.
Well, maybe that's the Atlantic Arc. Here in Brittany I'm right in
the centre of it.

Aiming at Open World, existing in Open World . . .
I'll end with a haiku:

> Around my Atlantic studio
> listen to it blowing
> the wind of the earth.

15

The Fronting Shore

If, throughout my life and work, I have chosen to concentrate so much on the Atlantic coast, it is for several reasons. First of all, I take 'seaboard' to be particularly significant space. We are close there to the beginnings of life, we cannot but be aware there of primordial rhythms (tidal, meteorological). In that space, too, we have one foot, as it were, in humanity (inhabited, inscribed, coded space), the other, in the non-human cosmos (chaos-cosmos, chaosmos) – and I think it is vitally important to keep that dialogue alive. It may be for reasons similar to those I have just evoked that in a text belonging to the tradition which I perhaps bear in my bones, an old Celtic text, *Imacallam in da thuarad* (The Talk of the Two Scholars), we read: 'The shore was always a place of predilection for the poets'.

Then, in the second place, I was born and raised on that Atlantic shore of Europe, more particularly, on the West Coast of Scotland, and I have its topography imprinted on my mind. I'm far from thinking that a poet's original landscape necessarily dictates his mindscape: if his intellect be at all energetic, he may well come to decide, beyond any 'homeland' fixation, that others are more interesting – but that West Coast of Scotland happens in fact to be interesting, extremely so. As Humboldt points out in *Cosmos*, what largely started up and quickened Greek thought was the topography of Hellas: the multiplicity of headlands and islands, the profusion of creeks and bays. Well, that West Coast of Scotland with its highly irregular outline and its 500 islands has a similar kind of topography, though, up to now, one can hardly say it has given rise to a comparably complex thought (but there have been beginnings,

202

the potentiality is always there – that is what I have been working at).

Lastly, now that we are beginning to hear again of the concept
'Europe', I think it will be as well for it to look to its West, not
only as to a breathing space, but as the locus (*topos*) of forgotten
movements and perhaps a new type of thought, a new sense of
culture, a new sense of *logos*. Perhaps Europe has been too
Mediterranean-oriented. But the greatest blockage does not lie
there – for from the Mediterranean, one can move out into the
Atlantic, as the Phoenicians did, as Pytheas did. No, the greatest
blockage lies in the ideology of national(ist) identity and in the
intellectual regression to culture-complexes that were productive
of those identities, which may be looked to as 'havens of stability'
in a time of cosmopolitan confusion, but which in fact can be no
more than half-way houses full of internal dispute, mere parlia-
mentary discourse and pathetic poetics.

In terms of civilization, the Atlantic West of Europe has been
marked by two characteristics which may seem totally antinomian, but which may be intimately connected. On the one hand,
there is isolation, indeed a kind of *negative destiny*; on the other,
the impetus towards industrialisation. Where the connection lies
is, I think, in this: when you have live minds, divorced – for
reasons of history and ideology – from any kind of earth-sense,
they will more towards invention: industrial invention. It is a
well enough known fact that the Scots were in the forefront of the
industrial movement, just as it is well enough known that their
discourse has tended to be marked by disputatious argument (an
'industrious logic', if I may say so, in place of which I would
propose an *erotic* logic). Now, just a few weeks ago, I was in
Glasgow, on Atlantic Quay, and it is a good vantage point to see
just how much has changed. We are, obviously, moving out of
the industrial phase of civilization, and moving towards a preoccupation with two activities felt at present as essential: information, and culture. Frobenius, in *The Destiny of Civilizations*,
foresaw this move some time ago. One of the theses he puts
forward in that book is that, after the mechanistic conquest of
the globe and the techno-economist civilization it set up and
spread, a 'great turning' must occur. Since it was largely Atlantic
seaboard peoples who brought about that techno-economist
phase, it was there, in the first place, we would see the end of

it and, perhaps, the beginnings of a 'world culture' that would correspond to the world economy. What would characterize this 'world-culture' would be: (1) an orchestration of all cultures, an original synthesis, and (2) the instauration of a type of thinking freed of (French) rationalism, (English) realism and (North American) materialism, a thinking that would go from 'the slavery of fact' to the 'freedom of the real', and that would be open to direct intuition, direct 'seizures' from the outside – which would require an 'oriental attitude'.

Whatever one thinks of Frobenius' analysis and programme (I myself find much of it extremely interesting), what is certain is that, in the context I saw myself involved in, while information kept being piled up (but with no adequate poetics to give it shape, *scape*), while cultural manifestations continued, indeed multiplied (it's a biological phenomenon: as extinction threatens, there occurs an agitational flurry), there was little or nothing in them that could with any justification be described as fundamental or foundational. Every nation, every 'cultural community', continued to persuade itself that it had worthy representatives and that something, if not important at least respectable, was going on, but the background was hollow.

This brings me to the notion of 'negative destiny'. I've already used it with regard to the Atlantic West, as culture-area, and I'll be speaking again in those terms shortly. But before coming back to that general landscape-mindscape, I'd like to use the term 'negative destiny' with regard to my own itinerary, not to say 'career' or 'destiny', seen as an attempt to get back beyond that hollowness. At one point in that itinerary, after publishing three books in London (the last of which was entitled *The Most Difficult Area*), aware not only of the narrowness of perspective and the lack of ground, but of the first signs of what I felt as a culture-circus, I decided to break with the cultural context that was, nationally and socially, 'mine' – let's say, British, or rather, English, with a Scottish coloration and tonality – and move into a negativity. This decision coincided with a move away from the Scoto-British context and an installation in the Atlantic Pyrenees. Concerned in this essay with lines and topography, I shall forego socio-personal detail, but let me just say that for nine years after leaving Britain in 1967, I maintained a literary silence, publishing nothing, concerned with that 'negativity' I have just mentioned, trying to work myself back into a ground. This went along with an exploration, or rather, an *experience*, of the Atlantic seaboard of South-West France, from say, the Basque country up to the marshes of Poitou. It is a land lying between sea and forest: a sequence of cliffs, dunes, fens, islands and pools. The noises one hears are the breaking of waves, the soughing of wind in pine-trees, the clean cry of a gull in blue emptiness . . .

But perhaps I should begin with a window – a geographical and philosophical window – in Pau. From my study window, I could see a great length of the Pyrenean chain, in front of me the Pic du Midi d'Ossau, the last great granite peak before the chain tails off to the West, towards the Pic d'Anie, on the edge of the Basque country, the Mont Orhy and la Rhune. The geographer I most read at that time, indeed the second tome of his *Géographie Universelle* had been a vade-mecum with me for years, was Elisée Reclus (anarchist as well as geographer, like Kropotkin – and the combination intrigued me), who, as chance would have it, was raised only a few miles from Pau, in Orthez. I remember reading a phrase of his with a little jolt of recognition: 'On many a peak of the Western chain one might imagine oneself in rainy Scotland'. I recall asking myself too if there was any linguistic connection between the Val d'Aran in the Pyrenees and the Aran Isles of Ireland (and the Arran in sight of which I had been raised on the West Coast of Scotland). I liked Reclus' evocations of the glaciers and torrents of the mountains, then of the iron-red sandstone of the Landes where, at one time (early nineteenth century) land was so cheap it was measured for sale by the length a voice could carry (I liked that association of voice and territory). I liked also what he had to say about the 'hydrographic complex' of the Atlantic coast, and about 'singing fish' at the mouth of the Garonne, anciently called Garumna and Garunda (I loved old names, toponymies and etymologies). It was in his pages too I first heard of the ferociously independent 'nine peoples' of the South-West, distinct from Gaul – and later saw the stone at Hasparren that marked this separation. I liked too his evocation of the Basques as adventurers and irreducibles, who had discovered the New World long before Columbus: 'In the Basque country, they say it was a man named Echaïd who discovered the New World'. I had the vague sensation of being in an area that Europe and history had lost sight of, but which had

retained connections with an archaic past and from there had
sprung towards a world to come, an area of strong geographical
realities, going from dark, stark rock to spaces of light.

Although, in my university studies, I had opted for modern
languages as against the classics (in which a professor of humanities, seeing the Latin I wrote, had wanted me to specialize), I still
had a kind of abstract hankering for a universal language, which
had of course at one time in Europe been represented by Latin.
That is why, in addition to simply contemplating pages of
mathematics (Poincaré, Riemann . . .), or again pages of Sanskrit
(I spent at least one summer writing *devanagari* script in the sand
of the Landes, thinking of Sanskrit as *sand-script*), I began to
read up all the Latin poets who had had some connection with
that territory.

There was, for example, Ausonius, writing from Burdigalia
(Bordeaux) to his friend Theon, who lived in a reed-roofed hut on
the Medoc promontory: 'What are you doing at this moment,
poet of the ends of the earth, you who plough a beach and farm
the sands, where Ocean reaches its limit and the sun sets?' It
was not so difficult, by extrapolation, to imagine the question
addressed to myself . . . Then there was Festus Avienus, the
author of that fascinating geographical poem, *Ora Maritima*,
which I translated as *Shores of the West*. Avienus had access to
information even Herodotus of Halicarnassus knew nothing of,
and his poem not only gives us a description of European lands
washed by the Atlantic, from Spain to Scotland, but offers
intriguing glimpses into the multiple and migratory origins of
the Spaniards, Portuguese, French, Germans and Danes. Starting
out from the Columns of Hercules at the mouth of the Mediterranean, Avienus moves up via Moon Island, the Galactic Gulf,
Promontorium Sacrum, the Pelagian islands and Cape Venus, to
the north shores called Oestrymnis, then comes back to the
Columns, follows the shores of Spain and Catalonia: Cape Venus
(another one), Palus Immensus, the island of Gymnesia (Major-
ca), Tarraco, Callipolis (Barcelona) to the Pyrenees, and from the
Pyrenees, via Candidum Promontorium and the delta of the
Rhodanus, to Marseilles, where the poem, originally intended
to go as far as the Black Sea, stops abruptly. We learn among
other things that it was the Tartessins, in the regions of Cadix,
who made, or who came to make, the tin trips to Cornwall for

the Phoenicians; we learn of early Celtic presence in Britain and of the marine nature of the culture. But above all we have a sense of delving into the archives of the world, following out the lines of little known coasts, receiving some kind of initiation into thalasso-theory (Berthelot in his commentary of the 1930s speaks of 'the logic of Atlantic navigation') and oceano-poetics, at least as experienced by a fourth-century Roman. And then, still keeping to the poets, there was Seneca of Spain, representing the farthest horizon as it were, with that strangely illuminated oceanic prophecy we find in the *Medea*:

> *Venient annis*
> *saecula seris quibus Oceanus*
> *vincula rerum laxet, et ingens*
> *pateat tellus Tythisque novos*
> *detegat orbes, nec sit terris*
> *ultima Thule*

'no Thule the ultimate Thule.' This was fourteen centuries before Columbus set sail from Palos . . . Seneca the Cantabrian I loved, not only for his 'new world' vision, not only for his exile (time, space, and silence!) but for his 'nature questions' (*Naturales quaestiones*) and for his style: that fast interchange between speaker and speaker called *stichomythia*. I experience most discourse as too heavy and too slow, and conceive of poetry as, along with other things, *fast thinking*.

If there were ancient poets, there were also ancient geographers: Strabo, Ptolemy, Pomponius Mela. In his *Description of the Earth*, Mela says that from Hispania the coast first of all follows a straight line then takes a great curve to the West. And that indeed is how it is, from Biarritz to the Point de Graves, then from Royan up to Brittany. Strabo, for his part, in the *Geographia*, speaks of 'the paroceanic region of Aquitania' – and the phrase delighted me. While Ptolemy (*Treatise on Geography*) describing 'the Aquitanic ocean', dwells on the changing line between earth and sea (i.e. the non-Mediterranean phenomenon of tides). Why waste time on ancient cartographies such as these which, compared with modern work in this field, are, to say the least, anything but exact? Well, for the reason already evoked: that there we have a sense of initial exploration, of tentative progression – which is what gives a parallel to the working of the mind. Then, for their simplicity. In all the 700 kilometres of territory between Spain and Brittany, Ptolemy mentions only six rivers, four harbours and four promontories. Yet we do not feel this as reductive. On the contrary, the very paucity of the locations gives us a sense of great misty, wavering space: they are like haiku in (Buddhist) emptiness. And let me say right away that I did not neglect modern maps – photographic documents, such as those aerial photographs showing the halibut and floundery shapes of submarine sands. Anything that would give me an augmented sense of the lie of the land (littoral morphology), and of sensitive movement along it, I worked with.

So, moving West from Pau ('good Friday, riding West' – a phrase, I think, of John Donne's), and then up along the celtogalatian coast: Biarritz (with a visit to the *Musée de la Mer*, for its exhibits of birds and its information on whales), Capbreton, the Etang de Léon (with its Courant d'Huchet like a miniature Mississippi), Mimizan, Biscarosse, almost lost in the sands (a seventeenth-century map: '*De sous ces Dunes il y avait une Paroisse qui est à présent couverte de Sables*'), Arcachon, Lacanau, Montalivet, the Pointe de Graves, the Cordouan lighthouse (like a white exclamation-mark out there in the mist!), La Tremblade with its piles of oyster shells, Rochefort, Oléron, the Pertuis d'Antioche, the Ile de Ré with its Whale Point (la Pointe des Baleines), la Rochelle with its museum of the Americas.

I spoke earlier of a window (in Pau) that was not only geographical, but philosophical. The notion of a 'philosophical window' is, of course, Hölderlin's, or at least derived from him (the famous letter to Böhlendorff of 1802: '. . . *das philosophische Licht um mein Fenster*'). Hölderlin I had studied in Glasgow, and again in Munich, long before I went to live in the South-West of France, and it is one of those coincidences and connections I mentioned earlier that I should have come up with him again in Bordeaux, where he was preceptor for a year, where (more precisely, at Lormont) he was 'struck by Apollo', and which inspired one of his finest and most significant poems, *Andenken*, which, again, I translated:

> There's a wild northeaster blowing
> The wind I love the best
> For a promise it is to sailors

Of high spirits and a fair passage.
But go now and give my greetings
To the beautiful Garonne
And the gardens of Bordeaux
Where the path goes along
By the steep banks and the brook
Tumbles into the stream, with oaks
And silver poplars looking nobly on . . .

Two principal ideas I had retained from Hölderlin were what
he called 'the free use of the national', and then the sense of being
the first to start something new since the Greeks. And the
geopoetical nature of his work is obvious enough, if only his
preoccupation with rivers such as the Rhein, the Main and the
Donau – though there was also Greece as mind-land, and the
New World vision of the poem 'Columbus'.

But it was not so much Hölderlin I read in Pau, but (again and
once more – after Glasgow, initial reading, and Munich, deepened
reading) Nietzsche and with him, Heidegger. Nietzsche's name I'd
always read as a kind of epitome of his thinking: first a negation
(*niet*), then an explosion, a deployment of energy (*zsche*). It's one
of those personal readings one does not bring out willingly in
public – something like a little private joke. It was with no little
surprise I saw this fun-phonetical reading of Nietzsche's name
aired on the very first page of Heidegger's *Nietzsche*, the book of
his lectures on Nietzschean thought given in Freiburg from 1936
to 1940. These were fatal years and anything concerning them
almost taboo. It's this taboo, the unwillingness to see the
Nietzsche-Heidegger complex as anything other than dangerous
and downright damnable, that is largely responsible for the
superficiality of European thought in the post-war years and
the general thinness of the culture. Let's try and look at the area
from a little higher up than the perspectives of the national-
socialist aftermath. Obviously, I won't be going into all this in
detail here. Within the context I'm trying to open, I'll only insist
on what I took, and take, to be the essential, culled from a whole
series of books with bleached covers and sand between the pages.

By 1887, when he drew up a programme for what he saw as
the final stages of his life-thought, Nietzsche was well into his
self-imposed exile or, since that is all too pathetic a word, let's

say, into the isolation he'd felt necessary for his work – an isolation inexorably turning into an alienation ('the desert is growing around me'). This 'exit' and the subsequent explorations he'd described in *The Wanderer and his Shadow*:

> So, ill, but determined to be my own doctor, I forced myself into a *climate of the soul* such as I had not yet experienced. I went abroad, into foreign lands, eager to approach what was strange to me . . . It was a long wandering, made up of research and transformation, a disgust with all heavy affirmations and negations, a ceaseless urge to move on. I adopted also a diet and a discipline that would enable the mind to travel far, fly high and always be ready for new flights.

The vocabulary is lyrical, unwonted in a philosopher – but Nietzsche was already the *artist*-philosopher, a new anthropological type. Hegel, with the encyclopaedia of world-history laid out before him, had said that art was no longer the highest manifestation of the intelligence, no longer a driving force in culture. That most art is decidedly not the highest manifestation of the intelligence is something Nietzsche would have no difficulty agreeing with – his numerous criticisms of 'poets' and 'poetry' are there as witness. As to 'driving force' (within a historical context), it was nothing like that Nietzsche looked for in art, but the phenomenon of *transparency*: 'The phenomenon of the artist is the most transparent'. And this itself could be true, in any strong sense (we are not talking about public confessions), only in the case of the artist who had gone not only to the limits of (Western) thought but to the limits of himself (at one point Nietzsche described himself as 'a poet – at the limits of the word'). Nietzsche's whole life-work can be seen as a *transition to transparency*. He had worked his way through Western philosophy. He had seen first of all the phenomenon of nihilism (life no value, being no meaning), resulting from the emptying out of metaphysics. Instead of revelling in that nihilism (or playing about in it), which a lot of art was going to do, or taking it as a basis for some kind of historical *Blitzkrieg* (which a certain politics was going to do), he'd tried to work back through metaphysics in order to open up another mindscape, in which there would be no 'beyond' (Platonism), no 'heaven' (Christianity), but a fidelity to the earth.

It was, I felt, that 'fidelity to the earth' which had not been given the time to get worked out fully. Instead, owing perhaps to personal exacerbation and exasperation, Nietzsche had stopped at the 'will to power' and the *Übermensch*, which seemed to me still 'all too human'. In his book *Beyond Good and Evil*, he had drawn up a list of 'situations' that had very much attracted my attention and excited my interest: 'Around the hero, everything becomes tragedy; around the half-god, everything becomes satire; around the god, everything becomes world'. The language, again, is too lyrical-metaphorical for my taste. But if for 'god', we substitute 'great poetic (or poïetic) thought', we could say that it was that Nietzsche did not get through to. He moves between satire and tragedy, part 'semi-god' (anti-Christ), part ontological hero (like Melville). 'World' remained on the horizon, a 'new world', of which, of course, *the* New World of socio-political terminology was (as Melville, who lived in it, also knew) only a caricature. I also had very much that idea of 'world' in view. But I was in no rush. I preferred *a*topia to *u*topia. What I retained from Nietzsche, in addition to his culture-analysis, was an æsthetics, summed up in one phrase: 'a sense of what is lasting, and few means' (*in der Dauer des Langen und Wenigen*). That did not mean, or did not necessarily mean, minimal art (though that could also be practised: I'm thinking again of haiku), but it did mean fidelity to the earth, an attention to minims, the move towards transparency, and an art in which the means are not over-elaborate, not over-obvious. What counted primarily was not 'craft' (that can be practised on all kinds of secondary bases), but a path, a wayfaring into primal space. This brings me to Heidegger, who takes over where Nietzsche broke off.

Moving out and down from Western metaphysics (and hence, *a posteriori*, from European ideology), Heidegger begins (by means of a 'beginning thought', *anfängliches Denken*) to explore 'more original districts'. Those may have particular names (such as Black Forest), but, fundamentally and globally, I'd like to call them *Westland*, a land where '*es west*', where 'there is being', a 'being' deeper than anything envisaged or experienced in ontology. In these districts, following 'paths that led nowhere' (*Holzwege*), Heidegger meets up with poets – poets such as Hölderlin (*was bleibt, stiften die Dichter*: 'only poetry exists on lasting ground') and Rilke (*lauter Raum reissend von weit herein*: 'pure

212   Kenneth White

space rushing in from afar'). If, for a start, he welcomed this
encounter as the occasion of a fertile dialogue, seeing poetry and
philosophy as two neighbouring but separate peaks, he gradually
came to see a closer connection, if not an identification. This
movement in his thought can be seen most clearly and most
succinctly in that little book written in 1947, *Aus der Erfahrung
des Denkens* ('from the experience of thought' – let's not forget
that in the German *Erfahrung*, there's *fahren*, travel). At one
point in that book, Heidegger says that there are three dangers
for thought: philosophical production (what goes on in the
'philosophical industry'); thought itself (the network of 'innate
ideas'); and, lastly, 'the song of the poet'. This latter danger is the
least of the dangers, is indeed a *salutary* danger – but it is still a
danger. Only a few pages later, however, in that selfsame little
book, a kind of *opusculum obscurum* (almost an example of
trobar clus), he is writing this:

This characteristic of thought, that it is poet's work, is still veiled.
Where it is revealed, it is largely seen as the utopia of a semi-
    poetic mind.
But poetry that thinks is the topology of being.
It indicates the place where being can deploy itself.

It can take a lot of culture-analysis, a lot of philosophising, to
get to this point, to this head-land (if I may say so), but once
there, the place does not call for philosophy, it calls for a
deepening of the experience, followed by a deployment. And
this is where Heidegger is very close to certain aspects of Far
Eastern, notably Buddhist thought.
    Nietzsche had been as much anti-Buddhist as he had been anti-
Christian – mainly because his knowledge of Buddhism came
through Schopenhauer, which made him see it only in terms of
quietism (a cessation of suffering). As such, it could only be a
half-way house, a sanatorium, and hence a hindrance to the
intensification of life he was out for. That a great deal of
Buddhism is this, I think no one who knows the least about it
would deny. But it is not all that. Over the centuries, its dialectics
deepened. It was said, for example, that if detachment was
necessary to avoid suffering, enlightenment meant the capacity
to detach one's-self from detachment. Likewise, *nirvana* (cooling
out – like swimming in nothingness) and *samsara* (performing

the round of daily existence) were seen less and less to be separate. The process does not perhaps *intensify* life (there is no doubt too much feverish heat in Nietzsche), but it *augments* it, it spaces it out. This is what Heidegger realised when he came across the writings of Daisetz Suzuki on Zen Buddhism. Seen from this comparative point of view, his work appears like a search for 'the original face'. And if he had known the book *Shashekishu* (Collection of sand and stones), written by Ichien Muju in the thirteenth century, he would have seen there the coming together of philosophy (*butsudo* – the way of Buddha) and poetry (*kado*) that was taking place in his own work. We can see it actually happening in that little book *From the Experience of Thought*, where so many of his notes are next door to haiku. In fact, I amused myself at one point (it was not *merely* an amusement) by translating them into haiku-form:

> Dawn silence:
> above the mountains
> sky clearing

> Through the rainclouds
> a ray of sunlight
> passing over the dark fields

> Early Spring;
> narcissi flowering here and there
> on the mountain meadows

> Summer flower
> and a butterfly
> balancing in the wind

> Winter night snowstorm –
> in the morning
> that quiet landscape

After this moment devoted to the topology of being, let us continue our deployment, our poetico-topographical peregrination, our *investigation* of Atlantic ontology.

We were standing there at La Rochelle, in front of the Museum of the Americas. All this South-West coast has always been in close touch with the New World. Right up from the grottos of Isturitz, with their marvellous intertwinings of salmon and deer,

among all those fringe-peoples and ghost-folk of mixed (Celto-
Iberian, etc.) identities: oyster-gobbers, tin-beaters, resin-gath-
erers, there have always been searchers and finders, travellers
following strange roads – the megalith road, then the tin road,
then the sea-road to new-found-lands. Wasn't Labrador originally Le Labourd? Didn't Jean Sébastien El Cano sail with
Magellan and come back, having gone wide-eyed round the
world? Didn't the first of all troubadours emerge from here:
Guillaume IX of Aquitania with his *amor lontana*? And think of
all those baroque visionaries and *alumbrados*. Think of Jean-
sans-Terre, last son of Alienor of Aquitaine. Of Champlain from
Brouage. Of the Jesuits (how many of them Basque!) in America.
Of the pirate Jean Laffitte of Dax, cruising in the Gulf of Mexico
and in the Lower Mississippi, coming to finance the printing of
Marx's *Communist Manifesto* . . . New worlds. Hadn't Pope
Innocent III dreamt of moving the Holy Roman Empire over to
the Atlantic – to create a Holy Oceanic Empire? But at bottom
there could be neither holiness nor empire in these *finisterras*, in
these multiple *puntas arenas*. Only ghost lands, empty lands,
over them that wild cry of the Basques, the *irrintzina*, that high,
raucous cry that fills the emptiness and goes tearing the space on
the horizon before ending in a kind of sinister laugh like, as Loti
says, the laughter of a madman . . .

At the end of metaphysics, faithful to the earth, trying to
follow out a path, it was the notion of 'world' that obsessed me:
'new world'. With America as reference, as the most recent
(failed) attempt. A great interest in it, especially in its beginnings,
and in upsurges of the primal thing here and there, but no desire
to get mixed up in the United States, get lost in the noisy
fairground, get stuck in the sentimental-moralistic sludge. It
was here, at the edge of Europe, that the real contours of a
new 'new world' were likely to be found. And, hadn't my own
native landscape, Caledonia, constituted the western frontier of
the Roman Empire?

I'd been living ten years in the South-West before I started
going back to Scotland. I'd left it with the notions of 'difficult
area' and 'white world'. The first of these terms meant the
kind of working-out I've just evoked via Nietzsche and Heidegger. The second had gone through several avatars. At first, it
had indicated simply a sensuous field, based on the series of

'whitenesses' that had caught my attention: quartz, pebbles, birch bark, gull wings, breaking waves . . . This had lead me into the Hyperborean world of shamanism . . . Then I'd found out that at the centre of Celtic culture there was an area named in Gaelic *finn mag*, in Brythonic, *gwenved*: white field, white world . . . Then in my studies of Buddhism, I'd come across the definition of supreme identity (or supreme being, non-identity): 'a white heron in the mist' . . . 'White world' was also connected with Nietzsche's idea of art as total transparency . . . When I started going back to Scotland, it was with all these notions in mind but, while keeping them as mental backdrop, with the desire to follow out *lines*, to lay out *topographies*, to write landscape-mindscape.

It was evident to me that, within the British context, the largest, most complete and most composed mind was, not Yeats, not MacDiarmid (however much I might be interested in parts of their work), but T. S. Eliot. Certainly I couldn't accept his Christian solution to the culture-crisis, but his *Waste Land* challenged anyone to find other ways out. Where I picked up from him was that injunction at the end of 'Cape Ann', one of the series of *Landscapes*: 'Resign this land at the end, resign it to its true owner, the tough one, the sea-gull, the palaver is finished.' So, I had T. S. Eliot in mind, but also, like anyone interested in 'scape', Gerard Manley Hopkins. No one had a finer sense of wilderness than this Jesuit ('I desire the wilderness'; 'Where is the wildness of the wilderness?'). Inspired (like the early Heidegger) by Duns Scotus, 'of realty the rarest-veinèd unraveller', Hopkins, with his notions of inscape and instress (the latter intended to actualize the natural inscape in the mind of the listener) had worked out a powerful poetics that interested me more in theory than in practice. In practice, I felt too much the intrusion of theology and a linguistic excess, almost a linguistic glut. In 1881, Hopkins was working at St Joseph's church in Glasgow. It was in that year, during a trip to the Highlands, that he wrote the poem 'Inversnaid':

This darksome burn, horseback brown,
His rollrock highroad roaring down,
In coop and in comb the fleece of his foam
Flutes and low to the lake falls home.

A windpuff-bonnet of fáwn-fróth
Turns and twindles over the broth
Of a pool so pitchblack, féll-frówning,
It rounds and rounds Despair to drowning.

Degged with dew, dappled with dew
Are the groins of the braes that the brook treads through,
Wiry heathpacks, flitches of fern,
and the beadbonny ash that sits over the burn.

What would the world be, once bereft
Of wet and of wilderness? Let them be left,
O let them be left, wildness and wet;
Long live the weeds and the wilderness yet.

This is a better poem than Eliot's 'Rannoch' (another of the
Landscapes), which gets bogged down in history, it is, especially
in the last stanza, one of Hopkins' strongest programmatic
statements, for once, too, the text is free of theology (though
Despair comes in with a moral heaviness). But one could well do
without the metaphor of the horse and the 'groins' of the braes,
and the versification, like the language, was too obvious. I
wanted something more discrete than this. Something closer to
prose. I wanted the *prose of the earth* – not history, or excited
lyricism. I am trying to indicate the approach to what I was going
to call 'Atlantic poetics', 'open world poetics', 'geopoetics'. But
let us follow the topography.

In the beginning, child and adolescent, my topographical area
had been a few square miles on the West Coast of Scotland: the
foreshore and back-country of an Ayrshire village, of which I
knew every rock and ridge, every clump of birch or pine – with
the island of Arran, an epitome of the whole of Scottish topography, on the horizon. But when I began coming back to
Scotland, while not forgetting that early landscape, what attracted me most was that line of mountain, Drumalban, running
from the Firth of Clyde right up to Cape Wrath, which is in fact
the main topographical feature of Scotland. Bede, in his *Historia*,
calls it the *dorsum Britanniae*, the back-bone of Britain, and
Fordun, in the *Scotichronicon*, speaks of 'high mountains stretch-
ing through the midst of the country, as do the tall Alps in
Europe, snow lying on them, boulders torn off beetling crags,

deep hollows'. It is an area of gulches and gullies, of high snowy
corries (*Coire an t-Sneachda*), and of plateaus like Rannoch
Moor where you can have the feeling that the Ice Age just
stopped yesterday, leaving everything in a strange light and a
tense, expectant kind of silence. In that word Drumalban, you
have the early name of Scotland: *Alba*. The etymology is
disputed. Some say it is connected with the Latin word *albus*,
white. Others say it is from the root you find in Alp, meaning
height. As I've already suggested, let us combine both derivations
and call it 'the high, white country'.

It seems incredible that the theory of glaciation only came to
the fore about 150 years ago, with Agassiz. But not so long ago,
there were intelligent people convinced that the world was
created (by God) in the year 4004 BC. And it's only recently that
concepts such as continental drift have come into our ken. Which
would suggest that there are plenty of other concepts to be
discovered, farther and deeper readings of the topographical
text to be made.

While walking the coast, while moving among the mountains,
with eye open for the flight of a ptarmigan, or a glint of sunlight
on a loch, I was reading all the pertinent books I could get my
hands on, looking both for information and for elements of a
writing. The blue booklets of the British Regional Geology were
constant companions: 'The islands and promontories along the
Western seaboard of Scotland are noted for records of intense
and prolonged igneous activity during early Tertiary times. At
that period, some forty million years ago, volcanic plateaus
forming part of a continental region must have extended con-
tinuously along the Western coast' (*Tertiary Volcanic Districts*,
1935). I read MacCulloch (*A Description of the Western Isles of
Scotland*, 1814), Hugh Miller (*The Old Red Sandstone*, 1841),
Archibald Geikie (*The Scenery of Scotland*, 1865), James Geikie
(*The Great Ice Age*, 1873), Heddge (*Geognosy and Mineralogy
of Scotland*, 1884), up to Craig (*The Geology of Scotland*,
Scottish Academy Press, 1965), Sissons (*The Evolution of Scotland's Scenery*, Oliver and Boyd, 1967), and many others. I read
also older, and often more extravagant books, such as Giraldus
Cambrensis' *Topographia Hiberniae*, that talks of 'Gurguintius'
(sounds like Gargantua) bringing 'Basclenses' (i.e. Basques) from
Spain to Ireland, or again, Martin Martin's *A Description of the*

Western Islands of Scotland (1716), where you have descriptions like that of 'Arran-Isle, its Etymology, Mountains, Bays, Earth, Stones, River, Air' and where Martin says in his Preface: 'There's a great Change in the Humour of the World, and by consequence in the ways of Writing'. And it's true that a great change was taking place back there in the eighteenth century, with its awakened interest in nature and in 'natural philosophy' (think of Buffon). But it had not been developed. No adequate global theory had emerged from its premises, little writing that was adequate 'prose of the earth'.

What I liked about Martin was his sheer delight in piling up facts: 'There is . . . there is . . . there is . . .' What I liked about MacDiarmid was his willingness to bring into his text great wads of information, but you could hardly be satisfied with his methods of holding it all together: 'As also', 'Even as' . . . What I liked about the scientific texts I read was the comprehension they provided of forces and forms, of networks and complex interactions, but the writing was so often inadequate if not clumsy, and a dimension always seemed to be missing – which is why, in the last chapters of some scientific books, there would be some mention of poetry; which is why some scientists maintain some kind of theology. All this information had to be integrated at a higher and/or deeper level. While walking the coast, while moving in the mountains, I was trying to work out a method, a methodology, which is to say (always breaking up the concepts, bringing them down to basics and primals) a *hodos* (path, way) and a *logos* (way of thinking, way of wording). A method and a poetics . . .

Since I settled in Brittany some years ago, on a coast marked by what in geology is called a 'centred complex', the work has been going on, perhaps in an even more concentrated way. When I say 'work', I always have two images, two models in mind. One is that of a coral reef: growing, in silence and obscurity, then emerging. The other is that of a glacier. A glacier is a very interesting phenomenon: it shapes and writes the landscape (read 'mindscape'). It accumulates at a centre, and moves out from there, taking its time, slow but sure. It has its own motive power, its own intrinsic energy, but it also uses all kinds of materials: the underside of an ice-sheet, the part that actually does the work, while the upper surface reflects the sky,

is like a sheet of great-grained sandpaper. It leaves erratics in its
tracks – you can find Scandinavian rock in Scotland, and Scottish
rock in the Azores. It advances, then retreates, then advances
again . . .

The working has meant, as always, 'walking the coast' – that
coastline that goes, say, from Penmarc'h up to the Abers country,
and from there all along the north coast of Brittany to the Ile de
Bréhat; or, more circumscribedly, more succinctly, simply along
the old coastguard path that skirts Lannion Bay. Within the
study (the *atelier atlantique*), in addition to continued readings
in the bio-, geo- and cosmo- sciences, linguistics and philosophy,
it has meant particular preoccupation with writers whom I
consider as 'Atlantic poets': Fernando Pessoa, Saint-John Perse,
the MacDiarmid of the 'raised beach' and, 'across the water',
Charles Olson – as well as, of course, my own writing, via poem,
way-book and essay, round the notion of 'world'.

Within recent years, there has been much talk of a European
region called the Atlantic Arc. This talk has gone on, up till now,
only in economic terms, hardly cultural and even less intellectual
ones – but it could happen (from that 'arc', an arrow, indications
to a new world . . .). Living right at the centre of that arc, I
consider my position as in some sense strategic, at least symbo-
lically so. Then too, these last few years, there has been a great
deal of interest in the dialectics of order and disorder, regularity
and irregularity (I am thinking for example of Thom's theory of
catastrophe), and in all kinds of 'complex frontiers' (there I am
thinking of Mandelbrot's fractalism – one of the early questions
of which was: 'What is the length of the Breton coast?'). As one
who for long years has described his sense of things as 'chaoti-
cist', I can only feel this mathematical work as water to my mill –
or rather to my glacier.

So, I keep walking the long coast, with all kinds of work in
progress, making for a livelier and more enlightened world.

Origins and Occasions

The Alban Project

This text was a lecture delivered at the symposium of the Scottish Centre for Geopoetics (affiliated to the International Institute of Geopoetics I set up in 1989): 'The Radical Ground – an in-depth exploration of the culture question', which took place at the National Library of Scotland in Edinburgh on Saturday, 16 November 1996.

The Archaic Context

This was written in Glasgow, in 1967. It was first published in my book of essays, *La Figure du dehors*, Paris, Editions Grasset, 1982.

A Shaman Dancing on the Glacier

This text was delivered as a lecture at the symposium 'Burns, Beuys and Beyond' organised by the Society of Scottish Artists and the Goethe Institute, which took place at the Goethe Institute in Glasgow, November 1990. It was subsequently published in *Artwork*, June–July 1991.

Tam o' Shanter: A New Reading

I wrote this study of what Burns called his 'standard performance in the poetical line' in Glasgow in 1966. I was re-reading a lot of Scottish literature at the time. Maybe also thinking of early days in Ayrshire. First published in *Scottish Literary Journal*, vol. 17, no. 2, November 1990.

Into the White World

Written in Glasgow, 1966. First published in the Amsterdam review *Raster*, VI/I lente 1972. Thereafter in *La Figure du Dehors*, op. cit.

The Birds of Kentigern

Written in Glasgow, 1967. First published in the review *Cencrastus*, Edinburgh, 1986.

Scotland, Intelligence and Culture

This was the keynote lecture I was asked to deliver at the Adcas (Advisory Council for the Arts in Scotland) conference in Edinburgh, June 1989.

The Scot Abroad

This text was a lecture delivered in Glasgow at the Celtic Connections Festival, January 1996. First published in *The Scottish Review*, no. 6, May 1996.

The Franco-Scottish Connection

This was a lecture delivered at the David Hume Tower, University of Edinburgh, November 1996, to commemorate the fiftieth anniversary of the French Institute in Scotland.

Looking Out: From Neotechnics to Geopoetics

This text was a send-off lecture for the Scottish Centre for Geopoetics, delivered at the British Council, Edinburgh, 25 October 1994.

Scotland, History and the Writer

This text was the introductory lecture to the international symposium on 'Historicity in Scottish Thought and Literature', organised by the Scottish Studies research group at the University of Grenoble, 15–17 March 1991. It was originally published in *Études Écossaises*, no. 1, Presses Universitaires de Grenoble, 1992.

The High Field

Written at Pau, in the Atlantic Pyrenees, 1975, this text was first published, under the title 'Taking off from Hugh MacDiarmid', in *Scottish Literary Journal*, vol. 17, no. 1, May 1990.

Talking Transformation

This text was written in Brittany, in March 1990. It was first published in *Cencrastus*, no. 40, Edinburgh, Summer 1991.

Kentigern on Atlantic Quay

This text was a lecture delivered at the University of Glasgow, 23 October 1994.

The Fronting Shore

This text was written in Brittany for a symposium on 'Regionalism, Nationalism and Internationalism' at the University of Tübingen, October 1990. First published, under the title 'The Atlantic Seaboard: poetic topology of the European West' in *Regionalität, Nationalität und Internationalität in der zeitgenössischen Lyrik*, Tübingen, Attempto Verlag, 1992.

Select Bibliography

Kenneth White's Work in English

First period, 1966–8

(published by Jonathan Cape, London)
The Cold Wind of Dawn, poems (1966).
Letters from Gourgounel, narrative (1966).
The Most Difficult Area, poems (1968).

Second period, since 1989

The Bird Path, collected longer poems (Edinburgh and London: Mainstream Publishing, 1989; also in Penguin paperback edition).
Travels in the Drifting Dawn, narrative (Edinburgh and London: Mainstream Publishing, 1989; also in Penguin paperback edition).
Handbook for the Diamond Country, collected shorter poems (Edinburgh and London: Mainstream Publishing, 1990).
The Blue Road, narrative (Edinburgh and London: Mainstream Publishing, 1990).
Pilgrim of the Void, narrative (Edinburgh and London: Mainstream Publishing, 1992).
Van Gogh and Kenneth White, an encounter, English version (Paris: Flohic Éditions, 1994).
Coast to Coast, interviews (Glasgow: Open World Editions and Mythic Horse Press, 1996).
Into the White World, two cassettes of poem readings (1992,

available from Scotsoun, 13 Ashton Road, Glasgow G12
8SP).

Kenneth White's Work in French

Récits, cheminements

Les Limbes incandescents, traduction Patrick Mayoux (Paris:
   Denoël, collection les Lettres nouvelles, 1976; nouvelle
   édition Paris: Denoël, 1990).
Dérives, plusieurs traducteurs (Paris: Laffont, Lettres nouvelles/
   Maurice Nadeau, 1978).
Lettres de Gourgounel, traduction Gil et Marie Jouanard (Paris:
   Presses d'aujourd'hui, 1979; nouvelle édition Paris: Grasset,
   les Cahiers Rouges, 1986).
L'Écosse avec Kenneth White (Paris: Flammarion, 1980; réédi-
   tion Arthaud, 1988).
Le Visage du vent d'est, traduction Marie-Claude White (Paris:
   les Presses d'aujourd'hui, 1980).
La Route bleue, traduction Marie-Claude White (Paris: Grasset,
   1983; Prix Médicis étranger, Livre de Poche 5988).
Les Cygnes sauvages, traduction Marie-Claude White (Paris:
   Grasset, 1990).

Poésie

En toute candeur, édition bilingue, traduction Pierre Leyris
   (Paris: Mercure de France, 1964).
Mahamudra, le grand geste, édition bilingue, traduction Marie-
   Claude White (Paris: Mercure de France, 1979).
Le Grand Rivage, édition bilingue, traduction Patrick Guyon et
   Marie-Claude White (Paris: le Nouveau Commerce, 1980).
Scènes d'un monde flottant, édition bilingue revue et augmentée,
   traduction Marie-Claude White (Paris: Grasset, 1983).
Terre de diamant, édition bilingue revue et augmentée, traduc-
   tion Philippe Jaworski, Marie-Claude White et l'auteur
   (Paris: Grasset, 1983).
Atlantica, édition bilingue, traduction Marie-Claude White
   (Paris: Grasset, 1986; prix Alfred de Vigny).

Les Rives du silence, édition bilingue, traduction Marie-Claude White (Paris: Mercure de France, 1997).

Essais, recherches

La Figure du dehors (Paris: Grasset, 1982; Livre de Poche, Biblio Essais 4105).
Une apocalypse tranquille (Paris: Grasset, 1985).
Le Poète cosmographe, entretiens (Bordeaux: Presses Universitaires de Bordeaux, 1987).
L'Esprit nomade (Paris: Grasset, 1987).
Le Monde d'Antonin Artaud (Bruxelles et Paris: Éditions Complexe, 1989).
Hokusaï, ou l'horizon sensible (Paris: Terrain Vague, 1990).
Le Plateau de l'Albatros (Paris: Grasset, 1994).
Le Lieu et la parole, entretiens (Pont-Aven: Éditions du Scorff, 1997).
Une strategie paradoxale (Bordeaux: Presses Universitaires de Bordeaux, 1998).
Les Finisterres de l'esprit (Pont-Aven: Éditions du Scorff, 1998).

Note

The French bibliography of White's work is to date the only complete one. The paradox of White's situation, and stance, is such that his work, written in English, except for the essays (mostly written in French), has appeared in French, and, substantially, in other languages (German, Dutch, Spanish, Italian, Bulgarian, Russian, Serbian, Romanian, Polish, Macedonian . . .) before it has appeared in English. This paradox may in itself be the sign of a tectonic displacement in European culture, a new mental cartography. In particular, a more Europe-oriented Scotland. In general, the opening, while not forgetting native sources (on the contrary, using them in a larger context, to which they have always aspired) of a field of life and thought outside and beyond all the localisms. Simple location is a thing of the past.